Legislatures and the Budget Process

Legislatures and the Budget Process

The Myth of Fiscal Control

Joachim Wehner
London School of Economics and Political Science

HJ
2005
W365
2010
WEB

palgrave
macmillan

First published 2010 by
PALGRAVE MACMILLAN

Palgrave Macmillan in the UK is an imprint of Macmillan Publishers Limited, registered in England, company number 785998, of Houndmills, Basingstoke, Hampshire RG21 6XS.

Palgrave Macmillan in the US is a division of St Martin's Press LLC, 175 Fifth Avenue, New York, NY 10010.

Palgrave Macmillan is the global academic imprint of the above companies and has companies and representatives throughout the world.

Palgrave® and Macmillan® are registered trademarks in the United States, the United Kingdom, Europe and other countries.

ISBN 978–0–230–21972–4   hardback

This book is printed on paper suitable for recycling and made from fully managed and sustained forest sources. Logging, pulping and manufacturing processes are expected to conform to the environmental regulations of the country of origin.

A catalogue record for this book is available from the British Library.

Library of Congress Cataloging-in-Publication Data

Wehner, Joachim.
    Legislatures and the budget process: the myth of fiscal control / Joachim Wehner.
        p. cm.
    ISBN 978–0–230–21972–4 (hardback)
    1. Budget—Case studies. 2. Fiscal policy—Case studies.
    3. Legislative bodies—Case studies. I. Title.
    HJ2005.W365 2010
    328.3'412—dc22

                                                                    2010011093

10   9   8   7   6   5   4   3   2   1
19   18   17   16   15   14   13   12   11   10

Printed and bound in Great Britain by
CPI Antony Rowe, Chippenham and Eastbourne

Contents

List of Figures and Tables

Figures

Tables

Acknowledgements

I owe enormous gratitude to a large number of people for their support of this research. Two individuals deserve special mention. In 1997, Warren Krafchik at the Institute for Democracy in South Africa (Idasa) asked me to conduct comparative research on the role of legislatures in the budget process. At the time, South Africa's first democratically elected parliamentarians had begun to rethink their role in budgeting and quickly discovered that they lacked relevant cross-national data and analysis. Initially intended as a little side project, this became the origin of my decade-long obsession with the topic. In 2003, I relocated to the UK and continued my work at the London School of Economics and Political Science (LSE), where in particular Patrick Dunleavy was the source of much inspiration, without which I would have written a very different book. Thank you both.

For their comments and suggestions, I would like to thank Elena Bechberger, Paolo de Renzio, Torun Dewan, Keith Dowding, Achim Goerres, Mark Hallerberg, Achim Hildebrandt, Simon Hix, Jouni Kuha, Valentino Larcinese, Michael Laver, Ian Lienert, Christian List, Martin Lodge, Deborah Mabbett, David Marshall, Roy Meyers, Ed Page, Carlos Santiso, Waltraud Schelkle, Rick Stapenhurst, Sally Stares, Mark Thatcher, Fred Thompson, Jane Tinkler and Andreas Warntjen. I resolved several country data issues with the help of Vasilios Alevizakos, Mario Arriagada, Jón Blöndal, Alexander Cirak, Gabriel Farfan-Mares, Gabriel Filc, Hajime Isozaki, Anna Kovacikova, Keiichi Kubo, Marcel Mihalenko, Rajagopalan Ramanathan, Vinod Sahgal, Carlos Scartascini, Mike Stevens, Francesco Stolfi and David Woodruff. Bernard Casey, Bernard Kittel, Thomas Plümper, Mike Seiferling, Bernard Steunenberg and Daniel Sturm helped with some econometric issues. Of course, all remaining errors are mine.

As part of the research for Chapter 6, I conducted a series of interviews in Sweden during May 2005 and received a number of written comments and clarifications. I thank Daniel Bergvall, Åke Hjalmarsson, Per Molander, Ove Nilsson, Johann Olsson and Dag Levin Sparr. In South Africa, I conducted interviews during March 2005 and February 2008. I thank Tania Ajam, Owen Barder, Francois Beukman, Cobus Botes,

Shaamela Cassiem, Neil Cole, Hildegarde Fast, Andrew Feinstein, Joan Fubbs, Nancy Gordon, Steve Gordon, Perran Hahndiek, Barbara Hogan, Louisa Mabe, Christina Murray, Nhlanhla Musa Nene, Adrienne Shall, Albert van Zyl, Len Verwey and Gavin Woods.

An earlier version of Chapter 3 was published in Joachim Wehner, 'Assessing the Power of the Purse: An Index of Legislative Budget Institutions', *Political Studies* Vol. 54 No. 4 (December 2006), pp. 767– 85, and is reprinted with the permission of the publisher (Blackwell Publishing Ltd.). The material on Sweden in section 6.2 as well as Figure 6.1 and the associated text were previously published in Joachim Wehner, 'Budget Reform and Legislative Control in Sweden', *Journal of European Public Policy* Vol. 14 No. 2 (March 2007), pp. 313–32, and are reprinted with the permission of the publisher (Taylor & Francis Ltd., http://www.tandf.co.uk/journals).

Several institutions deserve mention. The main dataset used in this book is based on survey work carried out by the Organisation for Economic Co-operation and Development (OECD). I am indebted to Michael Ruffner for patiently dealing with my questions about the 2003 Survey of Budget Practices and Procedures, and to Barry Anderson and Ian Hawkesworth for the opportunity to work on the update of the survey. The work presented in Chapter 3 was partly funded by the German Academic Exchange Service (DAAD). In London, the LSE provided a supportive environment to complete the research, in particular my colleagues in the Government Department, the MPA Programme, the Public Policy Group as well as the Political Science and Political Economy (PSPE) research group.

I dedicate this book to Aline.

List of Abbreviations

ANC	African National Congress
Idasa	Institute for Democracy in South Africa
IMF	International Monetary Fund
LSE	London School of Economics and Political Science
OECD	Organisation for Economic Co-operation and Development

1
Perspectives on Legislative Budgeting

The comparative study of political institutions has a venerable tradition in political science (Lijphart 1984, 1999; Weaver and Rockman 1993; Tsebelis 2002). Economists, too, have become increasingly interested in the policy effects of political institutions (for an overview, see Congleton and Swedenborg 2006a). Much of the focus in this literature is on fundamental constitutional choices, such as presidential versus parliamentary regimes, federal versus unitary states and proportional versus majoritarian electoral systems. For instance, Weaver and Rockman (1993: 10) regard the choice between presidential or parliamentary government as most fundamental for government performance. Similarly, Persson and Tabellini's (2003) widely discussed study of the economic effects of constitutions finds that presidentialism and plurality rule electoral systems result in lower levels of central government expenditure compared with parliamentary regimes and proportional representation electoral formulas.

As important as these contributions are, an exclusive focus on the grand design of polities risks missing crucial determinants of public policy outcomes. Fundamental constitutional differences are important, but to properly assess the impact of institutional arrangements on policy outcomes it is at least equally important to look beyond these broad systemic features into the more detailed machinery for policy making. The relative importance of these different institutions is contested. On the one hand, authors such as Cheibub and Limongi (2002: 176) argue that institutional effects are not mainly derived from macro-level constitutional fundamentals, but rather from 'the way

1

the decision making process is organized'. To the contrary, Weaver and Rockman (1993: 10) in their much-cited study of government performance diminutively dismiss 'secondary institutional characteristics' as having 'third tier' explanatory relevance, while describing the presidential–parliamentary distinction as the crucial 'first tier' explanation. I suspect that meaningful progress with this debate requires more focus on the institutional setting in particular policy areas (Bechberger 2007). This book offers precisely such a focus. It is dedicated to a particularly important aspect of legislative decision making, the annual allocation of public funds. I show that the structure of this process has substantively important consequences that rival the effect of any macro-constitutional distinctions.

With the term 'institutions' I refer to 'formal rules that have been decided in a political process' (Rothstein 1996: 145). This excludes concepts such as culture and social norms that might be regarded as 'informal' institutions. The stricter definition enables a focus on how formal political institutions, in particular constitutional features, affect public policy (Weaver and Rockman 1993; Tsebelis 2002). The 'new institutionalism' in political science is far from united (Hall and Taylor 1996). For instance, historical institutionalism emphasises path dependence and unintended consequences (Pierson 2000; Pierson and Skocpol 2002), whereas rational choice institutionalism, or the analytical politics approach, stresses the rationality of organisational choice in the context of addressing problems of collective action (e.g. Shepsle 1979). For large parts of the book, I draw on tools and insights developed with the analytical politics approach, in particular the literature on fiscal institutions, which I discuss further below.

Another conceptual clarification: the word budget can mean very different things to different people. For some, it represents an impenetrably dense collection of quantitative details: 'It's got a lot of numbers in it', George W. Bush put it.[1] Aaron Wildavsky somewhat more poetically summarises the multiple meanings of the budget as 'a prediction', 'a series of goals to which price tags are attached' and 'a contract' (Wildavsky and Caiden 2001: 1–2). The word itself developed from *bougette* or 'small bag' in old French. In England, it designated the leather bag in which ministers of the Crown carried financial plans to parliament[2] and eventually became synonymous with its contents. In the UK the word 'budget' now refers to the spring financial statement, which focuses on taxation measures.[3] In most countries, however, the term refers to the annual expenditure and revenue plans tabled in the legislature, and I use the word in this broader sense. According to Schick (2002: 20), one of the first legal definitions is contained in a French decree of 1862: 'The budget is a document which forecasts and authorizes the annual receipts and expenditures of the State' (see also Stourm 1917: 2). Although derided by Osborne and Gaebler (1992: 117) as 'useless and demeaning' because they 'suck enormous quantities of time away from real work', budgets remain ubiquitous in democratic governments across the world. A short historic detour is a helpful reminder of why this is the case.[4]

1.1 The evolution and decay of fiscal control

It took a series of long and often violent conflicts for the principle of parliamentary control of the budget to acquire the ubiquitous constitutional importance that it enjoys across democratic countries today. In medieval England, parliament sought to limit royal powers to impose taxes in order to curtail their ability to maintain a standing army beyond times of war and immediate threat (Harriss 1975). The principle of parliamentary consent to taxation gained constitutional recognition in the Magna Carta, a list of concessions to the barons that King John signed at Runnymede in 1215: 'No "scutage" or "aid" may be levied in our kingdom without its general consent.'[5] But this did not settle the matter. To evade expenditure control, a popular royal tactic was to resort to borrowing with the hope that parliament would subsequently consent to the raising of funds to repay such loans. In 1672, this led to the only state bankruptcy in British history when payments on loans from city bankers had to be suspended (Einzig 1959: 98). The Glorious Revolution brought a more decisive change. In the 1689 Bill of Rights, William III and Mary II had to accept 'That levying money for or to the use of the Crown by pretence of prerogative, without grant of Parliament, for longer time, or in other manner than the same is or shall be granted, is illegal.' However, at this stage there was still no such thing as an annual budget, and there was no comprehensive control of expenditures.

The idea of *public* finance with concomitant notions of accountability could not be established without a distinction between the property of the monarch and that of the state (Webber and Wildavsky 1986: 212). In England, the creation of the civil list put a decisive end to the tradition that the king should 'live of his own' (Smith 1999: 61–3). In 1698, parliament passed the Civil List Act that granted the Crown tax revenues of £700,000 per annum 'to meet the costs of the civil government and the royal establishment' (Smith 1999: 63). The monarch in turn relinquished most hereditary revenues. Originally, the list was intended to cover the financial requirements of the king and his household as well as the expenditure of the central civil government excluding debt charges. Expenditures for the civil administration were gradually transferred to the supply services and, later, the consolidated fund, in a process that lasted until 1830 (Einzig 1959: 149). This achieved the separation of public and royal expenditures.

After the Glorious Revolution, it was not long before parliamentary control spread beyond Britain. Ironically, parliament proved to have a short memory of the passions that could be incited by the unilateral imposition of fiscal measures. As imperial finances were stretched by the protection of vast colonial territories, parliament sought to force the inhabitants of the empire's North American possessions to contribute towards the defence of their territory. In 1765 it ordered the imposition of a tax on a stamp affixed to a range of documents including such essentials as newspapers and playing cards. This caused great discontent and led to a boycott of British goods by the colonialists. Despite a partial retreat by parliament, which abolished the 'stamp tax' and several other duties, the continued imposition of a duty on tea was sufficient to provoke unrest and ultimately led to the War of Independence. At the First Continental Congress in 1774 delegates from the colonies rejected 'every idea of taxation, internal or external, for raising a revenue on the subjects in America, without their consent' (Ford et al. 1904–37: 1:69). After the battle of Saratoga, parliament abolished the hated duty and resolved not to impose further taxes on America.

Legislative control remained incomplete as long as governments continued to enjoy extensive discretion in expending public revenues. By the beginning of the nineteenth century, the US Congress already constrained executive discretion through detailed line item appropriations, including strict limits on specific expenses such as firewood and candles in particular offices (Schick 2000: 11). This tradition has its origins in colonial times, when the colonialists were suspicious of governors they did not appoint and who they regarded as agents of the king in distant Britain. They thus devised stringent and humiliating control mechanisms including the annual voting of salaries, detailed specification of the objects and amounts of spending, as well as the reversion of unspent funds to the treasury at the end of the fiscal period (Webber and Wildavsky 1986: 365). However, such an advanced level of control was exceptional at the time.

The rise of modern budgeting in nineteenth-century Europe was linked to the Enlightenment idea that government, through conscious effort, could be made 'rational' (Webber and Wildavsky 1986: 323–6). France was first to develop modern expenditure control mechanisms, starting with the creation of the *cour des comptes* in 1807.[6] In the initial years of its operation, many audit reports were apparently 'lost in the library' of the National Assembly despite frequent but 'in vain' demands for them by parliamentary committees (Stourm 1917: 577). Since 1819 the assembly passed an annual law approving the execution of each budget, as the accounting officer was personally responsible for any misspent funds until a formal vote of 'granting discharge'.[7] The specification of detailed items of expenditure for each ministry became a legal requirement in 1831. By the middle of the nineteenth century, France had assembled the core elements of a modern budgeting system: a comprehensive written budget encompassing all revenues and expenditures, analytical procedures for estimating financial requirements, a standard fiscal year and the principle of annual authorisation, as well as a developed system of accounting and audit.

The control of expenditures evolved somewhat more haphazardly in Britain. The first known instance of parliamentary appropriation dates back to 1340, when a grant to Edward III was explicitly earmarked for 'the Maintenance and Safeguard of our said Realm of England, and on Wars in Scotland, France and Gascoign, and in no places elsewhere during the said Wars' (Einzig 1959: 79). To exercise some control over royal spending, particular sources of revenue were also frequently tied to specific expenses. However, parliamentary oversight of expenditures remained patchy until the creation of the consolidated fund in 1787 for the purposes of collecting revenues and disbursing all monies for the supply of public services: 'This broke the disorder caused by assigning particular taxes to special purposes and it provided the means of infinite expenditure control through comprehensive appropriation schedules' (Reid 1966: 57).

William Ewart Gladstone, who first became Chancellor of the Exchequer in 1852, was determined to force greater economy in public finance through more detailed controls. His approach reflected the orthodox economic thinking that started to shape fiscal policy by the middle of the nineteenth century, when the norm of balanced budgets became fashionable (Webber and Wildavsky 1986: 302). In 1861, based on his initiative, the Commons resolved to establish a Committee of Public Accounts (Chubb 1952: 32).[8] It was made permanent in the following year and tasked with examining the appropriation accounts (see Standing Order No. 148 of the House of Commons). The Exchequer and Audit Departments Act of 1866 required all government departments to produce such accounts for audit purposes and created the Comptroller and Auditor General by merging the *ex ante* function of authorising the issue of money to departments with a new *ex post* function of examining every appropriation account and reporting the results to parliament (National Audit Office 2001: 236). The Public Accounts Committee examined the first complete set of accounts in 1870 (Chubb 1952: 43). Gladstone's reforms established a model of *ex post* control that has spread throughout the Commonwealth (McGee 2002; Wehner 2003; Pelizzo et al. 2006).

The loss of veto power over financial legislation by the hereditary chamber was a final step towards the democratisation of the budget in Britain. The Commons considered the Lords unable to amend tax and spending bills by the end of the seventeenth century (Einzig 1959: 114). The formal removal of remaining veto power was triggered by the dramatic struggle over the 1909 budget of Chancellor Lloyd George, who sought increased tax revenues in order to pay for pensions and defence (Porritt 1910). When the Lords rejected the entire Finance Bill, this prompted the passing of the Parliament Act of 1911, the purpose of which was to debar the Lords from rejecting 'money bills'.[9] Since then, the supremacy of the elected chamber is firmly established. Nowadays, budgetary bicameralism generally requires second chambers with democratic credentials (Heller 1997; Patterson and Mughan 1999).

Parliamentary fiscal power in Britain was at its peak in the second half of the nineteenth century, when the Commons frequently amended spending and revenue proposals. Einzig (1959: 264–76) lists 26 government defeats over estimates between 1858 and the turn of the nineteenth century. However, parliament's budgetary function also started to fall into disrepute (Bagehot 1867: 154): 'The House of Commons – now that it is the true sovereign, and appoints the real executive – has long ceased to be the checking, sparing, economical body it once was. It is now more apt to spend money than the Minister of the day.'[10] Perhaps the first ever cross-national survey on budgeting practices, conducted by the Cobden Club during the 1870s, reveals discontent with parliaments in a number of countries. For instance, the French Finance Minister Léon Say complained that the budget equilibrium was being compromised 'by those very persons whose proper mission should be that of restraining the public administration, in the matter of expenditure, instead of encouraging the augmentation of its Budgets' (quoted from Probyn 1877: 49).[11] Legislative bodies had acquired a reputation for fiscal profligacy.

However, the zenith of fiscal power at Westminster was cut short by the emergence of organised political parties towards the end of the nineteenth century (Adonis 1993; Norton 1993). In the wake of the 1867 Reform Act the balance between the Commons and the cabinet began to shift, as governments became increasingly reliant on the approval of the electorate and parties sought to project a coherent image to the public (Mackintosh 1962: 161–209). The reform of parliamentary procedure became an issue as governments struggled to ensure the smooth passage of legislation and the timely voting of supply (Mackintosh 1962: 179–82). In 1872, the government obtained concessions that restricted the opportunity for amendments to the motion to move into committee of supply. A decade later, Gladstone proposed reforms that prohibited dilatory motions for adjournment, required speeches to be relevant and allowed a simple majority vote to close debates. This was followed in 1896 by the limitation of the number of supply days and the inauguration of the guillotine for the supply procedure (Einzig 1959: 245). Previously, each departmental vote had to be moved separately, which afforded ample opportunity for debate and tactical delays. These procedural adjustments made it easier for governments to get their proposals through the Commons.

In Britain, amendments to the estimates came to be regarded as fundamental challenges to the government during the beginning of the twentieth century. When in 1919 the Commons denied the Lord Chancellor funding for a second bathroom, Lord Birkenhead refused to move into his official residence. The government considered this incident so embarrassing that the Treasury initiated a seemingly innocuous but consequential change in procedure that moved the drafting of money resolutions, which are required for any new bill that would lead to an increase in public spending (Einzig 1959: 290–4), from the Public Bill Office of the Commons to the Treasury. Subsequent governments drafted more restrictive money resolutions, ending the practice of the preceding two centuries when they were sufficiently permissive to allow amendments. As successive governments became 'hypersensitive' to parliamentary challenges, every step in the financial procedure became linked to the question of confidence (Reid 1966: 77). The last government defeat over estimates was in 1921 over members' travel expenses. Nowadays, any amendment would be tantamount to a vote of no confidence.

Apart from the rise of disciplined political parties, other developments have also contributed to the weakening of traditional control mechanisms in many established democracies (Schick 2002). Following World War II, the expansion in public spending in many developed countries was fuelled to a large extent by an increase in entitlements, which in some cases are not subject to annual appropriations (Schick 2000: 52). More recently, many budget reformers promote the aggregation of previously separate items into larger categories, including lump sum appropriations to agencies, based on the idea that agency heads are best positioned to choose the appropriate input mix for their activities (Blöndal 2003: 15). In the extreme, however, this can make it 'impossible to determine what is actually happening with respect to a particular function or program' (Joint Committee of Public Accounts and Audit 2002: 4.50). Schick (2002: 31–2) concludes that

> the traditional role of the legislature as a restraint on the exercise of government power ... survives in most countries, though not as robustly as before. In a legal sense, the doctrine of control has not been impaired. Stripped to its essentials, it means that government may not spend more than authorised in law or for other than authorised purposes. *De facto* however, control does not mean the same today as it once did.

1.2　Existing theoretical and empirical work

A comprehensive assessment of legislative budgeting requires a less anecdotal approach than historical accounts provide. Indeed, theories of budgeting have evolved considerably over the past century (Kraan 1996: 1–8). The first milestone was Aaron Wildavsky's (1964) theory of budgetary incrementalism, according to which budgeting is so complex that decision makers largely forfeit a review of existing expenditure, referred to as the 'base'. Rather, 'this year's budget is based on last year's budget, with special attention given to a narrow range of increases or decreases' (Davis et al. 1966: 529–30). Incrementalism was a theory of organisational behaviour, rather than a theory specific to budgeting (Schick 1988b: 62). Although Wildavsky attempted to clarify his concept in later years (Dempster and Wildavsky 1979), incrementalism has been criticised as 'an extraordinarily elastic and elusive concept' (Schick 1983: 2; see also Meyers 1994). Wildavsky (1988) himself eventually abandoned the theory, as it became evident that its core ideas did little to explain budgeting in times of fiscal retrenchment (Bozeman and Straussman 1982; Rubin 1989).

Another theoretical approach is associated with William Niskanen (1971, 1973) and his theory of budget-maximising bureaucrats. Niskanen put forward a microeconomic theory of bureaucracy that dealt specifically with the interaction between bureaucrats and their legislative sponsor in the budget process. In his basic model, the institutional assumptions of asymmetrical information, bilateral monopoly and the power to make package proposals heavily favour spendthrift bureaucrats over their legislative sponsor (for some modifications, see Niskanen 1975). Later work in the public choice tradition explores some conditions that may facilitate greater legislative control (in particular Miller and Moe 1983; Bendor et al. 1985). Niskanen's book provided an intellectual foundation for the attack on big governments in the US and elsewhere (Hindmoor 2006: 152). His theoretical contribution was to bring the public choice approach to the study of budgeting, in particular the tools of microeconomic analysis, with its focus on methodological individualism, the rationality assumption, the search for equilibria and formal modelling. Yet Niskanen assumes a weak and passive sponsor, which some argue is 'extremely artificial' (Dunleavy 1991: 211). While relaxing the institutional assumptions helps to illuminate how alternative arrangements can yield more optimal results (Mueller 2003: 368), his account of the demand side remains underdeveloped.

For legislative scholars, a proper assessment of the design of the budget process is important for understanding the balance of power between different actors in a political system. Moreover, the control of financial measures is the original function of modern legislative bodies. Yet the cross-national study of legislative budgeting, despite some progress in recent years, is in a lamentable state. Legislative scholars have contributed a number of descriptive country studies of financial scrutiny, often laced with normative connotations.[12] Although the comparative study of legislatures has become more systematic in recent years, for instance through the work of Döring (1995a) as well as Döring and Hallerberg (2004), this does not yet extend to legislative budgeting. Perhaps the most substantial collection of country studies on legislative budgeting is decades old (Coombes 1976), and while it provides rich information on a few countries it lacks a rigorous theoretical basis that would make the studies comparable and enable an overarching perspective. Much of the legislative studies literature on financial scrutiny is outdated and methodologically unsophisticated.

Political economists have made a number of important contributions that are relevant for the comparative study of legislative budgeting. Following a period of economic crisis in the advanced industrialised countries during the 1970s, they displayed remarkably different speeds of adjustment. This puzzle prompted some scholars to explore determinants of fiscal policy beyond purely economic variables, such as the role of political parties (Roubini and Sachs 1989; Alt and Lowry 1994; Franzese 1999). Other authors argue that the key to understanding fiscal policy is the design of the budget process itself (Poterba and Von Hagen 1999; Strauch and Von Hagen 1999; Kirchgässner 2001). This fiscal institutionalist perspective has been influential with policymakers (Molander 1999). Compared with the legislative studies literature, this work is more quantitatively oriented and methodologically sophisticated, but its consideration of legislative aspects tends to be selective rather than comprehensive.

In addition to partisan and fiscal institutionalist theories, a more recent strand of constitutional economics has investigated the fiscal policy effects of fundamental features of the design of political systems (for an overview, see Congleton and Swedenborg 2006a). Empirically, this literature stands out for its use of large samples. However, the most important recent contribution to constitutional economics, by Persson and Tabellini (2000, 2003), focused on two constitutional aspects only, that is, electoral rules and forms of government. The authors 'leave out many potentially important constitutional features, including ... budgetary procedures' (Persson and Tabellini 2006: 85). The strengths of the constitutional economics literature are its attention to rigorous theoretical methods and quantitative analysis, but it adds little to our understanding of how legislative institutions shape fiscal policy.

The role of legislative budget institutions is also of increasing interest to policymakers. The 1990s saw a substantial number of developing and post-communist countries move towards democracy. This often required the wholesale redesign of political institutions, including legislative bodies. Their performance has come under the spotlight as donor agencies and international organisations seek to promote 'good governance' by enhancing accountability with initiatives that aim to 'strengthen' the legislative branch (Messick 2002: 1; see also United States Agency for International Development 2000; Hudson and Wren 2007). This concern fits into a broader debate on institution building in countries receiving foreign aid, in particular, as donors move from project-specific funding to general budget support (Stapenhurst and Pelizzo 2002; United Kingdom Department for International Development 2004; De Renzio 2006). The idea is to improve domestic oversight in order to fight corruption and enhance the effectiveness of aid (Santiso 2006). Yet it is far from clear what is required for 'strong' legislative financial scrutiny, and whether it really delivers the desired effect.

Paradoxically, many economists and public finance practitioners regard legislatures as fiscally dangerous and promote limiting their powers, while legislative strengthening is fashionable with legislative studies scholars and some actors in the development community. Part of the reason is that the latter are less concerned with ensuring prudent fiscal policy and more with promoting broader notions of democracy and development. Some legislative scholars boldly go as far as to claim that 'the presence of a powerful legislature is an unmixed blessing for democratization' (Fish 2006: 5). Similar assumptions are evident in the aid policies of some donor governments, who pledge to 'help make public institutions more accountable, for example by strengthening parliamentary ... oversight' (United Kingdom Department for International Development 2006: 27). Yet the empirical relationship between legislative oversight and democracy is poorly understood. Moreover, there may be side effects of 'strengthening' legislative bodies that should be more explicitly discussed. Is it possible to 'strengthen' legislatures without undermining prudent fiscal management, and if so, how? The urgency of advancing these debates calls for additional and more systematic analysis.

To sum up, the state of the literature and practical concerns generate a number of questions about the role of legislatures in public finance: how can we measure and compare legislative budgeting across countries? What factors explain cross-national variation? If countries differ in the way in which legislatures engage with the budget, how does this affect fiscal policy? What are the implications for institutional reforms? This book addresses these questions in an explicitly comparative framework focusing on the institutional design for legislative budgeting. More specifically, the aims of this book are (i) to establish and apply a framework for assessing the budgetary role of legislatures, (ii) to explore the determinants of cross-national variation in institutional arrangements and (iii) to assess empirically the impact of legislative budget institutions on fiscal policy.

1.3 Building on the fiscal institutionalist approach

In tackling these questions, I build on work investigating the effect of budget institutions on fiscal policy.[13] This work draws on the basic idea that spending will be higher when decision makers do not internalise the full costs of their actions. Weingast, Shepsle and Johnsen (1981) expressed this as the 'Law of 1/n' (see also Shepsle and Weingast 1981). In their model, expenditure x can be targeted at a particular geographical district where it produces benefits b, while costs c are shared equally across all n districts. This implies that the optimal level of spending for district i is achieved when its marginal benefit equals its marginal cost:

$$b_i'(x) = \frac{1}{n}c'(x).$$

The larger the *n* in the above equation the smaller the share of the tax burden considered in spending decisions. Hence, assuming universalistic logrolls, 'the degree of inefficiency in project scale ... is an increasing function of the number of districts' (Weingast et al. 1981: 654). In other words, the possibility to disperse costs and to target benefits engenders a pro-spending bias that increases with the number of decision makers.[14]

A number of studies support the prediction. Fiorino and Ricciuti (2007) and Bradbury and Crain (2001) find evidence of the predicted effect of legislature size on expenditures. Focusing on the executive arena, Perotti and Kontopoulos (2002), using a panel of 19 Organisation for Economic Co-operation and Development (OECD) countries over the 1970–95 period, find that cabinet size is a determinant of fiscal outcomes. Volkerink and De Haan (2001) investigate the fiscal impact of the number of spending ministers, that is, the total number of government ministers minus the minister of finance and/or the budget as well as the prime minister. This measure is associated with budget deficits in a panel of 22 OECD countries covering the years 1971–96. The most comprehensive cross-national study so far, using a global sample of 58 countries over a 24-year period, also finds a strong positive association between the number of spending ministers and central government budget deficits and expenditures (Wehner 2009).

Von Hagen and Harden (1995: 772–5) present a much-cited model that builds on the same idea, but which also yields concrete recommendations for the design of the budget process. They model decision making in a government consisting of several spending ministers, each of whom gets funds that are used to produce activities in order to achieve a policy target. While each has an interest in achieving their policy target and minimising the excess burden from taxation, each also receives a private utility gain from their budget allocation. Moreover, each spending minister only considers their constituency's share of the total excess burden.[15] If the budget process follows a bottom-up approach that allows each spending minister to separately draft a budget, so that the total budget consists simply of the sum of all bids submitted by the spending ministers, the aggregate budget outcome resulting from this bottom-up process is larger than the optimal total for the government as a whole.

Von Hagen and Harden (1995) go on to show that when a minister without portfolio, who has an incentive to consider the overall impact of excess taxation, is given strategic power vis-à-vis their colleagues in spending ministries, the resulting amount of total spending is closer to the joint optimum than under the bottom-up process. The model can be adapted to different contexts, such as legislative decision making, or where the process involves disciplined political parties in a coalition government (Hallerberg 1999; Hallerberg 2004: 22–7). The basic result is always that a spending bias will arise when decision makers do not internalise the full cost of their actions, resulting in 'fiscal illusion' (Von Hagen and Harden 1995: 772).

The fiscal institutionalist response to what is also referred to as the 'common pool resource' or 'fiscal commons' problem is to impose hierarchical budget institutions. These are institutional arrangements that centralise budgetary decision making in the hands of an actor who is more likely to consider overall costs than a spending minister, such as the finance minister or the prime minister, in order to contain free-riding and to safeguard fiscal discipline (Von Hagen 1992; Poterba and Von Hagen 1999; Strauch and Von Hagen 1999). This has spawned a substantial body of empirical work on the fiscal effects of budget institutions, for instance in Western Europe (Von Hagen 1992; Hallerberg 2004; Hallerberg et al. 2007), Latin America (Stein et al. 1998; Alesina et al. 1999; Hallerberg and Marier 2004) and more recently Central and Eastern Europe (Gleich 2003; Yläoutinen 2004; Fabrizio and Mody 2006).

While the institutionalist literature has contributed an important perspective on the determinants of fiscal performance, it also has limitations. Several formal models produce predictions about spending levels (Von Hagen and Harden 1995; Hallerberg 1999, 2004) whereas empirical work 'has consistently found an impact of budget institutions on fiscal deficits and debt, but almost as consistently has failed to find an association with government size' (Stein et al. 1998: note 35). A number of papers do not properly justify the use of other dependent variables when the theoretical discussion calls for the use of indicators of government size, in particular public spending. In this book, I develop a theoretical framework that generates predictions about the impact of particular institutional features on spending levels, and use three different cross-national datasets as well as case study evidence in order to test these.

Another limitation of the fiscal institutionalist literature, in the context of this book, is that it typically investigates only a limited range of legislative institutions. The most widely considered variable is legislative authority to amend the budget (Von Hagen 1992; Stein et al. 1998; Alesina et al. 1999). Another legislative variable considered in earlier studies is the sequencing of the voting process (Von Hagen 1992), but claims about its effects are contested (Ferejohn and Krehbiel 1987; Hallerberg and Von Hagen 1997). Crain and Muris (1995) consider how legislative committee structure affects spending levels. Other relevant features of the budget process, such as execution rules, are rarely considered from a legislative perspective. Moreover, in some of the empirical work the institutional variables are under-theorised or based on conjectures, such as the claim that the reversionary budget affects fiscal discipline (Alesina et al. 1999; Hallerberg and Marier 2004). In this study, I bring together a range of relevant variables in a more unified framework of legislative budget institutions than was previously available.

I accept the basic premise of the literature on common pool resources: budgetary decision making in legislatures is vulnerable to a pro-spending bias, which can be mitigated by institutional arrangements. However, it is far too simplistic to argue that any type of constraint imposed on the legislative process will improve fiscal performance. One of my contributions is to show that the effect of legislative institutions on fiscal performance needs to be analytically separated from understanding how institutional arrangements affect the range of outcomes available to the legislature. Many constraints do not unambiguously enhance fiscal discipline. Paradoxically, institutional arrangements may constrain legislative choice without affecting fiscal outcomes, and it is even possible for such constraints to have adverse effects on fiscal discipline. Only with clear predictions about the fiscal effects of legislative budget institutions is there a sound basis for empirically investigating their impact on public expenditures.

From an empirical perspective, this study is also more comprehensive in terms of countries covered than any previous research related to legislative budget institutions. Oppenheimer's (1983) literature review may be slightly outdated, but it still highlights the scarcity of research on the impact of legislatures outside the US on policies and budgets (see also Mezey 1983). It is in fact only more recently that innovative survey work by the OECD has started to address the lack of data on comparative legislative budget practices (OECD 2002b,

2006, 2007; OECD and World Bank 2003). I adapt and use these data to present the most broadly based comparative overview of legislative budgeting to date.

In doing so, I combine quantitative and qualitative methods.[16] Some recent research on fiscal institutions highlights the need to complement quantitative analysis with qualitative work (Hallerberg 2004; Scartascini and Stein 2009), but on balance this literature overwhelmingly uses quantitative methods. Sometimes, the variables of interest are only crudely operationalised. Among the possible advantages of case studies are that they allow us to appreciate the nuances and complexities of institutions, access better data and gain a deeper understanding of causal mechanisms (Gerring 2004; George and Bennett 2005; Bennett and Elman 2006). The debate about the pros and cons of quantitative and qualitative analysis in the social sciences is not new (Jackman 1985; Ragin 1987, 2000; King et al. 1996), but the choice of research techniques does not have to be exclusive. For instance, Lieberman (2005) propagates a 'mixed methods' approach to harness the respective strengths of different methods of inquiry. I use a case study approach to complement and deepen my quantitative analysis, which yields useful results about the interaction of different institutional features in terms of their effect on budget outcomes.

1.4   The structure of the book

In Chapter 2, I develop the theoretical basis for most of the empirical analysis in the book. I discuss a range of institutional arrangements and explore how they affect the budgetary choices available to the legislature. This analysis generates testable predictions about the impact of these features on fiscal policy. Chapter 3 moves on to empirical analysis. Using data from recent surveys of budget processes in the industrialised democracies, I translate the framework developed in Chapter 2 into a summary measure of parliamentary budget capacity, which I call the index of legislative budget institutions, and present the results for the national legislatures of all 30 OECD countries.

The following two chapters are dedicated to the analysis of these data. In Chapter 4, I first explore factors that account for cross-national variation in legislative financial scrutiny, focusing on colonial history, party political dynamics, other fundamental features of political systems, as well as the maturity of a country's democracy. In Chapter 5, I move to the core concern of the fiscal institutionalist research agenda, and systematically test the impact of various legislative institutions on fiscal policy outcomes. In this chapter, I use three different datasets. Of the two cross-sectional datasets, one contains detailed data for all 30 OECD countries from 2001 to 2005, while the second is more focused in terms of institutional features but almost three times larger in terms of observations, covering a global sample of 80 countries during the 1990s. The third dataset is a panel of 58 countries from 1960 to 1998, with which I explore indirect fiscal effects of legislative authority in budgeting.

Chapter 6 is dedicated to case study evidence on budget reform and legislative control. In this chapter, I address the question of whether legislatures can be both powerful as well as fiscally responsible, focusing on two countries – Sweden and South Africa – that have introduced variants of 'top-down budgeting' in the legislative process. Because Sweden implemented its reforms in the mid-1990s, I use data for the years prior to as well as after the reforms to explore the effect of these changes. The changes in South Africa are more recent but similarly fundamental, and I provide an initial assessment. Chapter 7 draws together the main conclusions.

2
Institutional Foundations of Legislative Control

Institutional arrangements fundamentally affect public policy and the balance of power between political actors. In this chapter, I survey a range of institutional elements that determine legislative control of public spending. This synthesis is important because the effect of one institutional feature may be balanced or neutralised by another (Scartascini and Stein 2009). Hence, a highly selective analysis may lead to unrealistic expectations about the impact of institutional arrangements on fiscal policy. It may also obscure the fact that similar aims can sometimes be achieved with different combinations of institutions. Some authors have developed models that incorporate aspects of institutional design discussed here with a focus on individual countries (Baldez and Carey 1999; Pereira and Mueller 2004). I outline a broader framework that provides a basis for cross-national analysis.

The focus here is on (i) how institutional arrangements influence the legislative-executive balance of power and (ii) how they affect fiscal policy outcomes. I consider how different types and configurations of certain fundamental budgetary decision-making rules constrain a legislature, by exploring the size and shape of its feasible set of choices. This approach also allows me to make testable predictions about the impact of institutional arrangements on fiscal performance, defined here in terms of the total level of expenditures. The analysis considers three sets of essential formal rules, namely those that regulate legislative amendments of the budget, reversionary budgets as well as executive flexibility during implementation. This is the approximate sequence in which these rules are relevant over the budget cycle, and hence I will introduce them in this order. Since budgetary decision making is not costless, I also consider aspects of legislative organisation that enable legislators to use their formal powers.

Of course, it is possible to argue that further variables merit consideration. In particular, some authors give great importance to executive veto authority in assessing legislative power over policy (e.g. Shugart and Haggard 2001: 75–7). I do not include executive vetoes in budgetary matters, for a number of reasons. First, this variable is system-specific. In some presidential systems, the executive has the power to veto a budget bill in its entirety (package veto) or individual items within a budget bill approved by the legislature (line item veto).[1] Such powers are virtually unknown in parliamentary systems of government. My approach considers essential features of budgeting that are relevant across both forms of government. In addition, there are very few presidential systems among the advanced industrialised countries, which are the focus of the empirical analysis in the following two chapters. Finally, the relevance of executive vetoes for fiscal performance is contested. Carter and Schap (1990) show convincingly that certain types of executive vetoes can be ineffective at containing spending (see also Holtz-Eakin 1988), although more recent work on amendatory veto authority in Latin America (Tsebelis and Alemán 2005) highlights the need for more nuanced analysis. For these reasons, I do not consider executive vetoes and refer interested readers to the relevant literature.[2]

In the following analysis, I make several core assumptions. First, I assume a two-dimensional policy space. A single dimension is insufficient to explore the effects of different versions of a constraint, such as types of amendment powers. The choice of two-dimensional space can of course be challenged as unrealistic, since most government budgets have more than two dimensions. In the US, for instance, Congress approves separate appropriation bills for different spending areas, each of which contains many line items.[3] However, two-dimensional space is intuitive in this context, since many fundamental budgetary choices involve trade-offs between two broad functional, economic or other spending categories: health versus defence, primary versus secondary education, current versus capital, discretionary versus mandatory and so on. Moreover, an extension of the analysis into *n*-dimensional space would be more complicated and less accessible. In two-dimensional space, the argument can be illustrated with the help of a straightforward diagrammatic exposition. Therefore, two-dimensional analysis is the logical starting point.

Second, I model both the executive and the legislature as unitary actors. I do not consider the interaction of the executive and particular members of the legislature (Huber 1996). Also, this analysis does not extend to dynamics within the legislature, for instance, between different chambers (Tsebelis and Money 1997; Heller 1997, 2001; Patterson and Mughan 1999). Nor do I cover intra-executive negotiations, such as between cabinet committees (Breton 1996: 98–111) or government departments and the central budget authority (Steunenberg 2005). This simplification facilitates analysis without challenging the key results. As Tsebelis (2002: 38–63) demonstrates, it is possible to approximate the ideal points of collective actors in spatial models. Moreover, this assumption allows me to focus on the main purpose of this analysis, to delineate a legislature's feasible set of budgetary choices within different institutional settings.

Third, I assume Euclidean preferences over the space of budgetary alternatives. This implies circular indifference curves in the two-dimensional space. Hence, for any set of alternatives actors prefer the one that is closer to their ideal point to the one that is further away. Circularity is a common assumption in spatial analyses. This assumption can be relaxed, although the implications are not always straightforward.

Fourth, I assume that the executive makes the first move and tables a budgetary proposal that has to be approved by the legislature. Without this assumption, amendment powers would not be important as the legislature could simply draft a budget according to its preferences. In practice, the task of drafting a budget for debate in the legislature is typically delegated to the executive.[4] While some legislatures retain formal powers to draft a budget on their own, few have the prerequisite technical capacity (Schick 2002). Von Hagen (1992: 41) notes that 'this possibility is of no practical importance'. The assumption of executive proposal power is very realistic.

2.1 Amendment powers

After the tabling of a budget, the scope for a legislature to shape budget policy is defined by its powers to amend the executive proposal. There are two broad classes of amendment powers, that is, unfettered and constrained. Amendment constraints can take a number of forms, but most common are constraints relating to the deficit, total spending and individual spending items (Inter-Parliamentary Union 1986: Table 38A). For now, I leave aside the possibility of non-approval. Some legislatures have no powers at all to amend the budget, which means that they may only accept or reject the executive's proposal in its entirety. I consider this particular scenario in the following section.

Unfettered powers imply that the executive budget proposal does not impose any kind of legally binding constraint on budgetary decisions by the legislature. In other words, there are in theory no numerical limits to the degree to which legislators can increase or cut the budget, or move funds around, during the approval process. The US president gained the power to co-ordinate the drafting of a budget and its submission to Congress with the 1921 Budget and Accounting Act (Webber and Wildavsky 1986: 411–16). However, the country's constitution ensures that the presidential proposal does not constitute a constraint on congressional action. Of course, legislators may face a number of *de facto* constraints in making budgetary decisions, both political and economic. For instance, markets may limit the ability of governments to borrow, international bodies may impose conditionalities or fiscal rules and the need to please powerful constituencies often limits taxing and spending choices. In legal terms, however, and in contrast with the arrangements discussed later, unfettered powers are most permissive.

Also relatively permissive are deficit-based restrictions on parliamentary changes. I use the term 'deficit constraint' when legislative amendments may not increase the deficit. In such cases, any spending increases have to be compensated by spending cuts elsewhere, revenue increases, or a mix of these two options. Article 220(1) of the Polish Constitution is an example of such a limit: 'The increase in spending or the reduction in revenues from those planned by the Council of Ministers may not lead to the adoption by the *Sejm* [the lower house of the national legislature] of a budget deficit exceeding the level provided in the draft Budget.' The analysis in this chapter will show that this type of limit may not always impose a hard budget constraint.

The term 'total spending constraint' describes rules that allow legislatures to make amendments as long as these do not lead to an increase in total expenditure, so that an increase of any item has to be compensated by commensurate reductions elsewhere in the appropriations, but not with revenue increases. In some countries, such types of changes are referred to as 'offset amendments'.[5] Article 134(6) of the Spanish Constitution provides an example: 'Every proposition or amendment which involves an increase in credits or a decrease in budget revenues shall require the agreement of the Government before its transmission.' In effect, the government can veto any amendment proposal that would increase expenditures (or decrease revenues). This superficially seems very similar to the 'deficit constraint' discussed earlier, but the analysis later will show that there can be a difference between these two types of constraints in terms of their fiscal policy impact.

At the restrictive end of legal provisions governing parliamentary changes to the budget, 'cuts only' constraints only allow a legislature to reduce individual items proposed by the executive, but not to increase them or to introduce any new items. In early eighteenth-century Britain, unexpected revenue surplus tempted private members (backbenchers) to secure a share of these funds for spending in their constituencies (Einzig 1959: 130–1). The Commons proceeded to resolve in 1706 'That this House will receive no Petition for any sum of Money relating to public Service, but what is recommended from the Crown' (quoted from Reid 1966: 36). The so-called financial initiative of the Crown has been enshrined in the standing orders since 1713. This limitation on the power of the purse is now an essential constitutional principle (May 1997: 770) that has been exported to many of the country's former colonies.[6] Paradoxically, while the British Parliament was at the forefront of claiming budgetary rights, it was also the first parliament to voluntarily cede the right to financial initiative (Inter-Parliamentary Union 1986: 1093):

> Parliament still respects this long-standing custom and practice and, as a result, it may not vote sums in excess of the Government's estimates. Consequently, the only amendments that are in order are those which aim to reduce the sums requested and have as their purpose the chance for Members to raise explanations before the sums in question are approved.

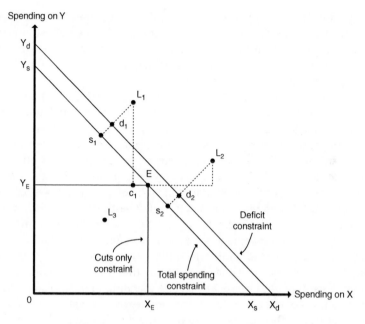

Figure 2.1 Amendment powers

Figure 2.1 explores the effects of these different types of amendment powers. The point labelled E identifies a hypothetical ideal budget of the executive and L_1 a hypothetical ideal budget of the legislature. In this case, the legislature wants somewhat less spending on item X than the executive, but substantially more on item Y, implying higher total spending. If the executive tables budget E, unfettered powers allow a legislature to move to any other combination, so it will choose its ideal spending package L_1. In contrast, with the power to cut, proposal E imposes a cap on each individual item so that the legislature's feasible set is the area $0Y_EEX_E$. If the legislature's preferred package is L_1, the closest feasible budget is now c_1.

In systems where the legislature can redistribute between items but not increase aggregate spending, the total amount proposed by the executive imposes an overall constraint, which is represented by the budget line with a slope of –1 that passes through E.[7] With such a constraint, the legislature can amend spending to any combination that is on the line or below it, but it cannot choose combinations beyond the line. The feasible set with a total spending constraint is the triangle $0Y_sX_s$, formed by the budget line and the two axes of the diagram. With a preferred spending package of L_1, the closest feasible budget with this type of constraint is s_1.

The impact of a deficit constraint on legislative amendments depends on how easy it is to cover spending increases with additional revenues. If legislators can easily augment revenues, for instance by making more optimistic economic assumptions, then the constraint imposed by a deficit limit is soft. There is some anecdotal evidence of legislators using 'spurious sources of revenue' in order to justify additional spending (Filc and Scartascini 2007: 168). For example, Tollini (2009: 12–15) describes the practice of 're-estimating' revenues in the Brazilian Congress, which legislators use to circumvent constitutional limitations on amendments (see also Blöndal et al. 2003: 118). On the other hand, if additional outlays would require tax changes with non-fictitious revenue implications then the deficit constraint may resemble that imposed by a total spending limit. In Figure 2.1, the softness of the deficit limit is represented by the gap between the budget lines imposed, respectively, by the total spending and deficit constraints. The larger this gap $(X_d - X_s \equiv Y_d - Y_s)$ the easier it is to 'discover' additional revenues, and hence the softer the spending constraint imposed by a deficit limit on legislative amendments. Put differently, with a soft deficit constraint, the budget line can be pushed further out, resulting in an expanded feasible set such as the one depicted by the triangle $0Y_dX_d$ with an associated budget d_1 that implies higher total spending than s_1. It is an empirical question whether deficit constraints are soft in practice, and to what extent, which I tackle in Chapter 5.[8]

The analysis with this combination of preferences yields several predictions: first, any of these limits on legislative amendments restricts total spending (L_1 implies higher total spending than c_1, s_1 and d_1). Second, expenditure constraints are associated with lower total spending than a deficit constraint as long as the latter is not completely hard so that revenues, and hence maximum total expenditure, are in effect fixed (d_1 implies higher total spending than c_1 and s_1). Third, 'cuts only' amendment powers lead to lower spending than an amendment rule that prohibits an aggregate increase (s_1 implies higher total spending than c_1).

Assuming that the legislature prefers higher spending than the executive on *both* items, as with the hypothetical ideal budget L_2, the first two predictions still hold (Figure 2.1 shows that L_2 implies higher total spending than c_2, s_2 and d_2 and d_2 implies higher total spending than c_2 and s_2, where $c_2 = E$). However, the third prediction no longer holds ('cuts only' powers result in outcome E, which implies the same amount of total expenditure as outcome s_2 with an aggregate spending constraint). Note that non-circular indifference curves may result in different predicted combinations of spending items, but the legislature would still have to comply with any amendment constraint as depicted.

Whether an amendment constraint bites depends on the relative preferences of the legislature and the executive. For instance, a fiscally conservative legislature with an ideal budget such as L_3 could approve exactly this budget no matter whether it has unfettered powers or is subject to any of the restrictions discussed so far. However, common pool resource theory suggests that a legislature has an in-built tendency to be relatively more profligate than the executive. This is because the pro-spending bias is an increasing function of the number of decision makers (Weingast et al. 1981; Von Hagen and Harden 1995). In practice, legislatures always have more members than there are spending ministers in the cabinet, and they also typically contain more parties than the executive. In short, even if the ideal budget of the legislature is less profligate than the executive's in some years, this is unlikely to be the case all of the time. Amendment limits should have a substantive long-run effect on fiscal policy.

In practice, there may be other considerations that limit the extent to which the legislature can amend the budget proposal. Most governments are to some degree constrained in their flexibility to vary the budget year on year. Public sector employment contracts and loan agreements typically impose long-term obligations on government, such as civil service pensions and debt servicing costs, and other factors such as demographic changes affect the rigidity of the budget (Heller 2003). In addition, there may also be powerful political considerations that protect parts of the budget from adjustment, for instance when the government has to ensure support from trade unions or other pressure groups by maintaining spending on certain programmes. As a result, a substantial proportion of spending may in practice be beyond the scope of the annual budget process and may be considered fixed in the short run. However, even if part of the executive budget proposal is predetermined due to such factors, it is still true that the feasible set is largest under unfettered powers, and is consecutively reduced by deficit, total spending and cuts only amendment constraints. As long as budgets are not completely predetermined by factors beyond the annual approval process, budget rigidity does not fundamentally challenge the analysis.

So far, this analysis assumes sincere voting. However, it is possible that actors anticipate the reactions of one another and behave strategically. This implies potential for compromise. I explore this possibility in Figure 2.2 for a legislature with a 'total spending' limit. As in the preceding analysis, proposal E would result in outcome s. The figure includes the indifference curve for the legislature in relation to s, represented by the circle centred on L and

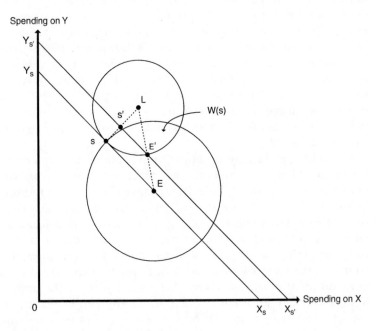

Figure 2.2 Amendments and strategic interaction

with radius Ls, which can be written as (L, Ls). The diagram also contains the equivalent indifference curve of the executive (E, Es). Both would benefit from moving to a point inside the winset of s, or $W(s)$, defined as the intersection of the two indifference curves, which contains all points that both the legislature and the executive prefer to s. More specifically, they would benefit from moving to a point in the winset and on the contract curve between E and L, which contains all Pareto-efficient outcomes. If the executive were to offer a budget such as E', just inside the winset and on the contract curve, both actors would be better off than with outcome s.

The illustration has general implications: first, executive agenda setting power is an increasing function of the radius of the legislature's indifference curve in relation to the relevant budget outcome with sincere voting, in this case Ls. Second, when a legislature is relatively profligate vis-à-vis the executive, any move along the contract curve away from E and towards L implies an increase in total expenditures – and vice versa. However, there is no guarantee that any compromise agreements can be sustained. Figure 2.2 shows that a possible problem with offer E' is that the legislature has a second-stage incentive to use its amendment powers to approve budget s', which it prefers to E'. This, however, leaves the executive worse off than with outcome s. The executive would be unwise to negotiate a compromise unless it can ensure that legislators are not going to renege and approve amendments following the tabling of the draft budget.

The main conclusion from this section is that amendment powers impact on the shape of a legislature's feasible set of budgetary choices. Restricted amendment powers limit the potential for legislative choice, since the budget proposal in effect fixes either a total expenditure ceiling, which can be more or less binding, or a ceiling on each item contained in the budget. In terms of fiscal performance, the analysis demonstrates that limited amendment powers contain public spending in a wide range of plausible scenarios.[9] Only a few procedures do not fit any of the four categories of amendment powers discussed earlier. Notably, some parliaments can only accept or reject spending proposals tabled by the executive. In this setting, the reversionary budget is of particular importance, which I discuss in the following section.

2.2   Reversionary budgets

The reversionary outcome takes effect when a previous budget has expired but a new one has not yet been approved. In most countries, there are provisions governing this circumstance in either the constitution or the organic budget law, although there are a few exceptions. Norway provides one example where there are no clear formal rules describing the consequences when approval is delayed beyond the beginning of the relevant fiscal year (OECD and World Bank 2003). However, such legal uncertainty about reversionary budgets is unusual (Lienert and Jung 2004; Dorotinsky 2008). Although there are variations and idiosyncrasies, it is possible to distinguish three broad groups of reversion scenarios across countries: zero spending, last year's approved budget or the executive budget proposal.

In some countries, spending reverts to zero when legislative approval of the appropriations is delayed beyond the start of the fiscal year. In the US, constitutional provisions prescribe that 'No money shall be drawn from the treasury, but in consequence of appropriations made by law' (article I, section 9, clause 7). This requirement can have powerful consequences. In late 1995 and early 1996, parts of the federal government shut down, as President Clinton and a Republican-controlled Congress failed to agree on spending cuts (Williams and Jubb 1996). This was one of the most dramatic budgetary crises in recent American history, but delayed appropriations are not exceptional (Meyers 1997). Over the fiscal years 1977–2000, Keith (2000: 4) documents 17 so-called funding gaps – the interval during a fiscal year when appropriations are not enacted into law, which triggers a shutdown of the affected agencies.

Some constitutions limit the severity of the consequences of non-approval by allowing reversion to the previously approved budget. For instance, when the annual budget has not yet been enacted at the beginning of the fiscal year, Germany's Basic Law allows the federal government to 'make all expenditures that are necessary: (a) to maintain institutions established by a law and to carry out measures authorised by a law; (b) to meet the legal obligations of the Federation; (c) to continue construction projects, procurements and the provision of other benefits or services, or to continue to make grants for these purposes, to the extent that amounts have already been appropriated in the budget of a previous year' (article 111(1)). These arrangements avoid the drama and large-scale disruption of government shutdowns. Still, reversion to last year's budget is inconvenient for the government of the day, as it can delay the implementation of new policy initiatives and investment projects.

Finally, some constitutional arrangements completely eliminate the possibility of any adverse impact of non-approval on the government by sanctioning the implementation of the executive proposal. For instance, the French Constitution states that 'Should Parliament fail to reach a decision within seventy days, the provisions of the [Finance] Bill may be brought into force by Ordinance' (article 47(3)). A somewhat less drastic version of reversion to the executive proposal allows the implementation of the draft budget for an interim period only, as provided in the Finnish Constitution (article 83). Such arrangements substantially reduce or eliminate the sting of non-approval by the legislature.

It is useful to start the analysis in the context of a legislature without any powers to amend the executive budget proposal. In this case the threat of non-approval would be the only mechanism with which legislators could attempt to extract concessions during the formulation of the budget. A legislature without any powers of amendment has two budgets to choose from: the reversionary budget or the executive proposal. If the reversionary budget is equal to the executive budget proposal, it would have no choice at all, and its action would be irrelevant for the outcome. In short, these conditions reduce the feasible set to a maximum of two points. If a legislature does have powers of amendment, then the outcome of non-approval is only attractive if it is more favourable than the outcome that can be achieved by amending the budget. Hence, for legislatures with amendment authority, the following analysis can also be used to complement and extend the discussion in the previous section.

Instead of tabling its ideal budget, the reversionary budget may induce the executive to make concessions. Strategic behaviour by the executive can avert the rejection or non-approval of its budget proposal and lead to a more favourable outcome from its perspective. In the absence of legislative amendment powers, the executive and the legislature are playing a veto game (Tsebelis 2002; Crombez et al. 2006). The executive has to move first and propose a budget, which the legislature can either accept or reject. If the executive proposal is rejected, the reversionary outcome takes effect. The executive has agenda setting power and makes the proposal at the closest point to its ideal budget that will receive legislative approval (Niskanen 1971; Romer and Rosenthal 1978). I assume that when the legislature prefers the proposal to the reversionary outcome, or when it is indifferent between the two, it will approve the proposed budget.[10]

Figure 2.3 depicts two hypothetical legislative ideal points, L_1 (profligate) and L_2 (fiscally conservative). It also contains a line representing all points that are equidistant to the executive's ideal budget E and a reversionary budget R. The point L_1 is closer to E than to R, as are all other legislative ideal points to the right of the dashed line, which implies that the executive will propose its ideal budget. On the other hand, L_2 to the left of the dashed line is closer to R than to E, and hence induces the executive to propose budget E' to

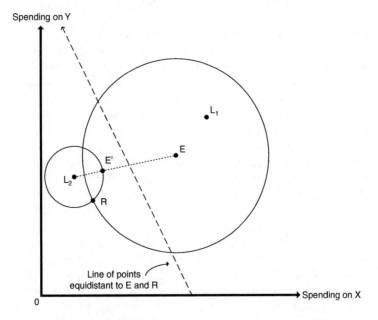

Figure 2.3   Reversionary budgets

avert reversion to the less favourable outcome *R*. More formally, with strategic interaction, the executive faces a minimisation problem in deciding which budget to table in the legislature. Its equilibrium offer *E** solves: minimise $|E - E'|$ subject to $|L - E'| \leq |L - R|$.

This illustration shows that the reversionary budget can affect the extent to which a legislature is able to extract concessions from the executive. The potential for concessions is a function of the distance between the reversionary budget *R* and the executive's ideal budget *E*, which is the radius of the indifference circle (*E, ER*). The closer these two points, the fewer the possible budgets that the executive prefers to reversionary spending. However, the legislature can only extract concessions if its ideal budget is closer to the reversionary budget than to the executive ideal budget, since the threat of non-approval is not credible otherwise.[11] The analysis also shows that the possibility of reversion to last year's budget or zero spending quite frequently may have no impact at all on the level of total spending, and in some scenarios it may even lead the executive to propose aggregate budgets that are smaller than it prefers. This finding contradicts the conjecture by Alesina et al. (1999: 258) that a 'weak' relative position of the government creates 'incentives to propose a larger budget, in order to ensure approval'. If the reversionary budget is south-west of the executive proposal, which is the most common scenario,[12] and the legislative ideal budget is north-east of it, which is likely when the common pool resource problem is endemic, legislators will always prefer the executive proposal to reversion. This variable is unlikely to have a systematic effect on public spending.

2.3   Executive flexibility during execution

Budget execution can afford the executive an opportunity to reshape the approved budget and to align it more closely with its preferred spending package. In other words, policy making may continue after the approval of the budget. National budget systems differ substantially in the degree to which they allow executive flexibility during the fiscal year (Hallerberg et al. 2001: 15–18). The applied literature promotes an increase in flexibility as a way to enhance operational efficiency (Blöndal 2003). At the same time, it cautions against undermining budget credibility through excessive in-year changes (Public Expenditure and Financial Accountability Secretariat 2005). As Alesina et al. (1999: 259) note, when the approved budget can be easily revised during its implementation, 'the entire budgetary process becomes less meaningful'. To date, few authors have explored the impact of execution rules from a legislative perspective (notably Pereira and Mueller 2004: 797). This section will demonstrate that execution rules have powerful implications for legislative choice. I analyse three principal ways in which budgets can be altered during execution: through transfers, cuts and increases.

Virement is the transfer or reallocation of approved funds between budgetary categories such as programmes. Some legislatures tightly control such changes. In the US, transfers between appropriation accounts require legislative approval, although Congress can grant transfer authority to specific agencies and has done so in 'rare cases' (Blöndal et al. 2003: 43). Elsewhere, appropriations are so highly aggregated that in-year shifts are effectively beyond parliamentary control. The Australian Parliament appropriates by outcome, that is, the intended impact of government activities. Theoretically, ministers cannot reallocate across different outcomes, only within the same outcome. However, outcomes are so vaguely defined that in practice ministers enjoy 'wide latitude' (Blöndal et al. 2008: 183).[13]

Figure 2.4 analyses the effect of unlimited virement authority, starting with sincere voting. If a legislature prefers a different amount of total spending than the executive, then unlimited virement authority allows the executive to shift allocations along the budget line so as to get the budget as close as possible to its preferred spending package within the total spending constraint set by the legislature, in this case resulting in v. If the executive and the legislature have the same ideal level of total spending, but disagree on composition, the executive would be able to use virement to implement its ideal budget. More generally, there is exactly one outcome for each level of total expenditure approved by the legislature. With sincere voting, any actual budget outcome would fall onto the line of virement-associated outcomes depicted in Figure 2.4. This line is made up of all spending combinations that are closest to the executive ideal budget E at any given level of total expenditure that the legislature approves.

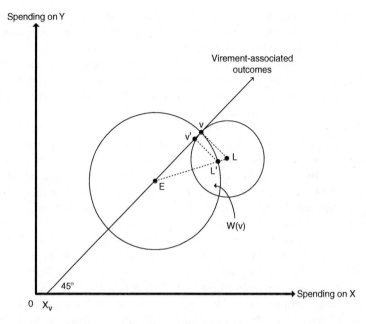

Figure 2.4   Executive flexibility and reallocation

The exact position of the line of virement-associated outcomes depends on the position of *E*. Note that this line does not go through the origin unless the executive desires exactly the same amount of expenditure on *X* as on *Y*. In the case of the ideal executive budget *E* as depicted in Figure 2.4, the executive prefers slightly more spending on *X* than on *Y*. Hence, the line runs from the origin to X_v and beyond that point has a slope of 1, passing through *E*. The significance of X_v is that at this point the slope of the line of virement-associated outcomes changes. If the legislature approved a total amount of spending that is less or equal to the amount X_v, an executive with the preferred spending package *E* would use unfettered virement authority to concentrate all spending on *X*. In sum, unfettered virement reduces a legislature's feasible set to the line of virement-associated outcomes, which contains exactly one feasible budget for each level of total expenditure. Also note that with sincere voting, virement affects the composition of public spending, but not its overall level.

Some budget systems attempt to strike a balance between legislative control and executive discretion through the imposition of numerical limits on reallocation during budget execution, for instance in New Zealand. Unlike its Australian counterpart, the New Zealand Parliament appropriates by output, that is, the goods or services supplied by the government. The 1989 Public Finance Act (section 26A(1)) allows the executive to reallocate up to five per cent of an amount of an 'output expense appropriation' to another such appropriation within the same departmental budget. Moreover, a clause that confirms such a transfer must be included in an appropriation bill. With restricted authority to realign spending, a rational executive will shift the budget as far as the numerical limit allows towards, and if possible onto, the line of virement-associated outcomes depicted in Figure 2.4.

Figure 2.4 also explores how outcomes are affected by strategic interaction. Both actors would be better off by agreeing on a point on the contract curve and inside $W(v)$. However, if the legislature offers L', the executive has a second-stage incentive to choose v'. The latter would leave the legislature worse off than outcome v. As discussed in relation to Figure 2.2, cooperation may not be sustainable. In addition, Figure 2.4 shows that strategic interaction also affects the total level of spending that results from virement. The executive is able to move the budget along the contract curve towards its ideal budget. In the case of a relatively profligate legislature, as in Figure 2.4, this implies lower public spending than with sincere voting. The converse holds for cases where the executive is relatively profligate.

Figure 2.5 explores two further implementation rules, which allow the executive to alter the size of the budget during execution. First, when the executive impounds funds it refuses to spend all or part of an appropriated amount, thereby reducing the size of the budget. This can take the form of deferrals (delays) and rescissions (permanent cancellations). Impoundment not only affects the total size of the budget, it also adjusts relative priorities unless all items are cut by the same percentage. Powers to impound are often a highly contentious device in budgetary politics. In the US in the early 1970s, President Nixon refused to spend large sums of congressional appropriations and claimed 'an inherent power to impound' (Schick 2000: 251). This prompted Congress to severely

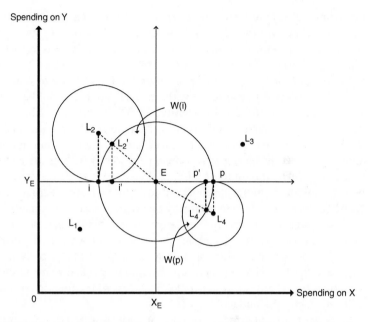

Figure 2.5 Executive flexibility and the size of the budget

limit impoundment authority by passing the Impoundment Control Act with the 1974 Congressional Budget Act. It required congressional approval for rescissions and allowed deferrals unless rejected by Congress.

While the US Congress tightly controls impoundments, executive authority to withhold funds during the execution of the budget is not uncommon. A recent study shows that most European Union member states allow the executive to carry over spending into the following fiscal year (Hallerberg et al. 2001: 15). End-of-year flexibility or carry-over, which is often promoted to achieve greater operational efficiency (Blöndal 2003: 24–5), is similar to impoundment in the form of deferral. Other countries impose cash availability limits on actual expenditures that give the executive substantial control over the disbursement of funds during the fiscal year, which permits rescission. In the UK, for instance, an appropriation act 'does not, by itself, authorise spending by individual departments' (Lienert and Jung 2004: 430). Rather, the Treasury has discretion over the actual release of funds. The budget systems in many of Britain's former colonies are similar in this respect (Stasavage and Moyo 2000; Lienert 2003).

Figure 2.5 illustrates the effect of unlimited impoundment power. A fiscally conservative legislature with an ideal budget L_1 would get its ideal budget, since there is no incentive for the executive to achieve a budget outcome that is even further from its preferred spending level. If a legislature's preferred spending package is L_2, then impoundment allows the executive to align spending on Y perfectly with its preferred spending level by impounding all funds in excess of Y_E. The executive will not impound funds appropriated for X because the legislature's spending level on this item is already below the executive's preferred level X_E. The resulting spending package i represents the best possible budget a legislature can get under these circumstances. If the ideal legislative budget is L_3, where spending on both X and Y exceeds the executive's preferred level, then impoundment will allow the executive to withhold any spending that is in excess of its preferred levels and get exactly the budget it wants.

More generally, Figure 2.5 shows that with unfettered impoundment authority the executive will cut any spending that falls outside the area $0Y_EEX_E$. Only legislative choices within this rectangle are protected from impoundment, as the executive would not cut spending even further below its preferred levels. Hence, a legislature's feasible set with unfettered impoundment authority contains all budgets to the south-west of E. Put differently, unlimited impoundment powers are 'cuts only' amendment powers in reverse. This time, it is the executive that has the power to cut and not the legislature, as in Figure 2.1, but the overall effect on legislative choice is identical. When impoundment powers are limited by some constraint, the executive will only be able to move the budget outcome some percentage towards the outcome it would have chosen without any constraint on impoundment.

In contrast to impoundment, what I call 'decree powers' allow the executive to augment the size of the budget during execution. With this term, I refer to a situation where the executive has the power to unilaterally disburse funds for expenditure over and above the amount authorised by the legislature. I borrow this term from the literature on presidential systems, where some chief executives can use decrees to authorise expenditures (Carey and Shugart 1998).[14] In many OECD countries, executive powers to increase spending are limited. However, even here there are sources of executive discretion that allow the augmentation of the approved amounts. In the UK, for instance, the 1974 Contingencies Fund Act allows temporary and urgent expenditures that have not yet been voted, up to two per cent of the budget of the previous year (section 1(1)). The use of a contingency fund dates back to the nineteenth century (Lienert and Jung 2004: 431) and a number of OECD countries have similar mechanisms for emergency expenditures. In Greece, Law No. 2362/1995 requires the submission of a 'supplementary or corrective budget' when actual revenues or expenditures deviate 'significantly' from those in the approved budget. However, an OECD study found that supplementary budgets are not submitted due to the permissive interpretation of these provisions by the executive (Hawkesworth et al. 2008: 25): 'There are often large deviations between the approved budget and actual expenditures, and overspending is not uncommon.'

Figure 2.5 also demonstrates the effect of unlimited decree powers. If a legislature's approved budget is to the south-west of the executive's preferred spending package E, such as L_1, so that a legislature's budget is lower on both items compared with the executive proposal, then the executive can use decree powers to top up spending on each item to exactly its preferred level. If only one spending item is below the executive's preferred level, as with L_4 for example, only this item will be topped up to the preferred level, resulting in outcome p. On the other hand, any approved budgets to the north-east of E, such as L_3, will be completely unaffected, as there is no reason why the executive should push the outcome even further away from its preferred budget. In short, with unlimited decree power all feasible budgets are to the north-east of the executive's spending proposal. With constrained decree powers, the executive will only be able to move the budget outcome some percentage towards the outcome it would have chosen with unfettered power to decree expenditures.

Figure 2.5 also explores the impact of strategic interaction on the outcomes associated with impoundment and decree powers. The relevant outcome is depicted as L_2' in the case of impoundment and L_4' in the case of decree powers. However, there is again a second-stage incentive for the executive to move away from the compromise proposal, which would result in i' and p' respectively, so co-operation may be difficult to sustain. In addition, note that the effect of strategic interaction on overall spending depends on the relative preferences of the executive and the legislature. In the case of impoundment, the example shows that strategic interaction can result in spending that is *higher* than would be the case without impoundment authority. This is the case when the executive is fiscally profligate vis-à-vis the legislature: in that case, a move along the contract curve towards E invariably means adding more spending on one dimension than is eliminated on the other dimension – and vice versa. In terms of decree powers, there is a similar finding. In the case depicted in Figure 2.5, the legislature is profligate relative to the executive, in which case the outcome with strategic interaction is *lower* than without executive decree powers. Paradoxically, there are constellations where executive power to increase spending *reduces* budgets, and the power to cut budgets *increases* them.

This analysis demonstrates the powerful effects of budget execution rules on legislative choice. Executive flexibility during implementation can be used to realign budget priorities away from those approved by the legislature (virement), or to reduce (impoundment) or augment (decree powers) the size of the approved budget. The use of impoundment and decree powers also is likely to alter relative priorities in the approved budget. Even with restricted executive flexibility, such powers reduce a legislature's feasible set of budgets. In other words, virement, impoundment and decree authority limit parliamentary control. In terms of fiscal performance, however, the effects of these arrangements are not straightforward. These predictions depend crucially on the relative positions of the ideal points of the legislature and the executive and on whether co-operation occurs. A correlation between these arrangements and overall levels of expenditure is unlikely.

This analysis could be extended by considering the implications of executive flexibility for legislative actions during the approval stage of the budget process (Pereira and Mueller 2004; Hallerberg, Scartascini and Stein 2009: 301–7). For instance, if legislators know that the executive can impound funds at a later stage, how does this affect their amendment decisions? One challenge for follow-up research is to develop a systematic analysis of these scenarios.

2.4 Legislative organisation and the use of formal powers

Extensive formal powers alone are unlikely to be sufficient to ensure legislative influence in the budget process. In particular, up to now the discussion has paid no attention to transaction costs in legislative decision making, which is unrealistic. A growing body of literature investigates the implications of transaction costs in political decisions (Horn 1995; Epstein and O'Halloran 1999; Huber and Shipan 2002). In a groundbreaking contribution, Horn (1995: 13–22) identifies several sources of transaction costs, including the time and effort necessary to reach legislative agreement, and the fact that agency problems make it costly for legislators to ensure executive compliance. In a budgetary context, decision-making costs may prevent legislators from fully exploiting their formal powers to shape the budget, and agency costs result in a gap between the approved and actual figures. However, formal powers can be complemented with organisational features that accommodate or reduce legislative transaction costs.

Sufficient time is an essential requirement for legislative decision making (Döring 1995b; OECD 2002a). Legislators need time to acquire information and to co-ordinate their budgetary actions. However, some budget processes do not fully accommodate these decision-making costs. For instance, some systems subject budgetary debates to 'guillotine' procedures that enforce the closure of parliamentary deliberation after a limited time period. This procedure helps governments to ensure the timely supply of funds but at the same time curtails parliamentary capacity to debate estimates in detail (Reid 1966: 70). During the budget approval stage the timing of the process has to allow legislators to scrutinise the government's proposal, formulate responses and to cut deals with their colleagues, otherwise the ability of the legislature to process amendments to the budget may be restricted.

Several international standards recognise the importance of time as an enabling factor for legislative scrutiny. The OECD Best Practices for Budget Transparency recommend that the budget should be tabled at least three months in advance of the fiscal year to enable meaningful legislative scrutiny (OECD 2002a: 8). The Public Financial Management Performance Measurement Framework, developed by various international bodies and bilateral aid agencies to assess budget systems in poor countries, is slightly less demanding. It gives countries a high score if the budget is tabled at least two months prior to the beginning of the fiscal year (Public Expenditure and Financial Accountability Secretariat 2005: PI–27). The Code of Good Practices on Fiscal Transparency of the International Monetary Fund (IMF) also demands 'adequate time' for the legislative review of the draft budget (IMF 2007a: 2.1.1) and the accompanying technical manual references the OECD's benchmark of three months (IMF 2007b: 47). There is strong consensus that time matters for budget scrutiny.

Committee structures play a crucial role in ensuring that legislatures have access to relevant expertise and time in order to extract, interpret and process information.[15] Notably, committees boost legislative productivity by enabling a division of labour (Mezey 1979). This can partly compensate for time constraints in the budget process. The efficiency gain in legislative throughput that a committee system can achieve is particularly important since the budget competes for time with regular legislation. In other words, division of labour through committees contains the opportunity cost of budget scrutiny in terms of other legislative measures. Second, committees allow the collective legislative body to reap information gains as a result of specialisation, reducing the cost of information acquisition (Krehbiel 1991). Powerful legislatures such as the US Congress take great care to despatch members to those committees where they act as conduits of information (Krehbiel 1990).

Committee expertise is not only crucial for scrutinising policy *ex ante*, but also to keep an eye on its execution (McCubbins and Schwartz 1984). Legislative approval only matters when budgets are actually executed as intended. Otherwise, budgetary drift allows the government to get what it wants irrespective of what the legislature has approved. Bawn (1997) finds that the costs of oversight of an agency are lower for members of a specialised committee with jurisdiction over that agency compared with non-members. Committees with a dedicated monitoring function, in particular those with a function to scrutinise audit findings, can also help to detect implementation failures and improve compliance (McGee 2002; Wehner 2003). Hence, legislatures with a well-developed committee infrastructure should be better able to contain agency loss. In sum, there is strong evidence that a well-developed committee system is 'at least a necessary condition for effective parliamentary influence in the policy-making process' (Mattson and Strøm 1995: 250; see also Longley and Davidson 1998).

When the quality of budget documentation is poor, it is difficult to ascertain the government's fiscal intentions and to exercise oversight (Von Hagen 1992: 35). To some extent a legislature can shift the cost of acquiring relevant information to the executive by requiring in statute the provision of information that meets international standards for fiscal transparency (IMF 1998, 2001, 2007a; OECD 2002a). The required information includes, among others, a comprehensive annual budget covering all operations of the government, medium-term estimates, regular expenditure updates during the financial year as well as a comprehensive and timely year-end report that is independently audited (Kopits and Craig 1998; Heald 2003). The IMF formally monitors fiscal transparency as part of its Reports on the Observance of Standards and Codes, an initiative launched in 1999 to promote the stability of the international financial architecture. This is not the only effort to enhance budget transparency. The International Budget Partnership, a non-profit organisation, has developed the Open Budget Index to strengthen accountability for the use of public resources (International Budget Partnership 2009). Legislatures are important potential beneficiaries of this campaign for greater budget transparency.

Transaction costs act as a barrier to the utilisation of the formal powers of a legislature. However, institutional arrangements can lower or accommodate transaction costs, in particular a generously timed budget process, a well-designed committee system and full access to relevant information.

2.5 Conclusions

Amendment powers, reversionary provisions and executive flexibility during implementation affect the size of a legislature's feasible set of budgetary choices. However, arrangements that constrain legislative choice may not always contain overall public spending. The theoretical case is strongest with regard to restrictions on amendment powers, which safeguard fiscal discipline in a large number of plausible scenarios. These predictions are tested empirically in Chapter 5. In addition, this chapter also highlights how time, committee expertise and information facilitate legislative utilisation of formal authority by reducing transaction costs.

It is possible to extend this analysis to particular combinations of rules and organisational features and to incorporate a wider range of budgetary actors, as propagated by Scartascini and Stein (2009: 5). This extension is certainly desirable, but the analysis of interactions between a large number of institutional features and political actors is complex. Such an approach is perhaps best pursued through in-depth country-level analyses of budget systems (see Pereira and Mueller 2004). The following three chapters are dedicated to cross-national analysis, but I return to this point in Chapter 6 of the book, where I analyse packages of institutional features in two countries that have carried out wide-ranging reforms of the legislative budget process. First, however, the challenge is to operationalise the variables discussed in this chapter.

3
Assessing the Power of the Purse

> *This power over the purse may, in fact, be regarded as the most complete and effectual weapon with which any constitution can arm the immediate representatives of the people, for obtaining a redress of every grievance, and for carrying into effect every just and salutary measure.*
>
> Publius, Federalist 58

The requirement for legislative approval of financial measures is a democratic foundation stone that is enshrined in constitutions around the world. Despite this widespread formal recognition, the actual budgetary role of national legislatures apparently differs sharply across countries. Members of the US Congress 'have long seen themselves as the bulwark against [executive] oppression' and their 'major weapon' is the constitutional requirement for congressional approval of appropriations (Wildavsky and Caiden 2001: 10). Scholars and practitioners agree that the US Congress is a powerful actor that can have decisive influence on budget policy (Wildavsky 1964; Schick 2000; Meyers 2001). On the other hand, the budgetary influence of legislatures is said to be marginal in several other industrialised countries including France and the UK (Chinaud 1993; Schick 2002). Existing comparative work on legislative budgeting contributes selected country studies (Coombes 1976; LeLoup 2004), but lacks systematic analysis on the basis of a common framework. Moreover, while the literature on the US Congress is extensive, legislative budgeting in parliamentary systems and developing countries in particular remains understudied

(Oppenheimer 1983). As a basis for more systematic comparative work, this chapter proposes and applies an index of legislative budget institutions that can be used to assess and compare the budgetary power of national legislatures.

A number of authors refer to the cross-national distribution of legislative power over the purse (Coombes 1976; Meyers 2001; Schick 2002), but few have constructed quantitative measures. Although some previous studies present indices of budget institutions, these pay only limited attention to legislative variables. Fiscal institutionalists are concerned with explaining fiscal performance, typically public debt and deficits, with the design of the budget process (see the review by Kirchgässner 2001). Most of this literature does not exclusively focus on the role of the legislature, but a broader selection of variables that are said to promote fiscal discipline in budgetary decision making. Von Hagen's (1992: 70) pioneering index includes one composite item on the structure of the parliamentary process that considers notably the amendment powers of a legislature. Alesina et al. (1996, 1999) construct an index of budgetary procedures with two out of ten variables as indicators of the relative position of the government vis-à-vis the legislature, namely amendment powers and the nature of the reversionary budget (see also Hallerberg and Marier 2004). Other studies focus exclusively on the fiscal effect of specific legislative institutions (e.g. Crain and Muris 1995; Heller 1997, 2001). Finally, from a legislative studies perspective, Fish (2006: 8) presents a parliamentary powers index, but only two out of 32 items relate explicitly to budgetary matters: one item on impoundment and another on control of resources for the operation of the legislature itself.[1] These contributions are important but of limited use for the purpose of comparing legislative capacity in budgeting.

Lienert (2005) offers a broader consideration of legislative budget institutions. His index of legislative budget powers, which is largely based on a draft version of the index presented in this chapter, covers five variables: parliament's role in approving medium-term expenditure parameters, amendment powers, time available for the approval of the budget, technical support to the legislature and restrictions on executive flexibility during budget execution. This work provides a step towards a more comprehensive comparative analysis of legislative budgeting, but it also raises some methodological issues. For example, there is hardly any variation on the first variable, the legislature's role in approving medium-term spending plans. Only one out of 28 legislatures in the sample formally passes a law on the medium-term strategy (Lienert 2005: 22). This lack of variation calls into question the usefulness of this item as a comparative indicator. In addition, the differential weighting of variables is not explicitly motivated. In short, what is missing so far is a broader measure of legislative budget institutions that is based on a thorough discussion of relevant indicators and methodological issues.

This chapter outlines a comparative framework to assess legislative budget capacity that can be applied, potentially, to any national legislature in a modern democracy. Based on the analysis in the preceding chapter, I suggest a series of variables that I combine into an index to measure cross-country variation in legislative budgeting and deliver an empirical application based on survey work by the OECD and the World Bank. A crucial assumption is that institutional arrangements reflect the budgetary power of a legislature. 'Control' is here defined as the power to scrutinise and influence budget policy and to ensure its implementation. As Wildavsky and Caiden (2001: 18) remind us: 'Who has power over the budget does not tell us whether or not the budget is under control.' The controversial question of whether legislative power over the budget is fiscally desirable is explicitly excluded from this chapter. I return to this question in Chapters 5 and 6, where I consider in some depth the fiscal effects of legislative budget institutions. The cross-national assessment in this chapter directly engages with the claim that a strong legislature, including in budgetary terms, is a necessary condition for democracy (Fish 2006).

I proceed as follows. The first section explains the selection of the variables included in the index and gives an overview of the data used. The second section discusses issues related to index construction and selects the most suitable method. I conduct a number of experiments to check the robustness of the index. The third section presents an overview of the results in the form of a ranking of legislatures. I use two approaches to validate the index. The first is to compare the resulting ranking with findings from case study literature and the second is to test the association of the index with an indicator of legislative amendment activity. The conclusion summarises the main results and highlights implications.

3.1 Variables and data

The construction of an index for the purpose of cross-national comparison requires the identification of essential differences. Invariably, some of the richness of qualitative analysis has to be forfeited to gain a tractable tool for comparative research, which is necessary to venture beyond particular cases in order to discover broader patterns. No single variable can be considered sufficient on its own and I make no claim to cover every potentially relevant variable. Following the analysis in the previous chapter, I adopt an approach based on assessing the *institutional capacity* for legislative control (Meyers 2001: 7). I argue that a critical number of institutional prerequisites, including formal authority and organisational characteristics, are necessary to facilitate budgetary control.

The data used here are principally from the 2003 Survey on Budget Practices and Procedures, which the OECD conducted in collaboration with the World Bank. The respondents were specially identified budget officials in each participating country. This survey provides data on legislatures in 27 out of 30 OECD members. The missing countries are Luxembourg, Poland and Switzerland. To complete the dataset, I added comparable data for these three countries from an update of the survey (OECD 2007), which I checked against additional sources (e.g. Staskiewicz 2002; Kraan and Ruffner 2005) to ensure that the relevant institutional features had not undergone major reforms since 2003. I double-checked all of the data as extensively as possible against information from online sources, such as finance ministry and parliamentary websites, as well as previous survey results (OECD 2002b) and country-specific sources. Where necessary, I sought clarification from country experts who are identified in the acknowledgements. In the following paragraphs, I discuss the specific data used for the construction of the index. The full dataset is reproduced in Table 3.3 at the end of this chapter and Table 3.4 details the construction of two composite variables.

Following Alesina et al. (1999: 257–8), all variables are coded on a range between zero (the least favourable from a legislative perspective) and ten (the most favourable). The maximum figure is divided equally between the categories. In the next section, I conduct some robustness checks to see whether this coding procedure significantly affects the ranking of legislatures compared with alternative methods.

The data appendix provides full details of the survey questions used to assign scores for each of the variables. Below, I indicate the score for each response option in square brackets. In a few cases where the arrangements cannot be neatly classified, I assigned the most accurate score (see Wehner 2006 for further details).

Amendment powers. As illustrated in Figure 2.1, the nature of formal powers to amend the budget determines the potential for legislative changes to the budget proposed by the executive. The survey asked respondents to indicate whether legislative powers of amendment are restricted, and if so, which form of restriction applies. I code the answers in accordance with the five categories of amendment powers analysed in the previous chapter, that is, the legislature may only accept or reject the budget as tabled [0], it may cut existing items only or has otherwise significantly contained amendment authority [2.5], it may shift funds as long as this does not increase aggregate spending [5] or the deficit [7.5] or it has unfettered powers [10]. Table 3.3 shows that 17 OECD countries have legislatures with unfettered amendment powers, whereas 13 impose various restrictions.

Notwithstanding a legislature's formal powers of amendment, in some parliamentary systems any change to the executive's draft budget is by convention considered a vote of no confidence in the government (e.g. Blöndal 2001a: 53). In effect, this confidence convention reduces legislative authority to a stark choice between accepting the budget unchanged or forcing the resignation of the government followed by fresh elections. On grounds of parsimony, I do not separately consider this variable. The confidence convention is most common in Westminster type systems, that is, Australia, Canada, New Zealand and the UK that, in any case, substantially restrict legislative powers to amend the budget (OECD 2002b: 159). As amendment powers are already included in the analysis, this suffices to signal legislative amendment restrictions.

Reversionary budgets. Under certain conditions explored in Figure 2.3, the legislature may be able to extract concessions by threatening not to approve the budget. The distance between the reversionary budget and the executive budget proposal affects the number of possible budgets that the executive prefers to reversionary spending. In the extreme case of reversion to zero spending, the executive is likely to prefer a compromise to the possibility of no supply and government shutdown. Conversely, when the executive budget proposal takes effect, the executive has no incentive to avert non-approval. Reversion to last year's budget typically constitutes an intermediate case. The survey asked about the consequences should the budget not be approved at the start of the fiscal year. I group the responses into four categories: the executive budget or highly punitive consequences such as new elections [0], vote on account [3.3], last year's budget [6.7] or no spending [10].

The second category requires elaboration. Historically, the English Parliament devised the tactic of voting appropriations near the end of the session so as to force economies on the Crown and to extract concessions (Einzig 1959: 55; Schick 2002: 18).[2] This historical rationale is now obsolete, but delayed approval nonetheless remains the norm.[3] Formally, supply would cease without an approved budget in place. In practice, however, the parliaments of the OECD Commonwealth countries routinely approve interim spending, in accordance with a procedure that is referred to as a 'vote on account' in the UK.[4] Some might argue that this procedure preserves the threat of reversion to zero spending, but in my judgement this practice is so standardised and predictable that it would be misleading to assign a score of ten. Table 3.3 shows that in ten OECD countries spending reverts to zero in case of non-approval, nine revert to last year's budget and four have 'vote on account' procedures. Seven countries have mechanisms to revert to the executive proposal or impose highly punitive consequences that in practice force timely approval.

Executive flexibility during implementation. Chapter 2 demonstrated that executive authority to transfer funds between items (Figure 2.4) or to withhold funds and initiate fresh funding (Figure 2.5) provides significant leeway to unilaterally alter the approved budget. In effect, such powers constitute amendment authority in reverse, and in extreme cases allow the executive to undo legislative choices during implementation. I use three survey items to construct a composite measure of executive flexibility. The OECD asked (a) whether there is scope for appropriations to be reallocated from one programme to another without parliamentary approval,[5] (b) whether the executive may withhold funds that are appropriated, but not available on a legal or entitlement basis, without legislative consent and (c) whether the annual budget includes any central reserve funds to meet unforeseen expenditures.

To construct the composite variable, I assign each answer to the above questions a score of 3.3 if it is negative, as a positive answer implies executive flexibility to vire, impound and authorise fresh funds respectively. The sum of the scores for each case can range between zero and ten and constitutes my indicator of executive flexibility during budget execution. Table 3.4 provides full details of the results. On the basis of this measure, the Swiss Parliament exercises most control over the execution of the budget. In 18 countries, legislatures have some control over budget execution but allow executive discretion to varying degrees and in different forms. On the other extreme, 11 countries obtain the lowest possible score, including the Australian and Greek examples discussed in Chapter 2.

Time for scrutiny. International standards for budget transparency recognise the importance of sufficient time to enable parliamentary scrutiny (OECD 2002b; IMF 2007a). The timing of scrutiny partly depends on how effectively a legislature can control its own timetable and the legislative agenda, but it may also reflect constitutional prescriptions. To measure the timing of the tabling of the budget, the OECD asked: 'How far in advance of the beginning of the fiscal year does the executive present its budget to the legislature?' and provided four response options: up to two months [0], up to four months [3.3], up to six months [6.7] and more than six months [10]. The US Congress is a clear outlier in this regard. It receives the presidential budget proposal in February, about eight months prior to the start of the fiscal year in October. On the other hand, legislatures in eight OECD countries receive the budget less than two months ahead of the beginning of the fiscal year, including all Westminster type systems.

Committee capacity. Chapter 2 highlighted the benefits of committees in terms of expertise, productivity and oversight. The survey asked about their role in budget approval, but it did not explicitly cover the role of committees in the audit process. Hence, I collected additional data on the latter aspect in a separate survey of parliamentary websites. To measure committee capacity, I distinguish the involvement of three sets of specialised committees and give equal scores [3.3] to each category, that is, a budget or finance committee, sectoral or departmental committees and an *ex post* audit committee. For instance, if a parliament uses a finance committee and sectoral committees for budget approval, as well as an audit committee for *ex post* scrutiny of audit findings, it gets the highest possible score of ten, and without any committee involvement a score of zero. Involvement of sectoral committees gets a score of 3.3 only if they have actual authority over departmental budgets, but not if they are merely consulted or submit non-binding recommendations while a finance or budget committee retains full authority. Also, if a legislature uses an audit subcommittee of the budget committee for the purpose of parliamentary audit, I assign half the available score for this item [1.7].

Table 3.4 reports full details on each of the committee variables. Only four OECD legislatures do not substantively involve a budget or finance committee in the approval process, while eight involve sectoral committees. Britain stands out among OECD countries for its lack of committee expertise during the approval stage.[6] More than half of the legislatures have specialised audit committee capacity. This involves a specialised audit committee in 11 cases and audit subcommittees as part of the budget or finance committee in six cases.

Access to budgetary information. Finally, Chapter 2 emphasised the importance for legislative scrutiny of access to comprehensive, accurate and timely information. Unfortunately, it was not possible to use the 2003 survey results to construct a reliable measure of the quality of budgetary information supplied by the executive, although some authors have attempted to do so (Bastida and Benito 2007; Benito and Bastida 2009; see also Alt and Lassen 2006). The Open Budget Index is a potential alternative data source, but it covers less than half of the OECD countries (International Budget Partnership 2009). However, the results of the Open Budget Index suggest that the overall quality of budgetary information among OECD members tends to be high in comparison with many other countries.

Instead of focusing on the executive supply of budgetary information, I focus on legislative access to independent analysis capacity. An executive monopoly on budgetary information can put the legislature at a severe disadvantage, as it is easy to manipulate budget figures and limit disclosure (Wildavsky and Caiden 2001: 78). Among the benefits of an independent legislative budget office are that it can help to simplify complexity and make the budget accessible for legislators, enhance accountability through its scrutiny of executive information and promote transparency by discouraging 'budgetary legerdemain' (Anderson 2008: 132; see also Engstrom and Kernell 1999). I use this variable as a proxy for legislative access to budgetary information.

The survey measured the size of specialised budget research units across countries, distinguishing legislatures without such research capacity [0] from those with a budget office of up to ten professional staff [2.5], 11 to 25 [5], 26 to 50 [7.5] and more than 50 [10]. I add the last category to acknowledge the uniqueness of the Congressional Budget Office in the US, which has about 230 staff (Anderson 2008). Seven other legislatures have smaller specialised budget units. I discuss several examples in the following chapter.

3.2 Constructing the index

Most indices of budget institutions take an additive form (e.g. Von Hagen 1992; Lienert 2005; Alt and Lassen 2006; Hallerberg et al. 2007). This approach has the benefit of simplicity, but it also implies certain theoretical assumptions that are often not explicitly discussed. The aim of this section is to make these assumptions explicit and to investigate the robustness of the results to the use of alternative aggregation methods. Recent work by the OECD and the European Commission Joint Research Centre (2008) has greatly advanced the methodology for the construction of composite indicators, especially for the purpose of cross-national comparison. Given the theoretical foundation provided by the preceding chapter, I do not adopt a statistical approach to index construction, but rather pursue a more theory-led approach to combining the variables under discussion.

The task of index construction raises, in particular, theoretical questions about the substitutability of components. The starting point for this discussion is the additive index. This most commonly used method consists of summing up all scores for a given case in order to derive the index score for that case. The simple sum index can be represented as a special case of the following formula (Alesina et al. 1999: 260):

$$I_j = \sum_{i=1}^{6} c_i^j.$$

The term c_i captures the value of component i, while j is a power term that can be adjusted to reflect different assumptions about substitutability. If $j = 1$, then we get the simple sum index. If $0 < j < 1$, this favours those with consistently intermediate scores over those with a mixture of high and low scores, that is, this approach assumes a limited degree of substitutability. Conversely, with $j > 1$, a greater degree of substitutability is assumed, since high scores are rewarded. In addition, it would be possible to allow differential weights for each of the components. However, in the absence of strong theoretical reasons, I do not pursue this possibility here.

To restrict substitutability, the components can also be multiplied. This aggregation method assumes that values of zero on any variable cannot be compensated at all. The multiplicative approach often generates highly skewed distributions because a single low score substantially drags down the index. Since the majority of legislatures included in this study have scores of zero on at least one of the components, this method does not yield useful results. Nor does it appear theoretically plausible to restrict substitutability to such an extent across all components. In addition, this method is highly sensitive to small mistakes in the data, which can lead to severe misrepresentation of the affected legislatures. These are strong reasons for rejecting the purely multiplicative approach for this analysis.

A third possibility is to blend the additive and multiplicative approaches to aggregation:

$$I_s = \prod_{k=1}^{2} s_k \text{ , where } s_1 = \sum_{i=1}^{3} c_i \text{ and } s_2 = \sum_{i=4}^{6} c_i.$$

Here s_k represents two sub-indices, each consisting of the sum of three different components, which are then multiplied. It is possible to again incorporate a power term into the formulas for the sub-indices, but most essential is the underlying approach. The rationale for this index is as follows. Variables one to three (amendment powers, reversionary budgets and executive flexibility) can be interpreted as formal legislative authority vis-à-vis the executive. Amendment powers and reversionary budgets are frequently stipulated in constitutions, and organic budget laws typically regulate flexibility during implementation (Lienert and Jung 2004). In contrast, variables four to six (time, committees and research capacity) are taken to represent the organisational capacity of a legislature. Assuming that a degree of both formal power as well as organisational capacity are necessary for effective scrutiny, this calls for multiplication of the two sub-indices. However, substitutability within each sub-index is more plausible. For instance, if committees are weakly developed, then this lack in division of labour might be compensated by using a lot of time to

Table 3.1 Spearman correlations between indices

	$j = 1$	$j = .5$	$j = 2$
$j = .5$	0.98	–	–
$j = 2$	0.95	0.88	–
s	0.98	0.97	0.91

Note: The table reports Spearman correlations between four indices, that is, I_s and three versions of I_j that use different values for j. The country scores were computed using the data reported in Table 3.3. N=30.

scrutinise the budget or by delegating scrutiny to a well-resourced parliamentary budget office. Similarly, even when amendment powers are limited, legislators may still extract concessions from the executive if spending reverts to zero in the case of non-approval.

Similar to Alesina et al. (1999: 261), I investigate the robustness of results with Spearman rank correlations between four different versions of the index. I use the simple sum index with $j = 1$ computed with the first formula and two other arbitrary numbers for the power term, that is, $j = .5$ (half the value of the simple sum version) and $j = 2$ (double the value), to consider the impact of different substitutability assumptions. I also calculate scores using the second formula based on the two sub-indices. All of the correlations between these four versions of the index are positive and very strong (see Table 3.1). The lowest coefficient is .88 between the two indices that use extreme values for j, which is expected. All other correlations exceed .9. Overall, the results are very robust. For this reason, in the remainder of the book I use the simple additive index computed with the first formula and with $j = 1$. Table 3.3 reports the resulting country scores.

3.3 A ranking of national legislatures

This section presents the index of legislative budget institutions and discusses the main results. For presentational purposes, I rescale the index to range between zero and 100. The resulting ranking is presented in Figure 3.1. To evaluate the index, I pursue two approaches. First, I briefly consider whether the results are broadly in line with case study literature. Second, I check the validity of the index by testing its association with a simple indicator of legislative amendment activity.

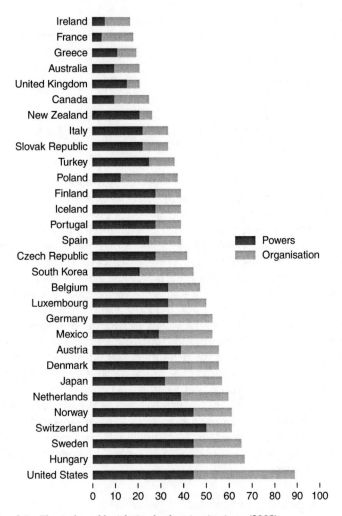

Figure 3.1 The index of legislative budget institutions (2003)
Note: Possible scores on the index of legislative budget institutions range from 0=no capacity to 100=full capacity. The powers sub-index combines the variables Powers, Reversion and Flexibility. The organisation sub-index combines the variables Time, Committees and Research. The index is based on additive aggregation. Refer to Table 3.3 and the data appendix for further details.

The US Congress emerges as an outlier by a substantial margin. Its score is more than three times greater than those of the bottom seven legislatures, predominantly Westminster systems. According to the index, the US Congress is the only legislature with the institutional foundation to exercise very strong influence over public finances. The importance of Congress in budgetary decisions is widely acknowledged. Aaron Wildavsky's seminal work on the politics of the budget process in the US is, in essence, a study of congressional policy making (Wildavsky 1964; Wildavsky and Caiden 2001). Although the US president submits a draft budget this does not bind Congress in any way (Schick 2000: 74–104). Oppenheimer (1983: 585) concludes a wide-ranging literature review with the observation that the US Congress is 'the most influential legislature' in policy making. The index produces results that are in line with this judgement.

On the other extreme, the British example is often said to epitomise the decline of parliaments (Einzig 1959; Reid 1966; Adonis 1993). Allen Schick (2002: 27) goes as far as to claim: 'Nowhere is the budgetary decline of parliament more noticeable than in Britain. ... [The] House of Commons, the cradle of budgetary democracy, [has] lost all formal influence over revenues and expenditures.' In 1998–9 the Procedure Committee of the House of Commons bluntly referred to its power over expenditure as 'if not a constitutional myth, very close to one' (quoted in Walters and Rogers 2004: 257). While we have no time series data to test the decline thesis, the index confirms that current capacity in the British Parliament is extremely limited. The rankings of other parliaments with a Westminster heritage are very similar, which again is supported by case study evidence. For instance, in Canada members have characterised legislative scrutiny of the budget as a 'cursory review' and 'a total waste of time' that involves 'futile attempts to bring about change' (quoted in Blöndal 2001a: 54).

Few national legislatures have been as extensively studied as the US Congress and the British Parliament, but nonetheless we can assess some other rankings against the available case study literature. Notably, the Danish, Norwegian and Swedish parliaments achieve relatively high scores on the index. This corresponds with literature that has pointed out the distinctiveness and relative strength of these parliaments (Arter 1984; Esaiasson and Heidar 2000). In addition, a large number of legislatures fall between the extremes of the US Congress and Westminster type parliaments. Notably, continental

European parliaments make up much of the middle mass on the index. Qualitative studies show that in a number of these countries, parliaments retain the capacity to exercise a limited level of influence on budgets (Coombes 1976; Eickenboom 1989; Leston-Bandeira 1999). It is beyond the scope of this chapter to present a full literature review. Still, this brief comparison with some of the case study literature suggests that the index generates a plausible ranking.

Apart from the aggregate scores, the results also show an interesting pattern in the relative balance between the formal powers of legislatures and their organisational capacity. Figure 3.1 distinguishes the contribution of each of these dimensions to the overall index. The dark shading indicates formal powers and the light shading organisational capacity. In only one fifth of all cases (six out of 30) does organisational capacity exceed formal authority in budgetary matters as measured on this index, that is, the legislatures of Australia, Canada, France, Ireland, Poland and South Korea. In some of these cases the difference between the scores on the two sub-indices is very small. This suggests that explanatory variables may impact asymmetrically on formal powers and organisational capacity. I explore this line of thought more fully in the following chapter and limit the remainder of the discussion here to further considering the validity of the aggregate results.

In addition to the comparison of the results against available country studies, the validity of the index can also be tested statistically. Given that the index captures institutional preconditions for legislative control, it should be associated with a measure of policy influence. One such indicator is amendment activity. The OECD asked whether the legislature generally approves the budget as presented by the executive. Ten out of the 30 legislatures in this sample generally approve the budget with no changes (refer to the last column in Table 3.3). More finely grained measures of amendment activity would be preferable, such as the number of amendments and their magnitude. However, comprehensive and reliable data at this level of detail are not available.

Also, it is true that a legislature may not have to amend the budget to impact on policy. Hidden actions such as a short phone call from a powerful committee chair to an executive official can be an important means of legislative influence (Meyers 2001: 7). Moreover, the executive may anticipate legislative reactions and fashion the draft budget accordingly, thereby reducing the likelihood of amendments

Table 3.2 Budget-amending and non-amending legislatures

	Amending	Non-Amending
Observations	20	10
Mean index score	47.7	34.9
Standard deviation	15.6	18.0

(refer to the analysis in Chapter 2). However, it might be naive to conclude that the absence of amendments indicates that the legislature is getting its way. An executive has no reason to be responsive to legislative preferences unless the absence of such consideration has consequences. For example, in the UK the last government defeats over estimates date back to the first half of the previous century.[7] It is possible to argue that legislative actors need to maintain a modicum of amendment activity in order to signal to the executive their capacity for more substantial revision should the draft budget not take sufficient account of their preferences.

Accepting the above premise, one would expect budget-amending legislatures to have more developed institutional capacity. I use a t-test to assess whether index scores are higher for budget-amending legislatures compared with those that do not amend the budget (Bohrnstedt and Knoke 1994: 139). Setting $a = .05$ for 28 degrees of freedom gives a critical value of 1.7 for a one-tailed test to reject the null. The data in Table 3.2 generates a value of 2, which falls within the rejection region. This supports the prediction that budget-amending legislatures maintain higher levels of institutional capacity for financial scrutiny.

The evidence in this section is mutually reinforcing and confirms that the index is a useful summary indicator of legislative capacity to influence budget policy. The overall ranking is broadly in line with case study literature and the index is positively associated with a simple measure of legislative impact on public finances. Not too much should be read into small score differences between national legislatures. Nonetheless, whether a legislature ranks towards the top, middle or bottom of the index conveys an overall perspective on the state of legislative budgeting in a particular country. Indeed, if the power of the purse is a *sine qua non* for legislative control in general, then the results also reflect the overall status of the legislature in the political system of a country.

3.4   Conclusions

This chapter has expanded the methodological toolkit for cross-national research on the legislative power of the purse. Previous efforts to construct quantitative measures of legislative budget power were either extremely limited in their coverage of relevant variables or neglected detailed discussion of related methodological issues. The index constructed here is robust and delivers results that can be checked against case study evidence and using statistical tests. It provides a sound basis for further investigating cross-national patterns in legislative budgeting, in particular their causes and consequences, which I investigate in Chapters 4 and 5 respectively. However, I do not suggest that quantitative analysis be a substitute for the detailed study of particular cases. Rather, there is an emerging debate on comparative research methods that argues strongly in favour of a carefully designed combined use of statistical and small-N approaches (Lieberman 2005). For instance, large-N analysis can provide the basis for a more deliberate choice of case studies, which in turn may deepen understanding and add important contextual variables. I return to this aspect in Chapter 6.

The findings of this chapter imply that we should not make overly simplistic distinctions between legislatures in parliamentary and presidential systems. Traditionally, the study of parliamentary systems has been biased towards a small number of European countries with mostly 'reactive' legislative bodies that exert minimal influence on policy and budgets (Oppenheimer 1983: 580). When the US Congress is compared with the British Parliament, for example, it may indeed seem as if there is an inherent difference between presidential and parliamentary systems in terms of the role of elected assemblies. However, the evidence here shows tremendous variation in the institutional capacity of legislative bodies in parliamentary systems of government in particular, as well as variation within a much smaller sample of presidential regimes. These results are in line with other comparative work on legislatures in parliamentary (Döring 1995a) and presidential regimes (Haggard and McCubbins 2001; Morgenstern and Nacif 2002). One important implication is that, rather than assuming that legislatures in parliamentary systems are inherently weak vis-à-vis their counterparts in presidential systems (Persson and Tabellini 2006: 92), analyses of the policy impact of institutions should not neglect more nuanced institutional differences. This important point will be pursued further in Chapter 5.

The ranking of legislatures also raises questions about the prerequisites for democratic governance. Despite widespread constitutional recognition of the importance of legislative control over the purse, this chapter reveals substantial variation in the level of financial scrutiny of government by the legislature among contemporary liberal democracies. The US Congress has an index score that is about three times greater than those of legislatures in the bottom quartile. Even allowing for US exceptionalism, the top quartile legislatures score twice as high on this index as the bottom quartile. These differences suggest that for some countries the power of the purse is a key safeguard against executive overreach, while others maintain a constitutional myth. This finding contradicts the assertion that a strong legislature, at least in budgetary terms, is a necessary condition for democracy (Einzig 1959; Fish 2006). Given that the authorisation of taxes and public expenditures is a primary function of the legislature in any democratic system, such an amount of variation among modern liberal democracies is perplexing. This raises the question why some legislatures maintain elaborate institutional arrangements for financial scrutiny while others essentially leave budgeting to the executive.

Table 3.3 Data for the index and amendment dummy

Legislature	Powers[a] a	Reversion b	Flexibility c	Time d	Committees e	Research f	Powers g = (a+b+c)/.6	Organisation h = (d+e+f)/.6	Index i = g+h	Amendments j
Australia	2.5	3.3	0.0	0.0	6.7	0.0	9.7	11.1	20.8	0
Austria	10.0	6.7	6.7	3.3	6.7	0.0	38.9	16.7	55.6	1
Belgium	10.0	10.0	0.0	0.0	8.3	0.0	33.3	13.9	47.2	0
Canada	2.5	3.3	0.0	0.0	6.7	2.5	9.7	15.3	25.0	0
Czech Republic	10.0	6.7	0.0	3.3	5.0	0.0	27.8	13.9	41.7	1
Denmark	10.0	6.7	3.3	6.7	6.7	0.0	33.3	22.2	55.6	1
Finland	10.0	0.0	6.7	3.3	3.3	0.0	27.8	11.1	38.9	1
France	2.5	0.0	0.0	3.3	5.0	0.0	4.2	13.9	18.1	1
Germany	10.0	6.7	3.3	6.7	5.0	0.0	33.3	19.4	52.8	1
Greece	0.0	6.7	0.0	0.0	5.0	0.0	11.1	8.3	19.4	0
Hungary	10.0	10.0	6.7	3.3	10.0	0.0	44.4	22.2	66.7	1
Iceland	10.0	0.0	6.7	3.3	3.3	0.0	27.8	11.1	38.9	1
Ireland	0.0	0.0	3.3	0.0	6.7	0.0	5.6	11.1	16.7	0
Italy	10.0	0.0	3.3	3.3	3.3	0.0	22.2	11.1	33.3	1
Japan	2.5[b]	10.0	6.7	3.3	6.7	5.0	31.9	25.0	56.9	0
Luxembourg	10.0	10.0	0.0	3.3	6.7	0.0	33.3	16.7	50.0	0
Mexico	7.5	10.0	0.0	0.0	6.7	7.5	29.2	23.6	52.8	1
Netherlands	10.0	6.7	6.7	6.7	3.3	2.5	38.9	20.8	59.7	1
New Zealand	2.5	3.3	6.7	0.0	3.3	0.0	20.8	5.6	26.4	0
Norway	10.0	10.0	6.7	3.3	6.7	0.0	44.4	16.7	61.1	1

Poland	7.5	0.0	3.3	6.7	5.0	12.5	25.0	37.5	1
Portugal	10.0	6.7	3.3	3.3	0.0	27.8	11.1	38.9	1
Slovak Republic	10.0[c]	0.0	3.3	3.3	0.0	22.2	11.1	33.3	1
South Korea	2.5	6.7	3.3	3.3	7.5	20.8	23.6	44.4	1
Spain	5.0	6.7	3.3	5.0	0.0	25.0	13.9	38.9	1
Sweden	10.0	10.0	6.7	6.7	2.5	44.4	20.8	65.3	0
Switzerland	10.0	10.0	10.0	3.3	0.0	50.0	11.1	61.1	1
Turkey	5.0	10.0	3.3	3.3	0.0	25.0	11.1	36.1	1
United Kingdom	2.5	3.3	0.0	3.3	0.0	15.3	5.6	20.8	0
United States	10.0	10.0	10.0	6.7	10.0	44.4	44.4	88.9	1

Note: Refer to the data appendix for variable definitions. A first version of the dataset (excluding Luxembourg, Poland and Switzerland) was published in Wehner (2006). The data published here include the following adjustments: (a) I use a more nuanced coding scheme for the amendment powers variable than in Wehner (2006). See data appendix. (b) There is a legal dispute about the extent to which the Japanese Diet can amend the budget (Sakurai 2004). According to Lienert and Jung (2004: 271), 'the general understanding is that the Diet cannot amend the government's budget proposal significantly'. To acknowledge the possibility of limited changes, and unlike in Wehner (2006), I assign a non-zero score in the dataset used here. (c) In the 2003 OECD and World Bank survey, the respondent from the Slovak Republic indicated that the National Council has limited powers to amend the budget. However, Gleich (2003) and Yläoutinen (2004) both indicate unlimited amendment powers, which I confirmed with the Ministry of Finance and the National Council of the Slovak Republic. I adjust the score accordingly.
Source: OECD and World Bank (2003), OECD (2007), parliamentary websites

Table 3.4 Construction of composite variables

Legislature	Withhold k	Virement l	Reserve m	Flexibility c=k+l+m	Budget n	Sectoral o	Audit p	Committees e=n+o+p
Australia	0.0	0.0	0.0	0.0	0.0	3.3	3.3	6.7
Austria	3.3	3.3	0.0	6.7	3.3	0.0	3.3	6.7
Belgium	0.0	0.0	0.0	0.0	3.3	3.3	1.7	8.3
Canada	0.0	0.0	0.0	0.0	0.0	3.3	3.3	6.7
Czech Republic	0.0	0.0	0.0	0.0	3.3	0.0	1.7	5.0
Denmark	3.3	0.0	0.0	3.3	3.3	0.0	3.3	6.7
Finland	3.3	3.3	0.0	6.7	3.3	0.0	0.0	3.3
France	0.0	0.0	0.0	0.0	3.3	0.0	1.7	5.0
Germany	0.0	0.0	3.3	3.3	3.3	0.0	1.7	5.0
Greece	0.0	0.0	0.0	0.0	3.3	0.0	1.7	5.0
Hungary	3.3	3.3	0.0	6.7	3.3	3.3	3.3	10.0
Iceland	3.3	3.3	0.0	6.7	3.3	0.0	0.0	3.3
Ireland	0.0	0.0	3.3	3.3	3.3	0.0	3.3	6.7
Italy	3.3	0.0	0.0	3.3	3.3	0.0	0.0	3.3
Japan	3.3	3.3	0.0	6.7	3.3	0.0	3.3	6.7
Luxembourg	0.0	0.0	0.0	0.0	3.3	0.0	3.3	6.7
Mexico	0.0	0.0	0.0	0.0	3.3	0.0	3.3	6.7
Netherlands	3.3	0.0	3.3	6.7	0.0	3.3	0.0	3.3
New Zealand	3.3	3.3	0.0	6.7	3.3	0.0	0.0	3.3
Norway	3.3	3.3	0.0	6.7	3.3	3.3	0.0	6.7
Poland	0.0	0.0	0.0	0.0	3.3	0.0	3.3	6.7

Portugal	0.0	0.0	0.0	0.0	3.3	0.0	0.0	3.3
Slovak Republic	0.0	0.0	3.3	3.3	3.3	0.0	0.0	3.3
South Korea	3.3	0.0	0.0	3.3	3.3	0.0	0.0	3.3
Spain	3.3	0.0	0.0	3.3	3.3	0.0	1.7	5.0
Sweden	3.3	3.3	0.0	6.7	3.3	3.3	0.0	6.7
Switzerland	3.3	3.3	3.3	10.0	3.3	0.0	0.0	3.3
Turkey	0.0	0.0	0.0	0.0	3.3	0.0	0.0	3.3
United Kingdom	0.0	3.3	0.0	3.3	0.0	0.0	3.3	3.3
United States	3.3	3.3	0.0	6.7	3.3	3.3	0.0	6.7

Note: Refer to the data appendix for variable definitions. A first version of the dataset (excluding Luxembourg, Poland and Switzerland) was published in Wehner (2006).

Source: OECD and World Bank (2003), OECD (2007), parliamentary websites

4
Explaining Cross-National Patterns

Existing literature is a poor guide for understanding why the role of legislatures in budgeting differs so fundamentally across countries. A number of quantitative cross-national studies use legislative institutions as explanatory variables, which is the topic of the following chapter. However, with few relevant exceptions (e.g. Pelizzo and Stapenhurst 2004; Lienert 2005), little attention has been given to legislative arrangements as dependent variables. With regard to legislative budget institutions more specifically, there are some interesting historical accounts of the evolution of financial scrutiny in particular countries (Stourm 1917; Coombes 1976; Schick 2002), but no structured review of broader patterns. One danger with the case study approach is to generalise on the basis of a small number of cases that may not be representative. For a long time, one serious obstacle to the study of cross-national differences in legislative budget institutions was the lack of comprehensive comparative data. Given the analysis in the previous chapter, this is no longer a reason to neglect the issue.

Here I use the index of legislative budget institutions introduced in the previous chapter as the dependent variable and explore why these arrangements differ substantially. This analysis is important in itself, but it also provides a useful background for the analysis of the effects of institutional arrangements. The chapter proceeds in three main steps. The first section outlines four propositions about cross-national differences in financial scrutiny arrangements and defines the relevant variables. The second section tests these propositions using multiple regression analysis. I also disaggregate the index into its two main sub-components in order to gain a more precise understanding of the associations under investigation. In the third section, I consider some broader implications and discuss reasons why some factors may affect certain institutional arrangements, but not others.

4.1 Exploring the determinants

This section considers possible explanatory variables to account for the cross-sectional variation in institutional arrangements. The nature of this chapter is exploratory and its ambition more modest than that of the following chapters, which connect with the theory developed earlier. Hence, the following paragraphs outline propositions rather than hypotheses. I consider four sets of possible explanations. These are based on very different assumptions about the durability of institutions and the power of political actors to shape the structures in which they operate. The first is the institutional replication proposition, which emphasises the durability and path dependence of institutions once they are established. Second, the separation of powers proposition is that legislative arrangements are a function of broader systemic parameters, notably whether a country has a presidential system of government or not. Both of these emphasise the importance of historical origins and choices. In contrast, what I call the partisan proposition assumes an ability of contemporary legislative actors to adjust institutional settings in their favour. Finally, I consider the proposition that there is institutional convergence of countries with similar levels of democratic maturity. Linked to each of these are relevant measures for the regression analysis in the following section.

The nature of institutions as 'enduring entities' is widely acknowledged in the political science literature (Rothstein 1996: 152). Given this potential durability, a look at history might reveal common homogenising factors among groups of countries. In particular, cross-national commonalities may be due to the transfer of institutional features from a colonial power to its colonies, and once in place this heritage may prove resistant to change (Acemoglu et al. 2001). This applies not only to fundamental constitutional distinctions, such as the choice between parliamentary and presidential government or the type of electoral system, but also the budgetary structures of a country. For example, Lienert (2003) observes significant differences between public expenditure management systems in anglophone and francophone African countries and Moussa (2004) traces the influence of the French public finance model on the country's former colonies. Hence, one implication of this line of thinking is the repli-cation proposition, according to which institutional arrangements in former colonies reflect those of the former colonial power.

A test of this proposition requires an indicator of colonial influence. In particular, I predict a negative association between being a former colony of the UK and the index of legislative budget institutions, given the British Parliament's low score on the index and its widely recognised marginalisation in financial matters (Reid 1966; Schick 2002). However, it is reasonable to expect colonial history to matter less as time since independence increases. For instance, important aspects of legislative arrangements for financial scrutiny in the UK evolved during the Gladstonian reforms in the 1860s (Einzig 1959). Countries that gained independence from Britain before this time are less likely to adopt similar arrangements. Moreover, the effect of institutional heritage may wear off as countries chart their own ways and respond to idiosyncratic domestic challenges. For such reasons, Persson and Tabellini (2003: 41) use a set of indicators that give more weight to colonial history in recently independent states. The argument also makes sense in the context of this sample, as the US developed a distinct style of legislative financial control even prior to independence and continued a unique path subsequently (Wildavsky and Caiden 2001: 26–30). However, as the four remaining former colonies (Australia, Canada, Ireland and New Zealand) are closer together in terms of the time of their independence, I use a simple dummy to indicate these four countries. The sample is too small to include similar variables to test the influence of French colonial rule or other such legacies.

The role of a legislature in policy making might also reflect the separation of powers in the political system. A core institutional debate in political science relates to the choice between presiden-tial and parliamentary regimes and its implications (Lijphart 1992; Weaver and Rockman 1993). Lijphart (1999: 117–18) highlights three defining attributes: chief executives in parliamentary systems rely on maintaining the confidence of the legislature in order to remain in office, are indirectly elected and govern collegially. In con-trast, their presidential counterparts have a mandate for a fixed time period, are popularly elected and constitute one-person executives.

Persson and Tabellini (2003: 97) use a more minimalist definition, according to which the only criterion is that the executive does not depend on the confidence of the elected assembly in order to stay in power. Others argue that such broad systemic categories are too crude to be meaningful (Siaroff 2003). These are ongoing debates, but important in this context is a frequently made and prominent argument that presidentialism may have systematic effects on the role of legislative bodies. For instance, Weaver and Rockman (1993: 14) express the view that parliamentary government gives rise to greater party discipline, which 'can turn the legislature into a rubber stamp for executive actions'. Conversely, if legislative–executive relations are more conflict prone under presidentialism, as in particular Linz (1990) has argued, one would also expect legislatures to have greater incentives to exercise higher levels of financial scrutiny. Lienert (2005) makes a similar argument in the context of legislative financial scrutiny.

To test whether the separation of powers affects legislative budgeting, I construct a dummy variable for presidential systems, for which I predict a positive coefficient. Even in this modest sample of 30 OECD countries, the classification of systems is not straightforward. According to Haggard and McCubbins (2001), only three of the 30 OECD countries are presidential: Mexico, South Korea and the US. Persson and Tabellini's (2003) definition implies that Switzerland should also be classified as presidential, since cabinet members there do not depend on the confidence of the legislature once elected. Strøm et al. (2003) concur that Switzerland does not have a parliamentary system. Here I adopt Persson and Tabellini's definition and classify the Swiss system as presidential, since its 'formal separation of powers has made both the executive and the legislature more independent' (Lijphart 1999: 35). However, the results should be interpreted with caution, given the small number of presidential systems in this sample and the contested definition of the concept underlying this variable.

Party political dynamics can either enhance or limit financial scrutiny. In the UK the emergence of organised political parties towards the end of the nineteenth century coincided with a decline in parliamentary influence (Adonis 1993; Norton 1993; Schick 2002). When party discipline is strong, an executive that commands a legislative majority is unlikely to face a fundamental challenge to its budgetary proposals during the parliamentary stage. The absence of a legislative majority, on the other hand, can lead to strong policy disagreement (Edin and Ohlsson 1991). As Messick (2002: 2) puts it: 'In all legislatures it is the party or parties out of power – the opposition – that has the incentive to oversee government. The more government incompetence, malfeasance or corruption that is revealed, the better the opposition's chances of winning the next election.'

Divided government or minority government in parliamentary systems, can be defined as 'the absence of simultaneous same-party majorities in the executive and legislative branches of government' (Elgie 2001: 2).[1] For a long time, the study of divided government was largely confined to the US, where shifting majorities among the branches of government and the two houses of Congress have caused severe budgetary gridlock (Williams and Jubb 1996). However, divided government also occurs in non-presidential systems (Laver and Shepsle 1991; Elgie 2001). Several studies with different samples have found that minority administrations account for about one third of governments in parliamentary systems (Strøm 1990: 8). Since legislative distrust of the executive is likely to be higher in the absence of a unifying partisan connection, I expect the persistence of divided government to increase legislative financial scrutiny.

To test this proposition I construct a divided government index, which is the ratio of years in which the government did not command a legislative majority in the lower house of the legislature. It covers the ten-year period immediately before the OECD and World Bank data on budget systems were collected (1993–2002).[2] I considered whether legislators from the party or parties in government held more than 50 per cent of seats in a unicameral parliament or in the lower house of parliament in the case of bicameral systems. Whenever this was not the case, I gave a score of one for that year, otherwise zero, and compiled the index by summing across the ten years for each country and dividing by ten. Possible index values therefore range between zero (never minority government) and one (always minority government). According to the data, 17 out of the 30 countries had experience with minority government at some point during this ten-year period. In systems that experience protracted spells of divided government, the legislative majority has an incentive to strengthen scrutiny, so I expect this variable to have a positive coefficient.

Finally, institutions are also embedded in a broader context and may reflect an evolutionary process (Goodin 1996). For example, we may expect convergence between countries with similar levels of economic development and democracy. However, the OECD sample by definition is already fairly homogenous, as membership of the organisation requires a country to demonstrate its commitment to an open market economy, democratic pluralism and respect for human rights. On the other hand, OECD countries differ markedly in terms of their experience with democracy, in particular since the last wave of accessions in the 1990s. Where experience with authoritarianism is relatively recent and democracy perhaps not yet fully entrenched, the capacity of legislative bodies to act as a check on the executive may be less developed, sometimes because executives actively undermine institutions that have potential to hold them to account for their actions (O'Donnell 1998).

To test whether democratic maturity is associated with legislative budget institutions, I use a measure of the age of democracy compiled by Persson and Tabellini (2003). In constructing this measure, they determine the first year of democratic rule. This corresponds to the first year of an uninterrupted string of positive yearly values of Polity scores until the end of their sample, if the country was also an independent nation. Foreign occupation during World War II is not counted as an interruption of democracy. The age of democracy is then defined as (2000 – first year of democratic rule)/200. Their variable ranges between zero and one, with the latter indicating a mature democracy. Refer to the data appendix for further details.

4.2 Empirical analysis

In this section, I test the above four propositions using ordinary least squares (OLS) regression. Some methodological notes and caveats are in order. First, OLS regression assumes a quantitative, continuous and unbounded dependent variable (Berry 1993: 45–9). I treat the index as a continuous variable, but its boundedness could produce nonsensical predictions, for example, negative values or values larger than 100. The logistic transformation can be applied to convert the index into an unbounded variable (for an example, see Demsetz and Lehn 1985: 1163). However, results with a transformed version of the index would be less intuitive to interpret, and in any case the substantive findings are very similar. Hence, I stick to the untransformed version of the index. Second, collinearity between the independent variables is a potential problem (Fox 1991: 21–31). However, the correlations between the right-hand-side variables are weak, that is, below .3 for this sample. Collinearity does not pose a problem.

Column (1) in Table 4.1 reports the results from regressing the index of legislative budget institutions onto the four explanatory variables, based on the full sample of 30 OECD countries. Every coefficient has the predicted sign and is statistically significant at the ten per cent level or higher. According to these results, British colonial heritage is negatively associated with legislative budget capacity, while the latter is positively associated with presidentialism, divided government and democratic maturity. Since each of the explanatory variables ranges between zero and one, the relative impact of these factors is directly comparable. Colonial heritage and the age of democracy are particularly influential. A switch from zero to one on these variables has about twice the absolute effect as a switch from fused to separate powers or from always to never majority government.

Table 4.1 The determinants of legislative budget institutions

Dependent variable	(1) Index	(2) Powers	(3) Organisation
Former British colony	−24.98	−19.61	−5.36
	(5.10)***	(4.51)***	(2.73)*
Presidential system	13.04	4.64	8.40
	(5.31)**	(4.92)	(4.95)
Divided government	12.59	5.52	7.07
	(6.86)*	(5.86)	(3.39)**
Age of democracy	21.67	16.03	5.64
	(11.36)*	(7.71)**	(6.50)
Constant	33.40	21.71	11.68
	(6.09)***	(4.45)***	(2.78)***
Observations	30	30	30
Adjusted R-squared	0.43	0.32	0.30

Note: OLS estimates with robust standard errors in parentheses. In column (1), the dependent variable is the index of legislative budget institutions (ranging from 0 to 100). In columns (2) and (3), the dependent variables are the powers and organisation sub-indices respectively (both ranging from 0 to 50). Refer to the text and the data appendix for further details.
*Significant at 10 per cent; **significant at 5 per cent; ***significant at 1 per cent.

To explore the impact of the explanatory variables on different components of the index of legislative budget institutions, and as a further check on the robustness of the results, I also used the two sub-indices developed in Chapter 3 and regressed them onto the set of explanatory variables. As discussed in the preceding chapter, the 'powers' sub-index captures the scope for legislative amendments, reversionary budget provisions and executive flexibility. It serves as an indicator of the formal authority of the legislature. The second sub-index sums the scores for the time, committee and research capacity variables. I use it as a measure of the organisational capacity of the legislature for financial scrutiny. Each of the sub-indices is rescaled and can theoretically range from 0 (no capacity) to 50 (full capacity), so that their sum equals the index of legislative budget institutions. By distinguishing these two institutional aspects, we gain a clearer understanding of which of these two distinct sets of legislative institutions are associated with the explanatory variables.

The results for the sub-indices are presented in columns (2) and (3) of Table 4.1, which reveal several noteworthy differences. In particular, the size of the coefficient for the former British colony dummy is substantially larger for the powers sub-index (column 2) than for the organisation sub-index (column 3). The results suggest that the impact of British colonial heritage on the legal framework for legislative budgeting is almost four times greater than its impact on legislative organisation. Both coefficients for British colonial heritage are significant at conventional levels. The result that colonial heritage has a strong effect on formal powers is in line with findings from a study by Lienert and Jung (2004), who compare the legal frameworks for budget systems and highlight a number of similarities among countries with a Westminster heritage, in particular, in relation to parliamentary authority over the budget.

On the other hand, presidentialism has no significant impact on either of the sub-indices, although the coefficient in column (3) is very close to statistical significance at the ten per cent level. The size of the coefficient for divided government is similar across columns (2) and (3), but it is only statistically significant for the organisation sub-index. On the other hand, the age of democracy predominantly affects legislative powers, where this coefficient achieves statistical significance at the five per cent level. Most of these associations are robust to the exclusion of the US, with the exception of the age of democracy, which falls short of statistical significance at conventional levels for either of the sub-indices when this case is excluded.

Substantively, this analysis finds strong evidence of the durability of legislative budget institutions, notably the strong effect of colonial heritage on legislative powers. The less robust effect of the age of democracy on legislative powers may capture constitutional fashions relating to the power of the purse, as this variable is highly correlated with the age of the current constitutional framework. In other words, strong parliamentary authority in budgetary matters may have been considered crucial for democracy among early democratisers, but less essential for countries that transitioned to democratic government more recently. This interpretation is supported by the fact that the age of democracy has no significant effect on legislative organisation. On the other hand, the association of presidentialism and divided government with legislative organisation suggests that political actors can to some extent shape legislative arrangements in a purposeful fashion in order to increase parliamentary control. This seemingly contradictory conclusion, that institutional arrangements are both durable and malleable at the same time, is discussed in more detail in the following section. While the models presented here account for a fair proportion of cross-national institutional variation, it is to be expected that part of the differences are due to country specific factors that are difficult or impossible to quantify, such as historical contingencies and political culture.

4.3 Fixed and variable institutional features

Although this analysis is of a cross-sectional nature, the independent variables raise interesting issues relating to institutional change over time. Some institutional arrangements can typically be adjusted more easily than others. For instance, constitutional features, several of which are captured in the powers sub-index, usually cannot be amended without the support of an extraordinary majority in the legislature. Because this requires a high degree of consensus that would be unusual in many contexts, fundamental constitutional reforms are extremely rare. This is true for parliamentary amendment powers, for instance, which are either hardly changing or time invariant in most countries (I present extensive comparative data on amendment powers in the following chapter).[3] Other institutional features are perhaps more variable in the short run. For instance, some aspects of legislative organisation are often an internal question, that is for the legislature to decide, and most standing orders can usually be amended with more ease than constitutional provisions. This makes variable features potentially more responsive to shifting political dynamics.

Anecdotal evidence illustrates that legislators seeking to strengthen their budgetary role may attempt to do so by adjusting variable institutional features in their favour. The best-known example, perhaps, is the overhaul of the budget process in the US with the Congressional Budget and Impoundment Control Act of 1974. Among a series of changes, the act reformed the legislative committee structure to facilitate fiscal decision making, severely curtailed executive impoundment authority by regulating rescissions and deferrals and shifted the beginning of the fiscal year from July to October to give Congress an extra three months to decide the budget (Wildavsky and Caiden 2001: 77–82). One of the most important legacies of these reforms is the Congressional Budget Office, which ended the presidential monopoly on budgetary information. Under the stewardship of its founding director, Alice Rivlin, the Congressional Budget Office sought to build a reputation for independent analysis that rivals the executive's Office of Management and Budget. More than 30 years after its creation, the Congressional Budget Office employed about 230 staff to carry out an extensive range of analytic tasks (Anderson 2008). The acrimonious nature of legislative–executive relations during the Nixon administration, a period of divided government, gave impetus to the reforms, which countered what had been a shift towards executive dominance since the introduction of the executive budget process with the Budget and Accounting Act in 1921 (Schick 2000: 8–22).

The US reforms of the 1970s were particularly far-reaching and in some respects exceptional. However, there are attempts at legislative reorganisation in other countries that illustrate the point, in particular a more recent wave of reforms that involve the establishment of legislative budget offices (Johnson and Stapenhurst 2008). In a number of countries, the creation of such analytic units is associated with a period of divided government or an increase in partisan competition that strengthens the incentives for a majority of legislators to scrutinise executive actions, in particular the handling of public finances. For instance, commentators for a long time regarded the Mexican Congress as 'the epitome of weakness' (Morgenstern 2002a: 9) despite its comparatively strong constitutional powers (Haggard and McCubbins 2001: 81). Since the emergence of competitive party politics and divided government in the 1990s the Mexican Congress has started to make amendments to the presidential budget proposal (Economist 2004). In the wake of these political changes, the Chamber of Deputies sought ways to strengthen its institutional capacity.

In 1998, these shifting dynamics of legislative–executive relations resulted in a cross-party agreement to set up a non-partisan unit to supply the Mexican Congress with independent analyses of public finances. This was the foundation for the establishment of the Centre for the Study of Public Finance (*Centro de Estudios de las Finanzas Públicas*). Ten years later, this unit had grown to the size of 50 employees, supporting Congress with research and monitoring in relation to revenues, expenditures, macroeconomic aspects as well as the further development of the public finance system. In 2006, it also acquired the task of costing the budgetary impact of legislative initiatives. As Santiso (2006: 85) remarks, 'the surge of legislative activism in the budget process in Mexico is partly the result of the emergence of an assertive opposition since the long-time ruling party, the Institutional Revolutionary Party, lost its parliamentary majority in 1997. It is probably not a coincidence that the Mexican legislative budget office emerged in 1998'. In Mexico, too, it was changes in the political environment that prompted legislators to reconsider variable institutional features.

A similar association holds for a number of other legislative budget units. In South Korea, the National Assembly set up its Budget Office in 2003, following – as in Mexico – a process of democratisation as well as an increase in partisan competition during the 1990s. The origins of this analytic unit date back to 1994, when the National Assembly created the Legislation and Budget Bureau within its secretariat. In 2000, this bureau was split into a legislative and a budget section. However, this was not enough to meet increasing legislative demand for independent scrutiny and analysis of budgetary information. In July 2003, South Korean legislators amended the 1948 National Assembly Act to make the Budget Office independent from the secretariat of the National

Assembly. Within about five years, its staff had grown to 135, the second largest such institution among OECD countries, providing research on the budget, including the costing of bills introduced by members, economic and revenue analyses, as well as programme evaluations.

While the largest legislative budget offices among OECD members are in countries with presidential systems (the US, Mexico and South Korea), which is in line with the regression results reported earlier, there are also examples of such units in parliamentary systems. For instance, the Canadian Parliament adopted the Federal Accountability Act in December 2006. Among others, the act created the position of the Parliamentary Budget Officer to provide the Senate and the House of Commons with 'independent analysis' of public finances, the estimates and economic trends, as well as research support to committees and estimates of the cost of legislative proposals when requested. Appointed in March 2008, Canada's first Parliamentary Budget Officer, Kevin Page, proceeded to create the infrastructure for this analytic unit. Similar to the experience of a number of other legislatures that created their own budget offices, this attempt to strengthen parliamentary financial scrutiny took place during a period characterised by a succession of minority governments starting in 2004.

The creation of legislative budget offices has been a major part of the evolution of financial scrutiny (Schick 2002; Johnson and Stapenhurst 2008). The common theme in the examples reviewed earlier is that these institutions were established following an increase in the tension between a majority of legislative actors and the executive. The demand for increased scrutiny is often, although not always, strongest among members of political parties other than those who form the executive (Messick 2002). However, while the motivation for the creation of legislative budget offices is deeply political in many cases, their credibility hinges on their ability to acquire a broadly shared reputation for objective, independent and non-partisan analysis (Anderson 2008). One lesson from the experience of the US is that the initial performance of these units is crucial, as it shapes their role for years to come. Establishing a reputation for credible analysis is a serious challenge, and such reforms are not always successful in unambiguously strengthening legislative control (Messick 2002).

The broader point in the context of this discussion is that a distinction between fixed and variable features provides a useful framework for understanding the scope for institutional reform in response to changes in the political environment, such as the emergence of divided government. This helps to shed light on the extent to which legislative actors have scope to purposefully shape institutional arrangements. Whether specific institutional features are fixed or variable in the short run does of course differ between countries, but features relating to legislative organisation are frequently variable and hence may respond to shifts in political dynamics. The distinction between fixed and variable institutions reconciles the seemingly contradictory assumptions of the institutional replication and partisan propositions by highlighting that some institutions are highly durable while others are malleable by contemporary political forces.

4.4   Conclusions

There are a number of plausible explanations as to why legislative scrutiny arrangements might differ between countries. This chapter considered four sets of propositions that related institutional features to colonial heritage, the separation of powers, partisan dynamics and the democratic maturity of a country. I investigated these using the index of legislative budget institutions as the dependent variable, as well as its two components introduced in the previous chapter, the powers and organisation sub-indices. The results suggest that colonial heritage is a powerful determinant of both legislative powers and organisation. Presidential government and divided government, on the other hand, mainly affect legislative organisation. Evidence that the maturity of democracy accounts for institutional differences in the industrialised democracies is less robust.

More specifically, former British colonies have lower index scores, whereas countries with a presidential system of government and a high incidence of divided government achieve higher scores. The impact of British colonial heritage is strongest on the component of the index that captures the formal powers of the legislature in budgetary matters, which in many instances has a constitutional basis that is typically very durable over time. Presidentialism is associated with higher levels of legislative organisation, but it has no impact on legislative powers. However, the sample is dominated by parliamentary systems, so it will be important to reconsider this issue with a larger sample of presidential regimes. The impact of colonial heritage suggests that some institutional features are highly durable, in particular constitutionally prescribed powers. On the other hand, the political dynamics associated with divided government and presidentialism can affect institutional features that are more variable in the short term.

5
Legislative Institutions and Fiscal Policy Outcomes

If legislative budgeting suffers from a pro-spending bias, what is the empirical evidence that institutional arrangements can contain this tendency? Since the 1990s, a number of studies, using different variables and datasets, have claimed that certain institutional features are conducive to maintaining fiscal discipline during the budget process in the legislature. This chapter provides an overview of the theoretical and empirical literature on the fiscal effects of legislative institutions and adds empirical evidence. While existing studies tend to focus on selected variables, the intention here is to present a more comprehensive overview and to provide additional assurances of the robustness of the findings through the use of multiple datasets and empirical approaches.

The most common empirical strategy in the fiscal institutionalist literature involves the use of composite indices of budget institutions (e.g. Von Hagen 1992; Alesina et al. 1996). A potential problem with composite indices is that they can obfuscate the impact of individual variables. Hence, this chapter adopts a more focused approach that puts individual variables at the centre of the analysis. I start with a summary review of the relevant literature and an initial look at empirical relationships between the identified institutional variables and the size of government. Such replication is increasingly acknowledged as essential for the credibility of research in the social sciences (Dewald et al. 1986; Herrnson 1995; King 1995).[1] It provides a check whether results 'travel' through time and space, and thus supports the search for underlying general results. I use this initial overview to set up a more detailed analysis of the relationship between legislative budget authority and public spending using a global sample of countries both in the cross section as well as over time.

5.1   A review of institutionalist hypotheses

The literature on the fiscal effect of budget institutions builds on the basic insight that spending will be higher when decision makers do not internalise the full costs of their actions (Weingast et al. 1981). This suggests that the spending bias in a legislative setting is potentially substantial: democratic legislatures are large decision-making bodies that typically encompass many special interests. For instance, individual legislators elected by geographical constituencies can internalise the benefits of a project, such as a bridge or road built in their district, while distributing the costs across all taxpayers. The same effect can occur in contexts where party discipline is strong, in which case political parties rather than individual legislators constitute the relevant decision-making units. For these reasons, the fiscal institutionalist literature generally regards powerful legislative bodies as fiscally dangerous and propagates institutional arrangements that centralise decision making in the hands of the finance minister or chief executive (Von Hagen and Harden 1995; Alesina and Perotti 1996). Here I take a closer look at the hypotheses about the fiscal impact of legislative institutions put forward in the literature.

In his groundbreaking and widely cited paper prepared for the European Commission, Von Hagen (1992) argues that institutions that weaken the role of special interests in the budget process affect fiscal performance. He develops three different versions of a 'structural index' that consist of up to four different items. Based on fiscal data for European Community countries in the 1980s, his empirical analysis finds support for the 'structural hypothesis' that a budget process with a dominating role of the finance minister vis-à-vis spending ministers, restricted parliamentary authority and limiting adjustments to the budget during implementation is strongly conducive to fiscal discipline. Item two of the structural index combines several components to assess the 'structure of the parliamentary process'. These indicate whether amendment powers are limited, changes to the budget are required to be offsetting, amendments can cause the fall of the government, all expenditures are passed in one vote and the process commences with a global vote on the size of the total budget.

Alesina et al. (1996) extend the geographical application of Von Hagen's (1992) work. They construct a ten-item index of budget institutions to classify budget systems as 'hierarchical' or 'collegial'. Using a sample of 20 Latin American and Caribbean countries, they find that more hierarchical budget institutions were associated with greater fiscal discipline in the 1980s and early 1990s. Alesina et al. (1996) sum two variables on amendment powers and the reversionary budget to construct their 'subindex three', which they argue measures the relative position of the government vis-à-vis the legislature in the approval stage, and find that it is a significant determinant of fiscal performance.[2] Hallerberg and Marier (2004) use a rescaled version of this sub-index to analyse the interaction of budget institutions and electoral incentives. They find that strengthening executive authority in the budget process is most effective at curbing deficits in countries with candidate-centred electoral systems. Cheibub (2006: 364) also draws heavily on these variables and finds that the effect of presidentialism on budget balances is conditional upon the budgetary powers of the president.

Von Hagen's (1992: 36) claim that the sequencing of budgetary decisions matters for fiscal policy outcomes has received particular attention in the literature. Ferejohn and Krehbiel (1987) formally demonstrate that a process that starts with a vote on total spending does not always contain the size of the budget relative to an item-by-item voting procedure. The empirical evidence is not entirely conclusive. Helland's (1999: 130–2) results for European countries challenge Von Hagen's intuition and Ehrhart et al. (2007) present experimental results that are consistent with Ferejohn and Krehbiel's (1987) model. On the other hand, Alesina et al. (1999: 270) interpret their evidence for Latin American countries to show that 'a voting procedure in which the level of deficits and in some cases the size of spending come first leads to more fiscal discipline than the alternative procedure in which the budget balance is determined at the same time or after the discussion on composition'. Moreover, many practitioners strongly believe that this sequence forces politicians to acknowledge the fiscal implications of their decisions by making trade-offs more explicit (Molander 2001: 42; see also Blöndal 2003; Kim and Park 2006).

As demonstrated in Chapter 2, the extent of legislative authority is strongly affected by how binding the appropriations are. A number of studies include the power of the executive to impound or withhold funds appropriated by the legislature and view it as a key mechanism for maintaining fiscal discipline during the implementation of the budget (Von Hagen 1992; Filc and Scartascini 2007; Hallerberg et al. 2007). The work by Pereira and Mueller (2004) on the Brazilian budget process also shows how executive authority to withhold voted funds constitutes a source of strategic power for the president. However, there is no consensus that impoundment authority is always conducive to ensuring prudent fiscal outcomes. Alesina et al. (1996: 13–4) offer a dissenting view: 'Intuitively, it would seem that the possibility of cutting the budget will result in smaller deficits. However, it is also possible that the government will not have incentives to submit a small budget if they can cut it later at their discretion. And later on, it may be difficult to cut it even if this was intended from the beginning.' My analysis in Chapter 2 also highlighted some possibly unexpected effects of impoundment authority. Hence, although many studies anticipate a positive effect of impoundment authority on fiscal performance, this relationship is not as straightforward as it may appear at first glance.

Legislative committees have also been linked to budget outcomes. Wildavsky in his early work famously described the Appropriations Committee of the US House of Representatives as 'a guardian of the Treasury' (Davis et al. 1966: 530). Schick (2002: 29) argues that to centralise responsibility in a budget or finance committee 'encourages examining the budget in fiscal terms', whereas to disperse authority across sectoral committees 'encourages a programme orientation'. Crain and Muris (1995: 319) similarly regard the consolidation of control within one committee as 'an institutional means to overcome the common pool problem' and 'a mechanism to contain spending pressures'. Using data for the American states, they find that the centralisation of spending decisions in a single committee indeed restrains expenditures compared with systems where decisions are balkanised across different committees. Focusing on the federal level, Cogan (1994) provides an interesting historical account of the fiscal cost of dispersing spending authority across committees in the US Congress. Dharmapala (2003, 2006) develops formal treatments of this topic. On balance, this suggests substantial agreement among scholars that the centralisation of committee authority in budgetary matters helps to contain spending.

In addition, a number of studies have investigated the impact of bicameralism on fiscal aggregates. Heller (1997: 486) argues that second chambers with budgetary powers increase the number of actors who can veto or modify legislation and this 'forces the government to include more spending in the budget than it would need to if the budget had to pass in only one legislative chamber'. Using a sample of 17 industrialised countries, he finds that deficits are higher in parliamentary systems with bicameral than those with unicameral legislatures (see also Heller 2001). However, with budget deficits rather than expenditures as the dependent variable, it is impossible to clearly distinguish his proposition that budgetary bicameralism leads to higher spending from the rival hypothesis that it can increase gridlock (Alt and Lowry 1994). Gleich (2003: 18) argues that bicameralism adds to the fragmentation of the legislature and hence contributes to a spending and deficit bias (see also Diaz-Cayeros et al. 2002). On the other hand, Ricciuti (2004) argues that bicameralism increases transaction costs and should lead to lower spending, but he fails to find empirical support for this hypothesis. However, Bradbury and Crain (2001: 322) do conclude that 'splitting the legislative branch into two chambers mitigates the fiscal commons problem'. Using subnational government data from the US, Gilligan and Matsusaka (2001: 79) find that the size of the upper house, but not of the lower house, has a consistently positive effect on expenditures and revenues. In short, the fiscal impact of bicameralism remains contested and may be more nuanced than implied in some of the literature.

This brief summary of related work identifies a substantial number of legislative variables that may affect fiscal policy outcomes. Most of these form part of the index of legislative budget institutions introduced in Chapter 3: parliamentary amendment powers, the reversionary budget, executive authority to impound legislative appropriations as well as the role of a budget or finance committee in the approval process. The theoretical analysis in Chapter 2 adds to this discussion, in particular the detailed predictions derived from the analysis of parliamentary powers to amend the budget proposed by the executive. In addition, the literature review identifies at least two other relevant variables, namely budgetary bicameralism as well as the sequencing of budgetary decisions, which deserve incorporation into the following empirical analysis.

5.2   Initial results

I pursue a two-step approach in order to combine different sets of quantitative empirical evidence into a single line of inquiry. In this section, I commence with a broadly based investigation into the association between legislative institutions and fiscal policy outcomes. I use the results as a basis for extending my empirical analysis in the following two sections, first across more countries and then across time. The dataset I use in this section contains the entire spread of legislative institutions highlighted earlier and in previous chapters. Based on the initial findings from this analysis, the following section focuses on selected legislative institutions and extends the empirical analysis beyond the advanced industrialised nations to a much larger global sample of both developed and developing countries. While each piece of evidence may have its potential weaknesses, this type of triangulation offers additional reassurances.

My first step in the empirical analysis again utilises the dataset developed in Chapter 3 of this book. To aid analysis, I normalise the index of legislative budget institutions, as well as each of its main components identified in Table 3.3 so that all scores on these variables range between 0 and 1. I add a simple dummy to indicate bicameralism, which I define in accordance with Heller (1997) as the existence of a second chamber with equal budgetary powers as the lower chamber of parliament. This definition excludes second chambers that have a negligible role or none at all in budgetary decisions. I also add a dummy to indicate the sequencing of budgetary decisions, drawing on data from the same survey utilised in Chapter 3 (OECD and World Bank 2003). The relevant survey item asked whether a legislature establishes aggregate expenditure ceilings before debating individual items (refer to the data appendix for further details). In some instances, the literature review earlier requires the use of elements of the composites constructed in Table 3.4, specifically the power to withhold appropriated funds as well as the use of a budget or finance committee. I create normalised versions of these two variables as well. In total, therefore, the institutional variables of interest in this dataset include the standardised index plus eight of its components and two other variables.

An assessment of the impact of legislative institutions on the size of government requires appropriate left-hand-side fiscal variables and data. One important choice relates to coverage, that is, whether to use data for central or general government. Moreover, databases differ in their inclusion of extra-budgetary entities, such as social security funds and other off-budget funds (Hogwood 1992: 34–7; Kraan 2004). Among the studies reviewed earlier, Von Hagen (1992) uses general government data, while Alesina et al. (1996) use central government data. Elsewhere, Woo (2003: 390–1) points out that central government data can be misleading when other parts of the public sector contribute substantially to fiscal outcomes. Perotti and Kontopoulos (2002: 196) also note that central government data do not capture spending at the subnational level that is mandated by the centre. To the contrary, Volkerink and De Haan (2001: 222) prefer central government data, arguing that most theories relate to central government. Persson and Tabellini (2003: 38) add data availability as a practical reason in favour of central government data, and further claim that these data are more reliable. Evidently, many justifications are plausible. In this section, I use general government data, whereas the following section uses central government data. While this choice is driven partly by data availability so as to maximise sample size and degrees of freedom, the fact that I vary the coverage of the dependent variable across different datasets also serves as a robustness check.

A related issue is the choice of appropriate indicators of 'fiscal discipline' or 'fiscal performance'. As with regard to data coverage, the literature offers a rather confusing variety of possibilities. Von Hagen (1992) considers gross debt, net lending (i.e. the negative of the conventional deficit) and net lending excluding interest payments (i.e. the negative of the primary deficit). Alesina et al. (1999: 263) use only the primary deficit as the dependent variable, arguing that it is less sensitive to inflation-induced increases in interest payments than the conventional deficit, and that it is a better indicator of the fiscal stance of the current government, whose interest payments are largely determined by previously accumulated debt. Stein et al. (1998: 129–31) use the institutional data from Alesina et al (1996), but test the effect on several dependent variables. Interestingly, they find no association between their measure of budget institutions and government size, but report the strongest and most significant impact when using the primary balance. Of the other papers reviewed earlier, Heller (1997) uses conventional deficits, while Crain and

Muris (1995) use the logarithm of state revenues and expenditures per capita. In sum, there is no agreement on what constitutes the most appropriate indicator of fiscal discipline.

The disagreement about appropriate fiscal variables for empirical testing cannot be explained with reference to differences in the underlying theoretical approaches. A number of models in the common pool resource tradition generate, in the first instance, predictions about relative levels of expenditures (Weingast et al. 1981; Von Hagen and Harden 1995; Hallerberg 2004: 22–8).[3] Von Hagen (1992: 32) justifies the use of the deficit as the dependent variable by assuming at least partly non-Ricardian taxpayers who shift some of the cost of today's consumption to future generations. Still, the most direct test of his initial model (Von Hagen and Harden 1995) is to consider the impact of institutional arrangements on levels of public spending. Similarly, Heller's (1997) model predicts spending levels, yet he uses deficits as the dependent variable for his empirical test. Perotti and Kontopoulos (2002: 193) go as far as to claim that 'often there is no theoretically compelling reason why political and procedural variables should affect the deficit, but certainly there are always reasons to expect them to affect expenditure'. To align my empirical analysis closely with the theoretical approach, this chapter investigates effects on public spending.

The size of the OECD sample is reduced by the unavailability of the required fiscal data for two countries, Mexico and Turkey, in the *OECD Economic Outlook Database* (OECD 2008). Due to the limited degrees of freedom, I keep the set of control variables to a minimum and include two basic controls for demographic structure (from World Bank 2007; see also Heller 2003; European Commission Economic Policy Committee 2006), as well as indicators of presidentialism and a majoritarian electoral system – two variables that Persson and Tabellini (2003) identify as primary determinants of fiscal policy outcomes.

To the basic set of control variables I add one by one my (standardised) institutional variables of interest. Table 5.1 presents the results. Column (1) includes the index of legislative budget institutions. The coefficient is large and significant at the five per cent level. In column (2) I include only the Powers variable, which also returns a large coefficient, with significance at the one per cent level. In column (3) I add Reversion and in column (4) Flexibility. The respective

Table 5.1 Cross-section estimates – OECD countries

	(1)	(2)	(3)	(4)	(5)	(6)	(7)	(8)	(9)	(10)	(11)	(12)
Index	13.38 (5.37)**											
Powers		8.33 (2.20)***										7.43 (3.26)**
Reversion			0.14 (2.71)									
Flexibility				0.52 (4.01)								
Withhold					1.35 (2.47)							
Time						9.51 (3.04)***						2.30 (4.35)
Committees							3.94 (4.38)					
Budget committee								3.50 (3.61)				
Research									0.38 (6.34)			
Ceiling										1.58 (1.94)		
Bicameralism											-1.84 (2.40)	

Presidential system	−11.79	−9.07	−7.35	−7.50	−8.29	−10.55	−6.87	−8.50	−7.43	−7.37	−6.12	−9.67
	(1.79)***	(1.97)***	(2.40)***	(2.46)***	(2.36)***	(1.76)***	(1.82)***	(2.04)***	(2.73)***	(1.64)***	(2.64)**	(2.07)**
Majoritarian elections	0.05	1.57	−2.00	−1.85	−1.20	−1.18	−2.24	0.11	−2.07	−2.16	−1.66	1.39
	(2.27)	(2.42)	(2.50)	(2.67)	(2.77)	(2.13)	(2.62)	(3.13)	(2.81)	(2.32)	(2.33)	(2.46)
Population 15–64	−0.68	−0.67	−0.99	−0.95	−0.83	−0.90	−0.99	−0.89	−1.00	−1.00	−1.03	−0.68
	(0.53)	(0.42)	(0.61)	(0.78)	(0.75)	(0.54)	(0.58)*	(0.60)	(0.60)	(0.58)	(0.60)	(0.43)
Population 65+	0.71	0.75	0.87	0.88	0.89	0.75	0.86	0.82	0.88	0.81	0.92	0.73
	(0.44)	(0.33)**	(0.48)*	(0.55)	(0.54)	(0.44)	(0.52)	(0.53)	(0.54)	(0.50)	(0.54)	(0.34)**
Constant	74.40	72.28	98.64	95.41	87.02	91.46	97.12	89.58	99.22	99.72	101.09	73.36
	(40.43)*	(29.46)**	(45.90)**	(59.43)	(57.17)	(39.80)**	(43.57)**	(46.25)*	(44.69)**	(44.16)**	(45.35)**	(30.66)**
Observations	28	28	28	28	28	28	28	28	28	28	28	28
Adjusted R-squared	0.51	0.64	0.42	0.42	0.42	0.53	0.43	0.44	0.42	0.43	0.43	0.63

* Significant at 10 per cent; ** significant at 5 per cent; *** significant at 1 per cent.

Note: OLS estimates with robust standard errors in parentheses. The dependent variable is general government outlays as a percentage of Gross Domestic Product (GDP). The results are for the period 2001–5. Mexico and Turkey are missing, as the *OECD Economic Outlook Database* does not report the relevant fiscal data (OECD 2008). All component variables of the index of legislative budget institutions, as well as the index itself, are rescaled to range between 0 and 1. The Ceiling, Bicameralism, Presidential system and Majoritarian elections variables are all dummies set equal to 1 to indicate the relevant institutional feature, 0 otherwise. Refer to the text and the data appendix for further details.

coefficients are far from significant at conventional levels. Entering Withhold as a separate variable, in column (5), returns a similar result. On the other hand, the coefficient on Time in column (6) has a substantively large coefficient, which is significant at the one per cent level. The results in column (7) to (11) show that none of the coefficients on the remaining variables come close to significance: Committees, Budget committee, Research, Ceiling and Bicameralism are not correlated with public spending levels. In the final column (12), I include Powers and Time simultaneously. The coefficient on the latter variable drops substantially in size, compared with column (6), and it is now far from significant. It turns out that these two variables are fairly strongly correlated with a coefficient of .6 for this sample of 28 countries. In other words, the coefficient on Time in column (6) is inflated by the exclusion of Powers from the model.

It is noteworthy that the coefficients on the two demographic controls have the predicted sign, although they are not always significant. An increase in the share of the population of working age decreases expenditures, while the opposite holds for the share of those aged 65 and older. Presidential government appears to have a very large negative effect on public spending. However, it should be noted that this sample only includes three countries that fall into this category, so this finding should not be over interpreted. In addition, and in contrast to the findings by Persson and Tabellini (2003), the effect of majoritarian elections is indistinguishable from zero across all models.

The results presented in this section indicate that only one of the legislative institutions discussed here has a direct effect on public spending, namely parliamentary powers to amend the budget proposal of the executive. This result is not surprising. First, the theoretical discussion in Chapter 2 suggested strongly that this institutional feature has sizable effects on expenditures. Second, while there is considerably less overlap with regard to most other variables, there is an impressive consensus in the literature on budget institutions with regard to the relevance of legislative amendment powers (Von Hagen 1992; Alesina et al. 1996; Yläoutinen 2004; Fabrizio and Mody 2006). In short, these findings are highly plausible as well as in line with existing empirical work. However, they are also vulnerable to criticism, since the sample size is small and cross-sectional evidence is particularly susceptible to omitted variable bias. Fortunately, having pinpointed the most relevant institutional feature provides a strong basis for a more targeted empirical inquiry that addresses these shortcomings.

5.3 Further cross-sectional evidence

Documenting the evolution of all of the earlier mentioned legislative institutions over a longer period of time as well as an even larger sample of countries is practically infeasible.[4] Fortunately, the preceding section helps to focus further analysis on the relationship between legislative powers of amendment and public expenditures, which enables the expansion of this inquiry in terms of space and time. I start by expanding the cross-sectional dataset of Persson and Tabellini (2003), which contains data for a diverse set of 80 countries averaged over the 1990–8 period. My key addition to this dataset is the inclusion of legislative amendment powers. The data presented in Table 5.2 were cross-checked extensively against relevant constitutional provisions. Since not all legislative amendment powers are codified in constitutions (Lienert and Jung 2004), I also consulted parliamentary standing orders, as well as surveys of legislative procedures or budget institutions conducted during or close to the relevant time period (see the sources indicated underneath Table 5.2 for a full listing). In quite a few cases, I discovered discrepancies between different data sources. Some of these are due to mistakes. Another reason is that surveys of fiscal institutions based on questionnaires administered to budget officials do not always clearly distinguish between formal rules and actual practice, which may lead to different interpretations and inconsistent responses. Here the focus is on formally codified procedures, which resolves such scoring issues. Where different sources indicated different results, I consulted country experts where possible.

Another difficulty arises when countries change their budget institutions during the period under consideration. However, the formal budgetary powers of national legislatures are remarkably stable and indicate a strong status quo bias (Stein et al. 1998: 21–5; Filc and Scartascini 2007: 168). The exceptions in this dataset are Argentina, Peru, Poland and New Zealand. Between 1990 and 1998, the first three countries moved from unrestricted to restricted amendment powers, while New Zealand only modified the form of its restrictions. More recent changes to legislative amendment authority in France (Chabert 2001), Romania (Yläoutinen 2004) and South Africa (see next chapter) fall outside the sample period used here.[5] For those countries where amendment powers changed during the 1990s, the Powers variable in Table 5.2 reflects the average score over the period.

Table 5.2   Legislative powers over public spending in the 1990s

Legislature	Constraint	Powers
Argentina	No increase of deficit[a]	0.86
Australia	Cuts only	0.25
Austria	None	1.00
Bahamas	Cuts only	0.25
Bangladesh	Accept or reject	0.00
Barbados	Cuts only	0.25
Belgium	None	1.00
Belize	Cuts only	0.25
Bolivia	None	1.00
Botswana	Cuts only	0.25
Brazil	No increase of deficit	0.75
Bulgaria	No increase of deficit	0.75
Canada	Cuts only	0.25
Chile	Cuts only	0.25
Colombia	Cuts only	0.25
Costa Rica	No increase of deficit	0.75
Cyprus	Cuts only	0.25
Czech Republic	None	1.00
Denmark	None	1.00
Dominican Republic	Other[b]	0.00
Ecuador	Total spending	0.50
El Salvador	Cuts only	0.25
Estonia	No increase of deficit	0.75
Fiji	Cuts only	0.25
Finland	None	1.00
France	Cuts only	0.25
Gambia	Accept or reject	0.00
Germany	None	1.00
Ghana	Cuts only	0.25
Greece	None	1.00
Guatemala	None	1.00
Honduras	None	1.00
Hungary	None	1.00

Table 5.2 Continued

Legislature	Constraint	Powers
Iceland	None	1.00
India	Cuts only	0.25
Ireland	Accept or reject	0.00
Israel	None	1.00
Italy	None	1.00
Japan	Other[c]	0.25
Latvia	No increase of deficit	0.75
Luxembourg	None	1.00
Malawi	Accept or reject	0.00
Malaysia	Cuts only	0.25
Malta	Cuts only	0.25
Mauritius	Cuts only	0.25
Mexico	No increase of deficit	0.75
Namibia	None	1.00
Nepal	Accept or reject	0.00
Netherlands	None	1.00
New Zealand	Cuts only[d]	0.25
Nicaragua	No increase of deficit	0.75
Norway	None	1.00
Pakistan	Cuts only	0.25
Papua New Guinea	Cuts only	0.25
Paraguay	None	1.00
Peru	Total spending[e]	0.56
Philippines	Total spending	0.50
Poland	None[f]	0.97
Portugal	None	1.00
Romania	None	1.00
Russia	None	1.00
Singapore	Cuts only	0.25
Slovak Republic	None	1.00
South Africa	Accept or reject	0.00
South Korea	Cuts only	0.25
Spain	Total spending	0.50
Sri Lanka	Cuts only	0.25
St. Vincent and the Grenadines	Cuts only	0.25
Sweden	None	1.00
Switzerland	None	1.00
Thailand	Cuts only	0.25
Trinidad and Tobago	Cuts only	0.25
Turkey	Total spending[g]	0.50
Uganda	Cuts only	0.25

(Continued)

Table 5.2   Continued

Legislature	Constraint	Powers
Uruguay	Total spending	0.50
United States	None	1.00
Venezuela	Total spending	0.50
Zambia	Cuts only	0.25
Zimbabwe	Cuts only	0.25

Note: (a) Restriction applied to the budget approval process from 1993 onwards (Section 28 of the 1992 National Public Sector Financial Administration and Control Systems Act; Alesina et al. 1996; Stein et al. 1998). (b) Legislative amendments require a two-thirds majority, unless they are initiated by the executive (Art. 115(3) of the 1994 Constitution; Alesina et al. 1996; Filc and Scartascini 2007). (c) There is a legal dispute about the extent to which the Diet can amend the budget (Sakurai 2004). According to Lienert and Jung (2004: 271), 'the general understanding is that the Diet cannot amend the government's budget proposal significantly'. (d) Since 1996 the Crown has a financial veto over amendments with more than a 'minor impact' on allocations or fiscal aggregates; previously as in the UK (Standing Orders 312–16; Inter-Parliamentary Union 1986; OECD 1998; Wehner 2006). (e) Restriction applied to the budget approval process from 1991 onwards (Alesina et al. 1996; Stein et al. 1998; Hallerberg and Marier 2004). (f) Deficit restriction since 1998 (Art. 220 of the 1997 Constitution; Gleich 2003; Yläoutinen 2004). (g) Restrictions apply in the plenary (Art. 162 of the 1982 Constitution; OECD 1998; Kraan et al. 2007). The governing party or parties have a constitutionally guaranteed right to appoint at least 25 out of the 40 members of the Budget Committee, where the amendment restrictions do not apply.

Source: Constitutions, parliamentary rules and standing orders, Inter-Parliamentary Union (1986), Von Hagen (1992), Döring (1995a), Alesina et al. (1996), OECD (1998, 2002b), Haggard and McCubbins (2001), Gleich (2003), Lienert and Jung (2004), Santiso (2004), Yläoutinen (2004), Filc and Scartascini (2004, 2007), International Budget Project (2006), Wehner (2006).

The observation that this particular institutional feature is extremely durable is helpful in addressing one of the most serious criticisms levelled at this type of research: the possibility of institutional endogeneity. While the literature acknowledges this potential problem, Fabrizio and Mody (2006: 14) highlight that the econometric challenge of 'identifying the exogenous component of fiscal institutions is hard' and 'a hurdle that no one has yet crossed' (see also Acemoglu 2005). The fact that fundamental reform of parliamentary amendment powers is extremely rare suggests that they are very costly to change. Anecdotal evidence supports the argument that fiscal performance has to be extremely unsatisfactory in order to overcome the status quo bias of budget institutions (Stein et al. 1998: 21–5). This is also illustrated by the accounts of the reform of legislative budget institutions in the following chapter. In Sweden, the trigger was an unprecedented macroeconomic crisis, while South Africa's redesign followed a fundamental regime change and even in these unique circumstances took more than a decade to negotiate. On balance, I conclude that the problems posed by the possibility of institutional endogeneity should not be exaggerated in this particular context. It is reasonable to treat legislative amendment powers as exogenous in at least the short to medium term (see also Alesina and Perotti 1996: 4).

The increase in sample size allows the inclusion of further control variables. Persson and Tabellini's (2003, 2004) control variables comprise the average of the Freedom House scores for political and civil liberties, the natural logarithm of the total population, the natural logarithm of per capita income, trade openness measured as the sum of exports and imports divided by GDP, the proportions of the population between the ages of 15 and 64 as well as 65 or older, a federalism dummy to account for decentralisation, a dummy indicating OECD membership prior to 1993 (except Turkey) and the age of democracy. Their main cross-sectional regression results also include three continental dummies as well as a set of indicators of colonial heritage, weighted by the duration since independence. The dependent variable is central government expenditures as a percentage of GDP. In this analysis, I adopt Persson and Tabellini's (2004) standard specification and investigate the effect of adding amendment powers to the model. I construct a new variable, Amendment limit, which is defined as 1–Powers, so that 0 indicates the absence of amendment limits and higher scores indicate restricted authority. This is more in line with the literature on fiscal institutions and it also facilitates the interpretation of the results with panel data. The data appendix contains further information.

Table 5.3 reports the results. I commence by adding Amendment limit to the baseline model. According to the estimate in column (1), a switch from unfettered legislative amendment powers to an amend-or-reject limit is associated with lower spending worth more than nine per cent of GDP. The result is significant at the

Table 5.3 Cross-section estimates – global sample

	(1)	(2)	(3)	(4)
Amendment limit	–9.18	–7.17	–7.94	
	(3.07)***	(3.02)**	(3.36)**	
Presidential system		–4.96	–6.13	–4.32
		(1.75)***	(2.42)**	(1.88)**
Majoritarian elections		–4.66	–3.34	–3.85
		(1.96)**	(2.51)	(2.00)*
Accept-or-reject limit				–7.95
				(2.92)***
Cuts only limit				–6.95
				(3.53)*
Total spending limit				–2.99
				(3.30)
Deficit limit				1.37
				(3.30)
Democracy	–3.31	–3.22	–3.95	–3.37
	(1.24)***	(1.22)**	(2.28)*	(1.30)**
Total population	1.01	1.21	2.02	1.30
	(0.82)	(0.73)	(0.93)**	(0.75)*
GDP per capita	0.21	–0.60	0.50	–0.20
	(1.86)	(1.98)	(2.54)	(2.09)
Trade	0.04	0.04	0.06	0.04
	(0.03)	(0.02)	(0.03)*	(0.02)
Population 15–64	–0.18	–0.22	–0.36	–0.19
	(0.34)	(0.35)	(0.42)	(0.37)
Population 65+	0.73	0.75	0.48	0.65
	(0.44)	(0.45)*	(0.54)	(0.48)
Federalism	–7.21	–6.17	–6.95	–7.37
	(2.54)***	(2.42)**	(2.81)**	(2.41)***
OECD	–1.20	–0.71	–0.89	–0.02
	(3.67)	(3.55)	(4.04)	(3.89)
Age of democracy	–6.30	–3.46	–6.04	–4.25
	(4.96)	(4.28)	(4.79)	(4.99)
Africa	–0.88	2.43	1.08	2.33
	(4.69)	(4.82)	(6.00)	(5.04)
East Asia	–4.98	–3.36	–7.77	–2.71
	(2.92)*	(3.09)	(4.50)*	(3.33)
Latin America	–7.02	–5.01	–4.69	–5.16
	(2.84)**	(2.61)*	(3.26)	(2.70)*
Spanish colonial origin	–3.05	2.39	2.71	–0.92
	(4.37)	(4.88)	(5.59)	(7.09)
British colonial origin	7.54	8.52	6.51	9.73
	(2.80)***	(3.09)***	(3.78)*	(3.78)**

Table 5.3   Continued

	(1)	(2)	(3)	(4)
Other colonial origin	–2.36	–3.08	–1.66	–3.69
	(2.76)	(2.59)	(3.02)	(2.84)
Constant	42.93	51.77	53.28	47.79
	(17.84)**	(17.12)***	(21.13)**	(20.04)**
Observations	80	80	64	80
Democracy threshold	≤5.5	≤5.5	≤3.5	≤5.5
Adjusted R-squared	0.63	0.65	0.65	0.65

* Significant at 10 per cent; ** significant at 5 per cent; *** significant at 1 per cent.
Note: OLS estimates with robust standard errors in parentheses. The dependent variable is central government expenditures as a percentage of GDP. The results are for the period 1990–8. Refer to the text and the data appendix for further details.

one per cent level. In column (2) I add Persson and Tabellini's (2003) main institutional variables of interest, here labelled Presidential system and Majoritarian elections. The coefficients suggest that both of these reduce expenditures by close to five per cent of GDP, the former significant at the one per cent level and the latter at the five per cent level. The coefficient on Amendment limit decreases slightly in size and achieves significance at the five per cent level. In column (3), I retain the same model but restrict the sample to countries with an average Freedom House score of 3.5 or smaller, applying a stricter definition of democracy. This leads to a drop in sample size from 80 to 64. In this reduced sample, the coefficients on Amendment limit and Presidential system both increase in size, relative to the results reported in column (2), and achieve significance at the five per cent level. In contrast, the coefficient on Majoritarian elections is no longer statistically significant at conventional levels. Taken together, these results suggest that parliamentary powers to amend the budget are at least as important as the form of government and the electoral system in determining public expenditures. Moreover, the size of the estimated effect of amendment powers is very similar to the results reported in Table 5.1.

The analysis in Chapter 2 predicted that overall spending decreases when amendment authority is restricted. In column (4), I distinguish between each type of amendment limit. In those countries that altered amendment powers during the sample period, I determine the relevant category on the basis of which arrangement prevailed the longest over the 1990–8 period. According to column (4), the coefficient on Accept-or-reject limit has the largest negative sign, implying a reduction in spending of almost eight per cent of GDP, and the estimated decrease for Cuts only limit is about seven per cent. The coefficient on Total spending limit implies a reduction of about three per cent worth of GDP, but in contrast to the former two this estimate is not significant at conventional levels. Finally, the coefficient on Deficit limit is positive and very far from statistically significant. Overall, these results are remarkably consistent with the analysis in Chapter 2. Also note that the coefficients on Presidential system and Majoritarian elections remain significant at the five and ten per cent levels, respectively, although their effect is somewhat smaller than in column (2). These results again confirm that amendment powers are a crucial determinant of public spending outcomes.

In terms of the control variables, Democracy has a consistently significant effect. Since Freedom House gives lower scores to more democratic countries, the estimate suggests that democracy is associated with increased demand for government spending. The large and highly significant coefficient on Federalism is not surprising, since the dependent variable here is central government expenditures; federal countries tend to have more decentralised provision of public services than their unitary counterparts (Lijphart 1999: 189). Some of the regional dummies and indicators of colonial origin also achieve significance across columns (1) to (4), controlling for some unobserved heterogeneity associated with geography and historical background.

An interesting additional result is that the introduction of parliamentary amendment authority into Persson and Tabellini's (2003, 2004) analysis affects, in particular, the estimated effect of the electoral system. The reason is that Majoritarian elections is rather strongly correlated with Amendment limit (the coefficient is .64), but not with Presidential system (.04). One possible explanation for this correlation is that majoritarian electoral systems were part of a broader package of institutional features that the UK bequeathed to its former colonies, which also includes the restrictive rules that characterise the Westminster Parliament. Indeed, it turns out that 29 of the 30 sample countries with majoritarian electoral systems (all except the US) impose limits on amendment authority. On the other hand, the remaining 50 countries with other electoral systems are almost evenly split between those that have amendment limits (24 cases) and those that do not (26 cases). Hence, some of the fiscal effects that Persson and Tabellini attribute to majoritarian electoral systems appear to be due to limits on legislative amendments, which are omitted from their analysis.

5.4 Conditional electoral budget cycles

The comparative political economy literature in the past two decades increasingly uses panel data, often primarily in order to increase the number of observations (Kittel 1999). However, since amendment powers are time invariant or rarely changing, depending on the sample, this raises methodological issues. Unit fixed effects are collinear with time-invariant variables and 'soak up most of the explanatory power' of rarely changing variables (Beck 2001: 285). Random effects models on the other hand assume that unobserved effects are a random sample drawn from a large population (Baltagi 2005: 35) and are often not appropriate in macro-comparative research. One possible approach in this context involves two-step regressions: a panel regression of the fiscal indicator on the time-varying control variables plus country fixed effects as the first stage, and a second stage using cross-section regression in which the estimated country dummies are regressed onto the time-invariant explanatory variables (e.g. Alesina et al. 1996: 21–2; Perotti and Kontopoulos 2002: 215). Plümper and Troeger (2007) refine this approach. Still, traditional cross-sectional analysis is often more suitable for investigating the direct effects of variables with no or very little variation across time. However, panel data can help to investigate how such variables condition the effect of other time-variant variables (Wehner 2010). This is the approach I adopt in order to harness the advantages of panel data.

Authors such as Frey and Lau (1968), Nordhaus (1975) and Tufte (1978) have investigated electoral cycles in policy making (for a review, see Franzese 2002). More recent is a growing focus on context-conditional electoral budget cycles. For example, Brender and Drazen (2005) discover that political budget cycles afflict only new democracies, but not established ones (see also Shi and Svensson 2002). Alt and Lassen (2006) find that deficits increase in election years when budget transparency is low, but that this effect is dampened by high transparency. Chang (2008) shows that electoral systems condition which types of outlays increase in election years: district-specific spending under single-member district systems and social welfare spending under proportional representation systems. This section makes a further contribution to this debate, drawing on the preceding analysis. My argument is straightforward: politicians have incentives to increase public spending in election years. However, the extent to which they can attempt to buy votes depends on whether they have sufficient authority to influence fiscal policy. In the context of this discussion, my hypothesis is that spending increases in election years only if legislators have unfettered powers over the budget, but not when their authority to increase expenditures is effectively curtailed. Amendment constraints can counteract the temptation for legislators to go on an election-induced spending spree.

The panel dataset includes data for 58 countries over the period 1960–98. As in the previous section, the dependent variable is central government expenditures. My explanatory variables of interest are Elections, an indicator for years of elections to (the lower house of) the national legislature, as well as Amendment limit. To test whether amendment powers condition the effect of elections on public spending, I include an interaction between these two variables in the model (Friedrich 1982; Brambor et al. 2006; Kam and Franzese 2007). I include a lagged dependent variable in all models to account for the path dependence of fiscal outcomes highlighted by Davis et al. (1966).[6] I use both country and year fixed effects to eliminate omitted variables bias from unobserved time-invariant features and common shocks, respectively.[7] The country fixed effects absorb all time-invariant controls included in the cross-sectional model.[8] I retain the controls for GDP per capita, trade openness and demographic structure. I do not control for democracy as this variable is very far from statistically significant. However, I do restrict the sample to countries with a positive score on the Polity index of democracy, using an interpolated version of this variable (Persson and Tabellini 2003: 285) to maximise sample size. The data appendix contains further details.

Table 5.4 reports the results. The model in column (1) omits the interaction term to establish a baseline result. The coefficient on Elections is almost zero and very far from statistically significant. Column (2) adds the interaction between Elections and Amendment

Table 5.4 Panel estimates – global sample

	(1)	(2)	(3)	(4)	(5)
Elections	0.01	0.42	0.56	0.36	0.50
	(0.12)	(0.20)**	(0.21)**	(0.21)*	(0.23)**
Amendment limit	–0.58	–0.29	–3.41		
	(0.59)	(0.63)	(3.73)		
Elections × Amendment limit		–1.01	–1.33		
		(0.34)***	(0.38)***		
Total spending limit				–0.30	–4.18
				(0.32)	(0.55)***
Deficit limit				0.07	0.23
				(0.31)	(0.33)
Elections × Accept-or-reject limit				–1.39	–1.75
				(0.62)**	(0.74)**
Elections × Cuts only limit				–0.66	–0.89
				(0.27)**	(0.31)***
Elections × Total spending limit				–0.20	–0.49
				(0.30)	(0.33)
Elections × Deficit limit				0.04	0.03
				(0.45)	(0.44)
Lagged expenditure	0.76	0.76	0.75	0.76	0.75
	(0.05)***	(0.05)***	(0.06)***	(0.05)***	(0.06)***
GDP per capita	0.63	0.66	1.11	0.66	1.08
	(0.64)	(0.64)	(0.93)	(0.64)	(0.93)
Trade	–0.02	–0.02	–0.02	–0.02	–0.02
	(0.01)**	(0.01)**	(0.01)*	(0.01)**	(0.01)*
Population 15–64	–0.05	–0.05	–0.05	–0.05	–0.05
	(0.06)	(0.06)	(0.08)	(0.06)	(0.08)
Population 65+	0.26	0.25	0.22	0.25	0.22
	(0.13)*	(0.13)*	(0.14)	(0.13)*	(0.14)
Elections | Accept-or-reject limit = 1				–1.03	–1.25
				(0.58)*	(0.71)*
Elections | Cuts only limit = 1				–0.30	–0.39
				(0.18)*	(0.21)*
Elections | Total spending limit = 1				0.16	0.02
				(0.23)	(0.24)
Elections | Deficit limit = 1				0.40	0.54
				(0.40)	(0.39)
Observations	1393	1393	1241	1393	1241
Number of countries	58	58	57	58	57

(Continued)

Table 5.4   Continued

	(1)	(2)	(3)	(4)	(5)
Country effects	Yes	Yes	Yes	Yes	Yes
Year effects	Yes	Yes	Yes	Yes	Yes
Polity threshold	> 0	> 0	≥ 6	> 0	≥ 6

* Significant at 10 per cent; ** significant at 5 per cent; *** significant at 1 per cent.
Note: OLS estimates with standard errors clustered by country in parentheses. The dependent variable is central government expenditures as a percentage of GDP. The sample period is 1960–98. Note that some variables relating to amendment powers are entirely time invariant in this sample, and hence their effect in non-election years cannot be estimated with a fixed effects specification (see endnote 8). Refer to the text and the data appendix for further details.

limit. The results indicate that central government expenditures increase by .42 percentage points of GDP in election years in the absence of any restrictions on parliamentary budget authority (i.e. Amendment limit = 0). This effect is significant at the five per cent level. The coefficient on the interaction term is negative, substantively large (about 1 percentage point of GDP) and significant at the one per cent level: an increase in Amendment limit significantly dampens the effect of elections. Column (3) shows that these results strengthen when I restrict the sample to observations with a Polity score of six or higher, that is, the group of countries that the Polity IV Project classifies as 'democracies' in accordance with its recommended three-part categorisation.

The interpretation of the interaction effect so far is incomplete, since the main results in Table 5.4 do not show the effect of an election on public spending for each possible value of Amendment limit (Brambor et al. 2006; Kam and Franzese 2007). To enable a more complete interpretation, column (4) in Table 5.4 reports results for each institutional group separately, distinguishing between each type of amendment constraint. Moreover, below the main results I include calculations of the estimated effect of elections for each type of amendment constraint. The results show that spending increases by .36 percentage points of GDP in election years when a legislature has unfettered powers of amendment (significant at the ten per cent level). According to the calculations reported below the main results, this effect increases slightly with deficit limits, to .4 percentage points, but without achieving significance at conventional levels. Where legislatures are subject to a total spending limit, elections increase spending by .16 percentage points, but this effect is again not statistically significant. On the other hand, in countries with cuts only and accept-or-reject limits spending *decreases* by .3 and 1.03 percentage points, respectively; both of these effects are significant at the ten per cent level. Column (5) shows that these results strengthen when I restrict the sample to observations that fall into Polity's category of democracies.

In sum, these results suggest that electoral cycles in public spending are conditional on legislative powers to amend the budget proposed by the executive. Only unconstrained legislators are associated with an increase in public spending during election years. The findings also support the earlier theoretical analysis and the cross-sectional evidence in this chapter that different types of amendment constraints are not equally effective in constraining a pro-spending bias. The results obtained here suggest that the more severe a constraint, the more it dampens the effect of an election on public expenditures. In fact, the data in Table 5.4 imply that some institutional restrictions can lead to a fiscal tightening in election years compared with non-election years. These findings add to the overall body of evidence assembled in this chapter, that legislative amendment authority in budgetary matters is an important determinant of fiscal policy outcomes.

5.5   Conclusions

The results in this chapter show that legislative effects on public expenditures are largely driven by one particular variable, that is, the power of legislators to amend the budget. In contrast, a number of other budget institutions highlighted in the literature do not appear to significantly affect the size of government. The finding that amendment authority has the most explanatory power among a range of legislative institutions discussed in the literature is very robust and confirms the theoretical analysis in Chapter 2. Put differently, many variables affect the budgetary power of the legislature, but most of these do not have a clear-cut impact on aggregate public expenditures. It is, however, important not to prematurely reject the possibility that institutional features other than amendment limits can enhance fiscal discipline in legislative decision making, which is why the following chapter revisits some of the mechanisms mentioned here and presents a more detailed assessment of them.

More broadly, the findings in this chapter serve as a warning not to oversimplify the debate about the fiscal effect of institutions to a few macro-constitutional distinctions. In a different context, Cheibub and Limongi (2002: 152–3) make this point succinctly when they argue that the performance of a political system 'cannot be entirely derived' from its fundamental macro-constitutional features. Rather, 'other provisions, constitutional and otherwise, also affect the way ... democracies operate, and these provisions may counteract some of the tendencies that we would expect to observe if we derived the regime's entire performance from its basic constitutional principles'. The results in this chapter support this line of argument by highlighting the need to pay careful attention to subtle nuances in institutional design, which can have substantively important consequences for public policy outcomes.

6
The Promise of Top-Down Budgeting

The analysis so far suggests the existence of a fundamental trade-off in legislative budgeting. It appears that legislatures cannot control the budget process and produce a prudent budget at the same time. For those who believe that elected assemblies should play an active role in budgeting, a legislative pro-spending bias may simply represent the cost of democracy, but this is unsatisfactory for those concerned with fiscal management. Can this tension be reconciled? Can legislatures be both powerful as well as fiscally responsible? This chapter is dedicated to discussing this possibility both theoretically as well as empirically. It throws the spotlight on *how* legislatures make budgetary decisions, rather than the limits of their formal powers.

The most promising attempts to reconcile legislative control of the budget process with prudent fiscal decision making involve top-down budgeting approaches. Blöndal (2003: 14–15) highlights the introduction of top-down budgeting as a key reform trend in the advanced industrialised economies over recent decades (see also Kim and Park 2006). It involves 'a binding political decision' about the total level of expenditures at the beginning of the budget process, followed by a decision on how to allocate these resources across the main sectoral spending areas such as health, education, defence and so on (Blöndal 2003: 14). At the executive level, this approach requires a strong role for the central budget authority in fixing the total size of the budget and broad sectoral allocations, but as a quid pro quo devolves detailed decisions on allocations within sectors to line ministries (Kim and Park 2006: 120). For example, the transport ministry might be subject to a strict overall expenditure ceiling imposed at the beginning

103

of the budget process, but within that exercise substantial autonomy over allocations to various programmes, involving decisions such as whether to prioritise roads over railways or airports (within the broad guidance of government policy, of course).

Several reforms have attempted to apply this type of process to legislative decision making. Perhaps the most famous attempt was the Congressional Budget Act of 1974, which introduced a process by which the US Congress could adopt a resolution to guide its budgetary decisions (Schick 2000: 105–38). A new set of Budget Committees – one each respectively in the House of Representatives and the Senate – were to consult other committees and develop a concurrent budget resolution with targets for budget aggregates and sectors. The Congressional Budget Office was created to support the budget committees in checking that the decisions of other committees complied with the resolution, which could be enforced with points of order. This process is well covered in the existing literature (e.g. Schick 2000; Wildavsky and Caiden 2001; Meyers and Joyce 2005). Instead, the empirical examples in this chapter draw on more recent but equally far-reaching attempts at procedural engineering in Sweden and South Africa, which have been less studied but are highly influential in their own right. This also counters any misperceptions that lessons learnt from the experience of the US Congress may be too unique to apply to other countries.

In the case of Sweden, prior to its budget reforms in the mid-1990s the *Riksdag*, the country's unicameral parliament, was widely blamed for contributing to poor fiscal performance. Commentators describe the role of the *Riksdag* in the old system as 'undisciplined' (Blöndal 2001b: 37). At the time, the need for change was strongly felt among parliamentarians and executive officials. Ensuing reform efforts culminated in the introduction of a new budget process in 1996 that also fundamentally reorganised the way the *Riksdag* deals with the state budget (Molander 1999, 2001). After about a decade of the new budget process, the Swedish reforms can be subjected to an interim assessment. While there are some good overviews of the overall package of reforms (Molander 1999; Blöndal 2001b; Hallerberg 2004: 153–68), this chapter adds a detailed assessment of the impact of these reforms on the budgetary role of the *Riksdag*.

More recent institutional changes to the legislative budget procedure in South Africa are no less far reaching. In the wake of its transition to democracy, the country had an opportunity to fundamentally reshape the role of its legislatures. The apartheid era parliaments had been feeble and discredited rubberstamps (Kotzé 1996). In contrast, the country's new constitutional framework promised 'dynamic and pro-active legislatures' (Murray and Nijzink 2002: 1). The first democratic parliament abolished apartheid era legislation and processed the fast-evolving public policy agenda of the new government (Calland 1999). At the same time, parliament itself was in a period of organisational change, including the implementation of a system of legislative committees (Calland 1997) and a new bicameral structure (Murray and Simeon 1999). One of the issues to be reconsidered by the democratic parliament was its role in the budget process. Section 77 of the 1996 constitution gave parliament the power to amend money bills, but required enabling legislation to regulate the process. In the absence of this legislation, parliamentarians could only approve or reject budgets in their entirety and they did not make a single amendment to money bills in more than a decade of democracy. This chapter documents the protracted debate over the reform and presents a first review of the outcome of South Africa's decade-long struggle to reshape the parliamentary budget process.

Cross-national quantitative research is often better suited to produce results that can be generalised, but in this context the case study approach has several strong advantages.[1] First, reorganisations of the legislative budget process of the magnitude I discuss here are rare, as they typically follow fundamental political or economic crises. Second, quantitative comparative research often treats budget institutions as exogenous (Alesina and Perotti 1996: 4).[2] Case studies are better suited to understand institutional change and to tackle the problem of institutional endogeneity that bedevils the fiscal institutionalist research programme (Poterba 1996: 10). Third, case studies can complement quantitative comparative research when they use more precise data than are available for larger samples of countries (Lieberman 2005: 440–1), such as the data on budgetary amendments in Sweden that I present later in the chapter. Moreover, they can enable a more nuanced understanding of how institutions affect public policy outcomes (Scartascini and Stein 2009).

The chapter is organised in three main parts. The first provides a theoretical framework for thinking about the different elements that constitute top-down budgeting, which makes an important distinction between sequencing and centralisation. I then consider the reform of Sweden's parliamentary budget process in the mid-1990s, including a discussion of the effects of the reform on budget outcomes. The third part turns to the South African reform, which is more recent but clearly exhibits the hallmarks of top-down budgeting. I conclude with an assessment of the potential of top-down budgeting to reconcile active legislative participation with prudent budgetary decision making.

6.1   Sequencing and centralisation revisited

In order to understand the potential effect of top-down budgeting, it is necessary to bring together work on the sequencing of budgetary decisions (Ferejohn and Krehbiel 1987) and the centralisation of budgetary decisions (Crain and Muris 1995). With regard to the former, the previous chapter highlighted Von Hagen's (1992: 36) initial suggestion that fiscal discipline is enhanced when a vote on aggregate spending precedes allocational decisions. However, Ferejohn and Krehbiel (1987) demonstrate that such a process may sometimes result in relatively large budgets. Their model assumes that the same group of legislators makes both the aggregate as well as allocational decisions, which is crucial for the outcome (Perotti and Kontopoulos 2002: 196): 'if the same agents decide at both stages, by backward induction they will take into account the likely allocations in the second stage when setting the total budget first'. As Ferejohn and Krehbiel's model cannot be clearly linked to any recommendations about which sequence to adopt in order to promote fiscally prudent decision making, Alesina and Perotti (1996: 12) conclude that its contribution is to provide 'a useful warning against oversimplifying the effect of certain procedures'.

Subsequently, Von Hagen revised his initial claim and argued that it is not a re-ordering of the voting sequence that is decisive, as it has no impact on the share of the tax burden that actors consider, but rather the centralisation of decision making (Hallerberg and Von Hagen 1997). This is the key to a more refined argument about the benefits of top-down budgeting: the effect of the two-step process in terms of fiscal discipline depends crucially on *who* makes the first decision on aggregates. More specifically, top-down budgeting is likely to systematically contain overall spending only when the initial decision on aggregates is delegated to actors who are more likely to consider total costs than those who decide individual spending items.

By clearly distinguishing sequencing and delegation, the debate on top-down budgeting can be linked to the work on legislative committee structures summarised in the previous chapter. Crain and Muris (1995) argue that with a balkanised committee setting, where partial spending decisions are distributed across a number of different committees, no one committee is responsible for the overall level of expenditure, which encourages free-riding. To illustrate their argument more concretely, Figure 6.1 presents stylised versions of the three main types of committee structures that parliaments in the industrialised democracies use for the budget approval process (see OECD 2002b: 164; Chapter 3). In what I call the 'dispersed' model, depicted on the left hand side of Figure 6.1, the different sectoral committees (labelled *SC*) make separate spending decisions over the parts of the budget that fall under their jurisdiction. With sectoral committees I refer to legislative committees that have responsibility for a specific sector of government activity, such as health, education or defence. This is in contrast to some types of committees with a government-wide remit, such as budget or finance committees. In the absence of binding constraints, such as hard expenditure ceilings imposed by law or limitations on parliamentary amendment powers, the literature on the common pool resource problem suggests that the dispersed committee structure encourages spending increases.

Figure 6.1 also illustrates two possible institutional fixes for the common pool resource problem in the form of the centralisation of the committee process. The 'hierarchical' model imposes a finance committee (labelled *FC*) at the centre of decision making that has the power to determine a total expenditure ceiling as well as sectoral

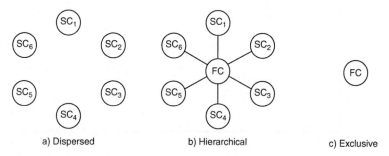

Figure 6.1 Committee structures for budgetary decision making

ceilings, which are binding for the sectoral committees. The latter still play a role in legislative budgeting, but in considering allocations within each sector they are forced to adhere to the ceilings established by the finance committee. A second solution is the 'exclusive' model, in which a finance committee is the sole decision maker and sectoral committees are excluded from the process. The latter two structures introduce centralisation and therefore would be expected to contain the common pool resource problem in the legislative arena.

Figure 6.2 illustrates the effect of sequencing with centralisation in a 'hierarchical' committee structure. Reverting to the two-dimensional budget space used for the analysis in Chapter 2 and in Ferejohn and Krehbiel (1987), it contains the ideal spending packages of three legislative committees, which for simplicity I assume to be unitary actors: the finance committee (FC), a sectoral committee responsible for spending area X (SC_X) and a sectoral committee responsible for spending area Y (SC_Y). We can think of these ideal points as representing the dimension-by-dimension median of the members on each

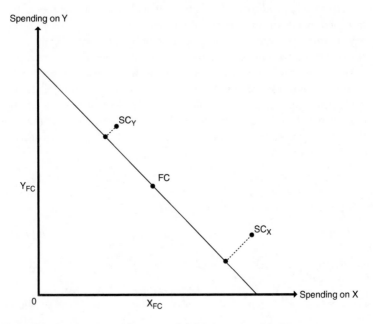

Figure 6.2 Sequencing with a powerful finance committee

committee. The argument by Crain and Muris (1995) suggests that members of the finance committee have institutional incentives to internalise the cost of budgetary measures, as they take an overall view of the budget, while members of sectoral committees on the other hand have fewer incentives to internalise costs and derive private benefits from spending targeted at their sector.[3] Hence, I assume that sectoral committees are relatively profligate vis-à-vis the finance committee, that is, their ideal package implies higher total spending, and that they prefer a spending mix in favour of the policy areas under their jurisdiction.

Under these conditions, empowering the finance committee to make an initial decision on the total size of the budget keeps spending low. If each committee could put forward an ideal level of total spending, then the level preferred by committee SC_Y would constitute the median aggregate budget size that could not be defeated by a majority of committee votes. This outcome contrasts with the illustration in Figure 6.2, where the finance committee imposes the aggregate constraint, which minimises total spending by ensuring the dominance of the low spenders. The imposition of the finance committee's preferences over the distribution of spending between items X and Y is also unlikely to be challenged. Here it constitutes the median of committee preferences projected onto the imposed budget constraint. The latter may not always be the case, but it is a highly plausible scenario from a perspective based on the common pool resource problem. This illustration highlights that it is not sequencing per se that contains the pro-spending bias, but rather the combination of a two-step process with a strong role for the finance committee in setting the fiscal policy agenda. With this in mind, the following two sections evaluate important examples of reforms of the legislative budget process that involved the introduction of top-down budgeting.

6.2 Sweden

Prior to the reforms in the mid-1990s, Sweden had a highly fragmented legislative budget process that lacked co-ordinating mechanisms. The government introduced parts of the budget in January. Over the following months, it would introduce further appropriations, sometimes comprising about a third of the overall budget, as they were being finalised. Appropriations were parcelled out to various sectoral committees of the *Riksdag* for consideration. The government typically tabled a supplementary budget to update its budget proposal at the end of April, based on revised macroeconomic forecasts. This kicked off a second round of scrutiny that again involved various sectoral committees with no overall co-ordination. Parliamentary approval proceeded on an item-by-item basis and was typically concluded in June, before the beginning of the fiscal year in July. Aggregate spending and the deficit were unpredictable until the very end of this process.

The piecemeal structure of the pre-reform process was also reflected in its balkanised committee authority. The various committees of the *Riksdag* have responsibility for both legislation as well as appropriations relating to their particular jurisdiction. A Finance Committee existed under the old system, but it had no special responsibility apart from scrutinising broad guidelines for budget policy. However, these did not contain any detailed expenditure targets. No single committee had responsibility for fiscal aggregates. Rather, sectoral committees deliberated without a hard budget constraint and consistently generated proposals to increase appropriations under their jurisdiction. As one official put it, under the old system members of sectoral committees felt a 'loyalty' towards their spending areas (author's interviews). Moreover, expenditure decisions were poorly co-ordinated with revenue measures that were mainly introduced in the autumn and dealt with in a separate Committee on Taxation. In short, prior to the reforms the committee process in the *Riksdag* resembled the 'dispersed' model in Figure 6.1.

The Secretariat of the *Riksdag* Finance Committee illustrates the outcome of budgetary decision making under the old system with a hypothetical example that is reproduced in Table 6.1. It is assumed that the legislature consists of three parties with none of them having an outright majority of seats. This reflects the fact that minority government characterised Swedish politics during the period under consideration here. Any two of the parties can form a coalition that commands a majority of seats. Table 6.1 details hypothetical proposals of the three parties and their net effect. Items that increase the deficit are given a negative sign and vice versa. In this case, all parties have deficit-neutral preferences, that is, the net effect of their proposed changes is zero. However, because each party represents different constituencies, they disagree about detailed decisions.

Given the preference constellation in Table 6.1, we can derive the outcome of a voting process that proceeds on an item-by-item basis.

Table 6.1 Hypothetical budgetary outcomes with item-by-item voting

Seat share	Government 40%	Party A 35%	Party B 25%	Outcome
Expenditure increase	−1000	−1000	−500	−1000
Revenue increase	400	0	200	200
Saving one	300	300	300	300
Saving two	300	0	0	0
Saving three	0	700	0	0
Net change	0	0	0	−500

Source: *Riksdag* Finance Committee

The first result is that the governing party and party A agree to increase expenditures. However, party B only consents to half the increase in revenues that the government proposes; the median wins. Third, all parties agree on saving one, but there is no majority for any further savings elsewhere in the budget. The overall outcome of the item-by-item voting process is given in the final column. Additional revenues and saving one cover only half of the new expenditures. The net effect is an increase in overall spending and a higher deficit, even though all parties agree on the desirability of fiscal discipline.

Efforts to reform the budget system took several years and were propelled forward by economic crisis. In October 1990 the *Riksdag* established a commission to review parliamentary procedures. Soon after, the country was hit by a pronounced macroeconomic crisis, which precipitated a dramatic deterioration of the general government financial balance. Against this background, the urgency of the investigation increased. In its deliberations, the commission also considered the unflattering findings of a study prepared by a Finance Ministry official (Molander 1992). It assessed Sweden's budget institutions on the basis of a framework developed in Von Hagen's (1992) work on budgeting in the European Community, and found that Sweden had the second worst set of institutions among 13 countries, only slightly ahead of Italy (see also Molander 1999: 202–8). The commission produced recommendations in June 1993.

The process of adopting the recommendations was cumbersome. The proposed reforms to the budget process required adjustments to the Riksdag Act, which meant that they also had to be considered by the Committee on the Constitution. In Sweden, parliamentary procedures have special importance and are more entrenched than in many other countries. Provisions fall into two categories, main and supplementary. Changes to the former require approval twice to become effective, before an election and thereafter. The reforms entailed adjustments to several main provisions in Chapters 3 and 5 of the Riksdag Act (Appendix II contains excerpts). The changes were submitted to parliament in December 1993 and received approval. Following elections in September 1994, in which the Social Democrats regained power from the centre–right coalition, parliament approved the amendments for the second time, thus paving the way for the implementation of the new process. The fact that approval was forthcoming despite a change of government underlines the broad consensus in favour of the reforms.

A range of reform measures were carried forward in the mid-1990s that are more fully discussed elsewhere (Molander 1999; Hallerberg 2004: 160–6).[4] The budget was reorganised into 27 'expenditure areas' that greatly systematised the presentation of appropriations (Blöndal 2001b: 57; see Appendix II). Sweden also moved from a 'broken' fiscal year, running from the beginning of July to the end of the following June, to the calendar year model (Tarschys 2002: 79). For transition purposes, the 1995/96 fiscal year was extended to cover 18 months. The reform of the budget process was combined with an extension of the electoral term from three to four years. In addition, Sweden got its first organic budget law (Government Commission on Budget Law 1996). The law greatly improved legal clarity and transparency, for instance by limiting off-budget expenditures and introducing gross budgeting. Open-ended appropriations used in particular for social benefit programmes were abolished. Finally, the restructuring of the budget process introduced top-down decision making, involving the determination of aggregate limits prior to allocational decisions.[5]

The move to top-down budgeting changed the sequence of the parliamentary process. Parliament would from now on vote first on budget totals before deciding individual appropriations. The first step was for a Spring Fiscal Policy Bill to propose aggregate expenditure ceilings for the upcoming budget plus two further years, as well as indicative ceilings or 'frames' for the allocations across the 27 expenditure areas. This bill was tabled for the first time in April 1996, preceding the presentation of the draft budget by five months. The Finance Committee was delegated responsibility for scrutinising the Spring Fiscal Policy Bill. Following parliamentary approval of the bill in June the executive would proceed to finalise a draft budget to be presented to parliament in September, more than three months before the beginning of the relevant fiscal year.[6]

It should be noted that the role of the Spring Fiscal Policy Bill was subsequently adjusted. Many parliamentarians felt that the process in the second half of the 1990s was too cumbersome and amounted to making budgetary decisions twice a year (Finansdepartement 2000). The Parliamentary Review Commission (2001: 9) recommended a refocusing of parliamentary deliberations on the draft budget in the autumn. As a result, the Spring Fiscal Policy Bill was altered to contain general guidelines for budget policy, but not fixed expenditure ceilings and indicative frames for the expenditure areas. Instead, the government used the Budget Bill in September to propose aggregate expenditure ceilings for the medium term, defined in nominal terms and covering all state expenditure and public pensions, excluding interest payments.

In conjunction with the two-step decision-making procedure, the reforms centralised the committee process along the lines of the 'hierarchical' model in Figure 6.1. The Finance Committee gained responsibility for the aggregate spending totals as well as frames for each of the 27 expenditure areas. Based on the work of the Finance Committee, the first parliamentary decision in the autumn sets the expenditure frames for the upcoming budget. Fifteen sectoral committees then have responsibility for between one and four expenditure areas and make allocational proposals within the approved ceilings. Sectoral committees may propose to shift funds between items within an expenditure area, but they may not breach the total set for that area. In effect, a hard budget constraint has been imposed on sectoral committees. Members on the sectoral committees initially resisted this change, but against a backdrop of fiscal crisis, the reformers assembled enough support for the new process to be accepted.

The specific voting procedure is crucial for understanding the effects of the new process. The report of the Finance Committee contains a proposal as well as reservations from the opposition parties that cover total spending, the allocation of expenditure across the different areas as well as revenue changes. These are treated as packages, unlike in the previous system where shifting majorities could form on individual items. With the reformed system, opposition proposals are eliminated until one main alternative remains (Molander 2001: 36). Under the Social Democratic administrations that followed the reforms in the mid-1990s, the opposition parties were ideologically fragmented and typically did not unite against the government, but only supported their own proposal. Under these conditions even a minority government can obtain the support of more than half of the members voting.[7] In practice, pre-budget consultations between the Social Democrats and their legislative allies, the Left Party and the Green Party, helped to ensure broader support.

By any standards, Sweden managed an impressive fiscal turna-round in the second half of the 1990s. The gap between general government revenues and expenditures had widened dramatically at the beginning of the 1990s, with the deficit exceeding 11 per cent of GDP in 1993. By the end of the millennium, macroeconomic condi-tions had stabilised and the government was back in surplus (OECD 2008). Previous studies suggest that the new budget process should be more conducive to the maintenance of fiscal discipline (Molander 1999: 207–8) and present tentative conclusions regarding its impact on the role of parliament (Blöndal 2001b: 42). Here I provide a more detailed assessment of the impact of the reforms on legislative budg-eting. I first consider what kind of changes can be observed, before discussing in greater detail to what extent they may be attributed to the new budget process.

Most studies on the effect of budget institutions use broad indica-tors of fiscal performance as the dependent variable, typically public debt or deficit measures. This makes sense for studies that consider the overall effect of budget institutions and use indices that com-bine a number of structural variables (e.g. Von Hagen 1992; Alesina et al. 1999). However, such broad indicators of fiscal performance make it difficult to isolate the effect of parliamentary institutions. With case studies it is possible to use much more fine-grained data than are typically available for quantitative cross-national research (Lieberman 2005: 440–1). Here I use two dependent variables that are very specific to the legislative budget process and allow a comparison of the budgetary role of the *Riksdag* prior to and after the budget reforms of the mid-1990s.

One indicator of the budgetary role of a legislature is the number of amendments made to executive proposals (Lienert 2005). While governments may anticipate legislative reactions and incorporate many of them into the budget prior to introduction, in particular in parliamentary systems where the executive relies on legislative support, the persistent absence of any amendments typically indicates a rubberstamp legislature (see Chapter 3). Figure 6.3 reveals that the number of amendments to the government's proposals for 11 budgets passed prior to the reforms (1985/86 to 1995/96) is substantially different from the following nine budgets (1997 to 2005). Prior to the reforms the *Riksdag* made on average 33 amendments, ranging between 63 in 1991/92 and 15 in 1995/96. Under the new process the mean is six, ranging between 17 in 2003 and none in four other instances including the two most recent budgets included in the analysis. The difference in the number of amendments between the pre- and post-reform periods is highly statistically significant ($t = 4.45$, $p < .01$) and indicates a substantial decrease in amendment activity following the reforms.[8]

When considering the difference in the number of amendments, some adjustments have to be borne in mind. On the one hand, the number of appropriations has been halved from a previous total of roughly a thousand to about 500 (Hjalmarsson and Jonsson 2003: 2). The reduction in part preceded the reform of the budget process. A smaller number of appropriations reduces the scope for parliamentary amendments to budgetary details. Nonetheless, even when post-reform amendments are double weighted to compensate for the halving in the number of appropriations, the adjusted level of amendment activity is still two thirds below the pre-reform average. Moreover, pre- and post-reform amendments are not fully comparable. Prior to the reforms almost all changes resulted in increased appropriations. Since any increases now have to be balanced by cuts elsewhere, this augments the number of amendments that are necessary for adjusting the budget. In short, the decrease in amendments is striking even when the reduction in the number of appropriations is taken into consideration.

To assess the fiscal impact of the parliamentary process, Figure 6.3 also indicates the net effect of amendments over the same period. Amendments to all of the budgets passed prior to the reforms resulted in net increases. The sums involved are relatively small compared to the overall budget, averaging 515 million Kronor and typically not exceeding approximately one per cent of the total. However, in many instances the government anticipated parliament's reactions

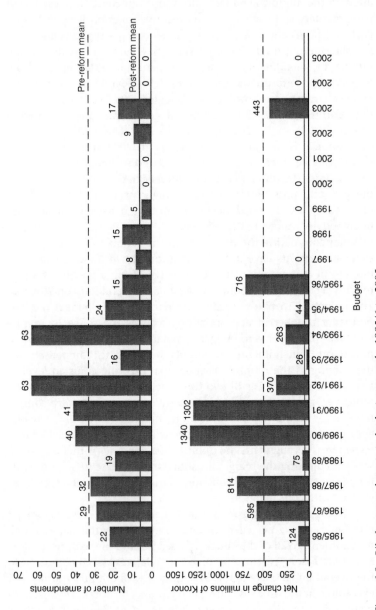

Figure 6.3 *Riksdag* amendments to budget proposals, 1985/6 to 2005
Source: Data from the *Riksdag* Finance Committee

and incorporated relevant demands into its proposals. The true net cost of parliamentary consent in the pre-reform period is therefore hard to determine, but it is almost certainly not fully reflected in these data. Even without this caveat it is clear that the *Riksdag* was unable to maintain fiscal discipline prior to the reforms and regularly increased spending. However, with the exception of 2003, there are no net increases in any of the years following the reforms, resulting in a post-reform mean of 49 million Kronor.[9] The difference in net change between the pre- and post-reform periods is statistically significant ($t = 2.78$, $p < .01$). In general, the parliamentary process following the reforms is characterised by greater fiscal discipline.

To what extent can these changes be attributed to the new budget process? The package voting procedure makes amendments more difficult. It compels opposition parties to be explicit about trade-offs by developing comprehensive alternatives to the government budget proposal. The impact can be illustrated with recourse to Table 6.1. In effect the new process proceeds column-by-column rather than row-by-row. Unless opposition parties unite and support a single alternative, the executive proposal emerges unaltered if it is pitched against any less popular opposition proposal. An evaluation of the new budget process by the Parliamentary Review Commission (2001: 8) confirms: 'The framework model has made it easier for a minority government to get its budget proposal through parliament, since it has made it more difficult for varying majorities to increase expenditures without financing the expenditures at the same time.' Moreover, the centralisation of aggregate decision making in the Finance Committee allows the imposition of a hard budget constraint on sectoral committees, which previously generated regular expenditure increases.

In addition, the extension of the electoral period that occurred at the same time as the reforms to the budget process may also have contributed to greater fiscal restraint. Empirical work on electoral budget cycles points to a negative relationship between the length of the electoral term and levels of public debt, suggesting that an extended time horizon induces politicians to pay more attention to the medium-term implications of their fiscal policies (Franzese 1999; see also Chapter 5). In Sweden, the budget reforms coincided with an extension of the electoral term from three to four years. It is not clear whether this was done deliberately on the basis of an assumption that a longer electoral term makes politicians more fiscally responsible. However, one official interviewed for this study highlighted that although this connection was not made explicit, 'those involved understood it perfectly well' (author's interviews). It is impossible to conclusively pinpoint the separate effects of these simultaneous institutional adjustments, but on balance the evidence indicates a cumulative effect in favour of fiscal discipline.

There are several possible alternative explanations that might be used to challenge these findings. Notably, a number of studies present evidence that minority government impacts on fiscal performance by delaying adjustment to economic shocks (Roubini and Sachs 1989; Edin and Ohlsson 1991; Alt and Lowry 1994). Policy outcomes may also be affected by the ideological orientation of the government (Hibbs 1977; Blais et al. 1993; Cusack 1997, 1999). Other authors find effects of the design of the electoral system (Milesi-Ferretti et al. 2002; Persson and Tabellini 2003; Hallerberg and Marier 2004). However, these alternative perspectives do not generate rival hypotheses, since these variables can essentially be treated as constants over the period under investigation. From 1985 to 2005, Swedish governments consisted of Social Democratic minority administrations, with the exception of the interval between 1991 and 1994, when the party briefly lost power to a centre–right minority coalition. Similarly, the electoral system has been based on proportional representation, with only some modifications (Bergman 2004: 205–6). In short, these alternative accounts do not challenge the procedural hypothesis under investigation.

However, while the reformed institutional arrangements support the maintenance of fiscal discipline, they cannot be regarded as its 'ultimate' or 'fundamental' cause (Gerring 2005: 175–6). Rather, the politicians and officials who initiated the reforms had strong preferences for more prudent fiscal policy (Levy and Lovegrove 2009). The new arrangements were deliberately chosen to achieve this objective in a process that included consideration of fiscal institutionalist research (Molander 1992). Because no party or group of parties controlled the required majority to reform the system on its own, institutional change would never have been possible without strong cross-partisan consensus about the aims of reform, which was forged in a context of economic crisis. As one senior budget official cautioned, it is problematic to relate the improvement of public finances to any specific instrument, but rather 'underlying attitudes and values that changed, and that influenced the result ... and the methods chosen'. In other words, budget institutions are endogenous; the institutional arrangements were shaped by the preferences of politicians who favoured greater fiscal discipline.

This is reflected in consistently strong support for fiscal sustainability at the highest political level. The reform was designed at a time when the then Finance Minister, Göran Persson, used pre-budget consultations with opposition parties to stabilise the budget process (Hallerberg 2004: 165–6). After becoming Prime Minister in 1996, Persson (1997) published a book that made a personal commitment to fiscal prudence. His government's objective was that public finances, comprising central and local governments plus the pension system, show a surplus of two per cent of GDP over the economic cycle (Ministry of Finance 2005: 4). Following the 2006 elections, it remains to be seen whether the achievements of the reforms are dependent on continuity of political leadership or whether fiscal discipline has been hard-wired into the system.

Lastly, the focus of this chapter is not meant to suggest that the improvement in overall public finances should be entirely attributed to the revised legislative process. Several other factors played a role as well. Favourable macroeconomic conditions in the second half of the 1990s certainly aided fiscal recovery. Moreover, the reforms also strengthened the role of the Finance Ministry during executive negotiations, putting it in a stronger position to contain demands from spending ministries compared with the pre-reform process. Since the introduction of expenditure ceilings they have always been adhered to. On the other hand, although the reforms coincided with Sweden's entry into the European Union, this played 'at best a secondary role' in spurring the reforms, which were 'a direct response' to economic crisis (Hallerberg 2004: 167). These and possibly other factors are all important for a wider analysis of public finances in Sweden, but they do not affect the conclusions reached here about the impact of the institutional adjustments on legislative budgeting.

6.3 South Africa

South Africa's 'negotiated revolution' (Sparks 1995) brought an end to apartheid, a system of racial segregation, when the African National Congress (ANC) gained a decisive victory in the country's first democratic elections in 1994. In government, the former liberation movement had to face multiple pressures that were difficult to reconcile. On the one hand, it had an ambitious service delivery agenda that promised to address past injustices (African National Congress 1994). At the same time, the ANC also had to reassure the business community and to re-establish fiscal credibility in order to enhance foreign investment (Department of Finance 1996; for critical perspectives, see Michie and Padayachee 1998; Weeks 1999; Streak 2004). Prior to the 1994 elections, the consolidated general government deficit had deteriorated to nine per cent of GDP, and the budget remained markedly unbalanced in the first few years of democracy (South African Reserve Bank various). In this context, budget reform had the potential to reconcile the demands for service delivery with the need for fiscal consolidation.

With the appointment of Trevor Manuel as Minister of Finance in April 1996, South Africa embarked on an ambitious set of reforms of the budget process. Among these were the implementation of a new system of intergovernmental fiscal relations in 1997, based on the Constitution's three-sphere structure comprising the national government, nine provincial governments and local authorities (Abedian et al. 1997, Wehner 2000). In December 1997, the then Department of Finance published the first Medium Term Budget Policy Statement, a pre-budget report containing the policy framework for the upcoming budget and the two following 'outer years' (Department of Finance 1997). The introduction of a medium-term framework enhanced the capacity of the Minister of Finance to ensure reprioritisation, initially away from defence and towards social expenditures, within strict aggregate limits on spending (Walker and Mengistu 1999). The 1999 Public Financial Management Act modernised the legal framework for budgeting (Fölscher 2007; see also below). These and other reforms earned South Africa praise from the IMF (2003: 18), which commended the country for its 'impressive track record in budgetary management', as well as favourable assessments by independent budget analysts (Fölscher et al. 2000; Fölscher 2002).

The new constitutional framework demanded a range of changes to the budget process and included several specific requirements for legislation (Walker and Mengistu 1999: 48). Among these was section 77(2) of the Constitution: 'An Act of Parliament must provide for a procedure to amend money Bills before Parliament.' Section 77(1) defined a money bill as a bill that 'appropriates money or imposes taxes, levies or duties'.[10] In a first attempt to address the constitutional demand for regulation of the parliamentary budget process, the Department of Finance produced a draft Money Bills Amendment Procedure Bill, which it prepared for tabling in parliament in late 1997. The memorandum attached to the draft bill reveals the attitude that prevailed in the executive at the time. In dramatic language, the memorandum emphasised the need to 'maintain the integrity of the budget and the tax system' and argued that the right to amend money bills 'cannot be an unfettered right' so that 'government is not paralysed in the process'. This wording reflects the emphasis on budgetary consolidation that marked the early years of Manuel's tenure as Minister of Finance, who perceived parliament as a potential fiscal threat.

The content of the draft bill reflected this attitude. The crucial provisions in part one (section 4) would have severely curtailed parliamentary amendment authority. In the National Assembly, only the Finance Committee was to be given authority to propose amendments to money bills. There was no provision for individual members or other committees to table amendment proposals. Moreover, the draft bill required the Finance Committee to give seven days' notice of any proposed amendment and the Minister of Finance would have a right to address the committee prior to it tabling any amendments. The implications of these procedural hurdles are stark in the context of the National Assembly Rules applicable to money bills at that time, which required any such bill to be referred to the Finance Committee on the day of its introduction (rule 290). Moreover, the Rules limited the period for Finance Committee consideration of money bills to 'a maximum of seven consecutive Assembly working days' and required the committee to report to the house before the expiration of this deadline. With these time restrictions, a requirement for seven days' notice for amendments would have all but eliminated any realistic possibility of changes.

In addition, the draft bill sought to prohibit most types of amendments. Without the written consent of the Minister of Finance, the Finance Committee would not have been allowed to table any amendments that increase total spending or spending on a 'vote' (an appropriation for a particular department or government entity), or that introduces a new expenditure item. Hence, it only would have been possible for parliament to reduce expenditure on existing items. Amendments relating to revenues would have been even more restricted. Parliament would not have been allowed to alter the rate, base or time of imposition of a tax, levy or duty, to introduce any new measures or to grant exemptions from proposed measures.

In essence, the draft bill would have allowed the Minister of Finance to veto any substantive amendments to revenue provisions.

The draft bill faced strong opposition within parliament as well as civil society (Krafchik and Wehner 1998). The Congress of South African Trade Unions (1997), despite its electoral alliance with the ANC, strongly condemned the proposal: 'The restrictive content of the proposed Bill ... is a result of the lack of consultation and public discussion. ... In fact, the proposed Bill limits the rights of parliament to such an extent that it would appear to undermine the spirit, if not the letter, of the constitution's commitment to parliamentary oversight of the budget.' A number of ANC parliamentarians were also uneasy with the executive's emphasis on fiscal consolidation and sympathised with demands by the trade unions for a more interventionist role by the legislature. After all, the ANC's policy platform for the 1994 elections, the Reconstruction and Development Programme, called for an end to 'unnecessary secrecy in the formulation of the budget' and the establishment of 'a Parliamentary Budget Office with sufficient resources and personnel to ensure efficient democratic oversight of the budget' (African National Congress 1994: 6.5.8). So unified was the criticism of the draft bill that it was withdrawn and never formally tabled. The trade unions decided to boycott parliamentary hearings on the budget until parliament received meaningful powers of amendment.[11]

Although there was little progress towards a resolution of the issue in the following years, other legislative developments somewhat strengthened parliamentary control. In 1999, the Public Finance Management Act replaced the inherited patchwork of ten different Exchequer Acts and gave effect to various sections in the financial chapter of the Constitution. Several provisions of this act enhanced oversight, for instance a requirement for budgets to include performance information in the form of 'measurable objectives' (section 27), numerical limits on executive discretion to reallocate funds between programmes during the financial year (section 43)[12] and regular in-year reporting (section 32). This legislation was also noteworthy for the way in which the Portfolio Committee on Finance took the lead in rewriting the bill, including the insertion of these and many other provisions (Feinstein 2007: 71). Yet the debate on parliamentary amendment powers remained unresolved.

This was followed by a prolonged stalemate within the ANC. On occasions, the divisions within the party on this issue became visible to the public. In June 2001, Barbara Hogan, then the Chairperson of the Portfolio Committee on Finance, announced that parliamentarians and the Finance Minister had come to an agreement on parliamentary amendment powers with regard to money bills (Ensor 2001). The tabling of new legislation appeared to be imminent. However, soon afterwards there were press reports of Hogan's resignation, which cited as a main reason her frustration about the lack of progress towards more substantial parliamentary involvement in the budget process (Ensor 2002). Hogan did continue as Chairperson of the Portfolio Committee on Finance, but the incident highlighted deep intra-party divisions about fiscal policy and the nature of legislative–executive relations.

Almost ten years after the failed attempt by the Department of Finance to advance the required legislation, little concrete progress had been made in reshaping the legislature's budgetary role. Several parliamentary initiatives had considered the issue and formulated broad principles (Corder et al. 1999; Ad Hoc Joint Sub-Committee on Oversight and Accountability 2002). Parliament had created a Joint Budget Committee in 2002, but it operated in a vacuum due to the unresolved issue of its budgetary authority and as a result struggled to establish a meaningful role for itself – a case of what Calland (1997) described as 'all dressed up with nowhere to go'.[13] As one parliamentarian put it, the issue had evolved into a 'never ending battle' with 'endless renditions of the bill that just went nowhere'. During this period, some Treasury officials started to talk about scrapping the constitutional requirement for legislation on the amendment of money bills as one possible option for resolving the stalemate (author's interviews).

Several political changes enabled the tabling of legislation on parliamentary amendment powers in 2008. One was the replacement of the Speaker of the National Assembly, Frene Ginwala, in 2004. Calland (2006: 111) describes her as 'executive-minded' and cites a parliamentarian from the ruling ANC: 'As a manager she was despotic, and resented the growth of the committee system, over which she had insufficient control and which thereby sapped power from the plenary, where she did have full control.' Ginwala was strongly opposed to giving parliament budgetary amendment powers. According to another parliamentarian, she had been 'the biggest blockage' to the resolution of this issue (author's interview). A second factor was the leadership battle and subsequent realignment of power within the ruling party. During the ANC's Polokwane conference in December 2007, the then president, Thabo Mbeki, lost his bid to remain party leader to his rival and former deputy, Jacob Zuma. Zuma's victory was immediately felt in parliament, where it precipitated a change of guard. Prior to the Polokwane conference, ministers dominated the Political Committee of the ANC, but changes in January 2008 brought in Zuma supporters with substantial parliamentary experience.[14] The balance of power within the party had shifted in favour of strong parliamentary oversight. These changes paved the way for the National Assembly to formally instruct the Portfolio Committee on Finance to report a bill by mid-August.

A draft Money Bill Amendment Procedure and Related Matters Bill appeared in the Government Gazette in July 2008. Instead of the Joint Budget Committee, it required a committee in each chamber to consider macroeconomic and fiscal policy as well as all amendments to money bills (section 4). The Minister of Finance was to submit to parliament 'draft budget allocations for each programme within a vote as approved by Cabinet' at least three months before the budget (section 5). Approval of 'the fiscal framework' and the annual Division of Revenue Bill, regulating transfers and grants to the provinces and local governments, was required prior to the consideration of any amendments to the budget (section 6). The draft bill did not contain specific limits on amendments, but required members to motivate these with reference to a list of 11 items, starting with 'the relevant fiscal framework adopted by Parliament' (section 7). Ministers were to be given 30 days for comments before committees could consider adopting amendments. The budget committees would be required to report within four months after the introduction of the relevant money bill. If parliament failed to adopt any amendments within this period, it would have to adopt the bill as tabled. Finally, the draft bill provided for the establishment of a Parliamentary Budget Office as part of the parliamentary administration (section 8). These proposals envisaged a substantial restructuring of the budgetary role of parliament, but they were also imprecise in some important aspects, notably the definition of 'the fiscal framework' as well as the distinction between the revenue and expenditure side of the budget.

Following public hearings, the Portfolio Committee on Finance revised the draft and formally tabled the Money Bills Amendment Procedure and Related Matters Bill in the National Assembly. The bill was approved with minor modifications and became law in April 2009. The legislation clarifies several aspects, compared to the earlier draft. Notably, it defines the fiscal framework as comprising aggregate spending and revenues (budgetary and extra-budgetary), as well as borrowing, interest and debt servicing charges and the contingency reserve (section 1). It also clearly distinguishes the revenue and expenditure sides of the budget and assigns responsibility for them to different sets of committees. The scrutiny of macroeconomic and fiscal policy as well as revenue measures falls to the existing finance committees, whereas a new set of appropriations committees, one in each house, are to scrutinise spending and the intergovernmental division of revenue (section 4).

The act establishes a clear sequence of decisions. It tasks portfolio committees with producing 'budgetary review and recommendation reports' for each department (section 5), prior to the adoption of reports on the Medium Term Budget Policy Statement by the finance and appropriation committees (section 6). The reports on medium-term policy may include recommendations to amend the fiscal framework or the division of revenue should they remain 'materially unchanged' in the budget proposal tabled towards the beginning of autumn. The approval of the annual budget starts with the adoption of the fiscal framework and revenue proposals (section 8), followed by the Division of Revenue Bill (section 9) and finally, the relevant appropriation bill (section 10). The Minister of Finance has the right to respond to proposed amendments within at least two, three and ten days, respectively. Any affected cabinet member can also respond to amendments to appropriations. The act requires any changes to appropriations, revenue measures and the division of revenue to be consistent with the adopted fiscal framework and several guiding principles, which are reproduced in Appendix II. This sequencing of decisions, coupled with the central role of the financial committees in aggregate decisions, establishes a top-down process.

The act also includes new instruments for parliamentary control, which had not been in the gazetted draft bill (section 10). Drawing on their knowledge of legislative budget processes in other countries, acquired over a decade of grappling with this thorny issue, parliamentarians inserted a clause which allowed other committees to recommend to an appropriations committee that an item be appropriated 'conditionally' so as 'to ensure that the money requested for the main division will be spent effectively, efficiently and economically'.[15] Incidentally, the only amendment of the National Assembly to the bill removed a limitation on the sum of money that could be appropriated conditionally. In addition, the act allows other committees to advise the appropriations committees that money be appropriated 'specifically and exclusively' for a particular main division within a vote, thereby suspending the virement rules in the Public Finance Management Act (section 43) for specific items. These provisions enable tight control over budget execution.

Finally, the act also significantly overhauls the provisions on the establishment of a Parliamentary Budget Office (section 15). Notably, it stipulates as the main objective of the office 'to provide independent, objective and professional advice and analysis to Parliament on matters related to the budget and other money Bills'. While the draft bill envisaged the office to be established by the Secretary to Parliament as part of the parliamentary administration, the act gives the finance and appropriations committees the duty to recommend to their respective houses 'a person with the requisite experience, qualifications and leadership skills' to be appointed as director and at the same level as the top rank of the public service. The director can only be removed from office in case of 'misconduct, incapacity or incompetence' as attested by the appointing committees and with the adoption of a resolution to that effect by both houses. The independence of the Parliamentary Budget Office is underscored with a requirement for the director to report 'any inappropriate political or executive interference', as well as an entitlement to a transfer from the parliamentary budget. The act creates the basis for an independent and well-resourced analytic unit to support the new process.

For more than a decade after the adoption of a democratic constitution, the budgetary role of the South African Parliament remained undefined as the ruling party was unable to reconcile conflicting visions of legislative involvement. The 1997 draft bill on the amendment process for money bills would have severely curtailed legislative authority to an extent that many parliamentarians deemed unacceptable. Without a doubt, the adopted legislation is a major milestone and a leap forward in the evolution of South Africa's democratic institutions.[16] On the one hand, the choice for unfettered amendment powers, additional tools to control the execution of the budget, well-defined financial committees and the creation of the Parliamentary Budget Office constitutes a clear break with a restrictive Westminster heritage. At the same time, the legislation puts in place carefully designed procedural safeguards, in particular a committee structure similar to the 'hierarchical' model in Figure 6.1 and a top-down sequencing of decisions as analysed in Figure 6.2. The effectiveness of these procedures in containing the common pool resource problem may not be revealed as long as the governing party commands a secure majority in the legislature. Their true test is likely to be in a more fragmented political context.

6.4 Conclusions

The hope of many budget reformers is that top-down budgeting injects greater fiscal discipline into budgetary decisions (Blöndal 2003). However, the analysis in this chapter adds to Ferejohn and Krehbiel's (1987) caution against a naive belief in the disciplining effect of sequencing by itself. The latter alone cannot force fiscal actors to internalise a larger share of the cost of their actions. Rather, key to the effectiveness of sequencing in containing a pro-spending bias is its combination with the delegation of decision making authority on aggregates to a set of actors who are likely to internalise a larger share of the cost than those making choices about individual spending items. In a legislative setting, this role can be played by finance and budget committees. The assessment of the Swedish experience strongly supports this argument. South Africa's reformed legislative budget procedure also combines sequencing with centralisation, although in this case the effectiveness of these arrangements is yet to be tested.

The findings in this chapter show that a wider range of legislative institutions deserve attention in efforts to redesign the budget process in order to improve fiscal performance. Although it may appear so at first glance, this conclusion does not contradict the empirical findings in the previous chapter. Rather, substantively important direct effects of legislative institutions are likely to be rare. The implication is that research ought to focus more on their interaction. Much of the literature on fiscal institutions does not pay sufficient attention to the possibility of conditional effects, with notable exceptions such as Pereira and Mueller (2004) as well as Hallerberg, Scartascini and Stein (2009). The findings of this chapter are also encouraging, because the proposition that the curtailment of amendment powers is the only way to achieve fiscal sustainability is normatively problematic for those who regard the legislative power of the purse as a democratic fundamental. Moreover, it may not always be possible to adjust constitutional provisions on amendment powers. Under such circumstances, a carefully designed top-down decision-making process, combining sequencing with centralisation, can be a viable alternative approach to strengthening fiscal discipline.

The analysis further raises complex questions about the exact nature of parliamentary control. At first glance, it implies an inverse relationship between legislative influence on budget policy and the maintenance of fiscal discipline. This suggests that effective parliamentary control has to entail that the legislature is able to control itself. In Sweden and South Africa, the procedural constraints discussed in this chapter are essentially self-imposed, which in the final analysis makes it difficult to argue that legislators have lost budgetary control. In the Swedish case, individual parliamentarians, in particular those on sectoral committees, had to relinquish some influence over budget policy compared with the pre-reform system. The same does not hold for South Africa, because the institutional changes must be compared against a very different status quo, where no parliamentarian had any formal authority to alter budget policy. The broader point is that any such reform affects the power relations between political actors (Wildavsky 1961). In this context, the changes affect not only executive–legislative relations, but also the existing patterns of intra-legislative interactions.

While the literature on budget institutions favours 'weak' legislatures as fiscally beneficial, the contours of a somewhat more careful interpretation emerge from this chapter: the possibility that legislatures can be, at the same time, both powerful, by retaining full control of the design of the budget process, as well as constrained, by self-imposing institutional devices that support fiscally prudent choices. Of course, we have good reasons to be deeply sceptical about the ability of politicians to impose effective fiscal constraints upon themselves (Primo 2007). The evidence presented here suggests that this possibility is not entirely utopian, but it may be rare. Sweden's macroeconomic crisis, and the advent of democracy in post-apartheid South Africa, provided exceptional windows of opportunity for institutional redesigns that may have been impossible in less than extraordinary circumstances. Hence, ultimately most important are the preferences of those who get to design rules and procedures. The challenge for reformers is to use such rare opportunities to make wise institutional choices.

7
Beyond the Myth of Fiscal Control

> *The finance of the country is ultimately associated with the liberties of the country. It is a powerful leverage by which English liberty has been gradually acquired. ... If the House of Commons by any possibility lose the power of the control of the grants of public money, depend upon it, your very liberty will be worth very little in comparison. That powerful leverage has been what is commonly known as the power of the purse – the control of the House of Commons over public expenditure.*
>
> William Ewart Gladstone, 1891
> (quoted from Einzig 1959: 3)

> *Parliament does have control in the sense that the Government cannot obtain funding from the public purse without Parliament's consent. ... [A] wide range of financial information is made available to the House each year. But this is, at present, the limit of the House's power: if not a constitutional myth, it is close to one.*
>
> House of Commons Procedure Committee, 1998
> (quoted from Walters and Rogers 2004: 257)

This book had three main aims: (i) to establish and apply a framework for assessing the budgetary role of legislatures, (ii) to explore the determinants of cross-national variation in institutional arrangements and (iii) to assess empirically the impact of legislative budget institutions on fiscal policy. I consider each of these in turn, followed by a discussion of the relevance of my findings in the context of the broader institutionalist research agenda in political economy.

7.1   Diverging trajectories

The emergence of modern legislatures is inextricably intertwined with the struggle for democratic control of public finances (Stourm 1917; Einzig 1959). The institutional foundations of legislative control emerged over a number of centuries and are shaped by local context. Yet different legislatures at different times have grappled with essentially similar issues relating to their formal powers, organisation and access to information. This provides a basis for constructing a comparative framework to measure the extent to which the institutional prerequisites for legislative control are present.

In analysing the effect of institutional arrangements on legislative budgeting, I distinguished two types of impacts: on legislative control on the one hand and budget outcomes, in particular spending levels, on the other hand. The size of a legislature's feasible set of budgetary choices is affected by a range of institutions, including constraints on its power to amend the budget, the nature of the reversionary outcome as well as executive authority to alter the approved budget during implementation. However, only restrictions on amendment powers contain aggregate spending in a wide range of plausible scenarios. Moreover, the use of any formal legislative powers is likely to involve transaction costs. These can be accommodated or lowered if the organisation of the legislative process maximises the time available for budget scrutiny, enables a division of labour and the development of expertise through a well-designed committee system and ensures full access to all relevant information. These institutional prerequisites affect the extent of legislative control of budget policy and provide a framework for comparative empirical work.

The index of legislative budget institutions reveals very different degrees of legislative control of public finances. The top quartile legislatures score at least twice as high as those in the bottom quartile. Moreover, there is a substantial amount of variation between the extremes, as suggested by the more recent comparative case study literature in the legislative studies tradition. This finding challenges the claim that legislative financial control is fundamentally important for democracy (Einzig 1959; Fish 2006). This claim seems impossible to reconcile with the fact established here, that legislative bodies in democratic countries are so differently equipped for financial scrutiny.

This raises questions about the trajectory of legislative budgeting. Until the nineteenth century, the struggle in many countries was to achieve full parliamentary control of the budget (Stourm 1917). Once this was achieved, however, legislatures took very different paths. Documenting developments in Britain and France respectively, Einzig (1959) and Stourm (1917) were writing at times when they regarded the golden age of fiscal control as a thing of the past. In the US, however, there is much less of a clear-cut trajectory of decline. Congress at various points ceded power to the executive, but later struggled to strengthen fiscal control. According to Schick (2000: 8–35), Congress dominated budgeting until the triumph of the executive budget movement with the 1921 Budget and Accounting Act, which inaugurated a period of presidential dominance. However, following a souring of legislative–executive relations under the Nixon presidency, the 1974 Congressional Budget and Impoundment Control Act signalled congressional resurgence (see also Wildavsky and Caiden 2001: 69–92). Hence, while in broad terms the initial trajectory of legislative budgeting in these countries was shared, with a common goal to achieve legislative fiscal control, developments from about the nineteenth century onwards became much more diverse. Taking a comparative snapshot of legislative budgeting today, as in Chapter 3, the US on the one hand and the UK as well as France on the other emerge as polar cases, with most of the cross-national distribution between them.

It is uncertain whether younger and emerging democracies will follow the same path as these pioneers of legislative budgeting. For one, the context of legislative scrutiny has changed in many countries. The origins of the battle for legislative fiscal supremacy in the UK and the US owe much to the fact that these bodies sought to impose limitations on unelected executives (Einzig 1959; Harriss 1975). The fiscal leash was a rare mechanism to impose some degree of accountability and control. Nowadays, more governments than ever before are accountable via the ballot box (Huntington 1991), so this historically important driver of fiscal scrutiny is less applicable. Although the historical golden age of legislative budgeting may have little to offer as a model to newer democracies, there is still substantial variation in the budgetary role of legislatures, even among countries with similar levels of democratic maturity.

7.2   Shaped by history and current politics

So which factors might account for this variation? Testing a range of plausible explanations, I found robust evidence that British colonial heritage and divided government affect legislative arrangements for financial scrutiny. Legislative budget institutions are shaped by both long-term and more immediate factors. This might seem contradictory at first glance, but not when considering that different elements of the institutional setting are likely to be affected by different factors. Legal frameworks, and constitutional provisions in particular, are often deeply entrenched and slowly changing (Lienert and Jung 2004). This implies a greater importance of long-term causes such as colonial history in shaping these aspects. The key mechanism is institutional replication (Lienert 2003). In particular, the UK bequeathed very similar rules to its former colonies that greatly limit the potential for legislative influence on public finances. On the other hand, legislative organisation and demand for information are more variable in the short term, which explains why they are sensitive to more immediate political dynamics, notably occurrences of minority government. When partisan control differs across the legislature and the executive, there is greater parliamentary demand for scrutiny (Messick 2002).

The analysis to some extent challenges the hypothesis that presidential and parliamentary systems are inherently different (Lijphart 1992, 1999). The index of legislative budget institutions highlights a substantial range of financial scrutiny capacity among parliamentary systems. While presidentialism does affect a country's score on the index of legislative budget institutions, this result is driven by an outlier – the US Congress. Lienert's (2005) work similarly challenges the overriding importance of this macro-constitutional distinction for the budgetary role of the legislature. One reason why the regime distinction may be overrated is that legislative research for too long excessively focused on two 'paradigmatic cases' (Cheibub and Limongi 2002: 168), the UK and the US.

Many researchers failed to grasp the full range of variation in legislative influence among both types of systems until the work by Shugart and Carey (1992) and Döring (1995a). With regard to legislative budgeting, these are good reasons not to prematurely accept the notion that fundamental differences exist between these extremely broad and diverse groups of countries.

While this study identified factors that account for some of the cross-national variation in legislative budget institutions, we can only speculate why this variation might be sustained without undermining democratic government. Does the absence of effective legislative scrutiny of the budget mean that governments are less accountable? Perhaps not necessarily. One possibility is the functional equivalence of other mechanisms in holding government to account. In medieval England, parliamentary control of the purse was the most essential and effective tool for controlling the Crown (Harriss 1975). In contrast, modern parliaments have a wide range of 'oversight tools' at their disposal (Pelizzo and Stapenhurst 2004). These include committee and plenary hearings, commissions of inquiry, parliamentary questions and question time, interpellations as well as access to supportive external bodies such as ombudsmen and supreme audit institutions. It may well be that some of these can be substituted for parliamentary control of the budget. Alternatively, the very nature of financial control may have shifted from *ex ante* scrutiny to *ex post* review and accountability (Schick 2002: 33–5). It is likely that parliaments periodically assemble new packages from a changing menu of oversight tools, occasionally abandoning some and honing new ones instead.

7.3   The fiscal cost of legislative power

A number of studies claim that legislative institutions such as amendment powers, the reversionary budget, top-down voting procedures and bicameralism affect fiscal policy outcomes. Most of the empirical work to date has been based on small samples of countries from selected geographical regions. This book presents the first comprehensive evaluation of the effects of legislative institutions on public spending. I found no evidence in support of most of the relevant fiscal institutionalist hypotheses, except that countries where the legislature has unfettered powers to amend the budget proposal of the executive have higher levels of public expenditures. The effect is statistically significant and substantively large, amounting to several percentage points of GDP. This finding holds across a number of different operationalisations of this variable as well as different datasets and empirical approaches. Legislative amendment powers are a primary determinant of fiscal policy outcomes.

Chapter 5 has several significant implications for further empirical work. It underscores the importance of replication for the credibility of quantitative research in this particular area as well as in the social sciences more generally. Two decades after Dewald et al. (1986) highlighted the embarrassing impossibility to replicate many empirical results in a leading economics journal, replication is arguably more crucial than ever before but remains both undervalued and undersupplied (Hamermesh 2007). In political science, the use of quantitative methods in arguably the leading journal of the discipline 'skyrocketed' during the 1960s and has since become increasingly sophisticated (Sigelman 2006: 467). This makes replication, and in particular what Hamermesh (2007: 1) refers to as *scientific replication* (i.e. using a different sample, different population and similar model) even more fundamentally important. Chapter 5 highlights how exactly this approach can at the same time help to focus, challenge and confirm research. This is an essential process for enhancing the credibility of empirical political science research that cannot be valued enough (King 1995).

The analysis also has important implications for empirical research on fiscal performance. Crucially, greater attention needs to be paid to the dependent variable. If a theory generates predictions about expenditure levels, then empirical tests should report results with spending as the dependent variable. Further motivation ought to be provided if other indicators of fiscal performance are used instead. If the results with the most plausible indicator are not strong, this should be transparently reported and discussed. Examples of this in the relevant literature (notably Stein et al. 1998) are too rare. One likely reason is that the social sciences tend not to value 'negative results' (Lehrer et al. 2007), which is a problem that also afflicts other disciplines (Hebert et al. 2002). Unless fiscal indicators are tightly linked to the theoretical argument, there remain grounds for suspicions that they are chosen to support particular theoretical stances, rather than to evaluate them empirically.[1]

The analysis of top-down budgeting in Chapter 6 relied on more in-depth qualitative work, and in the case of Sweden very specific data about the parliamentary impact on fiscal policy. It suggests that institutional arrangements other than amendment powers can nonetheless impact on fiscal discipline in a legislative setting. However, procedural subtleties are hard to capture in cross-country quantitative indices, for example how Sweden's approval process pits pairs of alternative packages of budget proposals against one another and favours the package backed by the largest voting block. The chapter highlights that it is not the sequencing of budgetary decisions in itself that matters but the centralisation of the decision over aggregate budget totals, which again is not captured in crude cross-national indices that score voting sequence alone. This finding is entirely consistent with the theory of the common pool resource problem in budgeting (Hallerberg and Von Hagen 1997). In this way, qualitative work can help to clarify exact causal mechanisms, which in turn has the potential to feed into constructing better cross-national quantitative measures. Moreover, this work shows that the achievement of fiscal discipline need not necessarily come at the price of emasculating the legislature, as long as the latter maintains control over the design of the budget process.

Future work on the budgetary implications of institutional arrangements should go beyond their relationship with indicators of fiscal performance. The literature on fiscal institutions typically ignores the possibility that there may be trade-offs between different budgetary objectives. A rare exception is the work by Stasavage and Moyo (2000), which highlights a trade-off between the reduction of deficits and allocative as well as operational efficiency (see also Campos and Pradhan 1996). Only recently has the quality of public expenditures received greater attention. Scartascini and Stein (2009: 13) argue that the traditional focus on fiscal sustainability should be complemented with an expanded focus on efficiency, adaptability and representativeness. They pioneer this approach with studies of eight Latin American countries (Hallerberg, Scartascini and Stein 2009). A future challenge is to gather more systematic evidence of how legislative budget institutions, and budget institutions more broadly, affect such a wider set of outcomes and what the trade-offs between these are. It is quite likely that this extended focus will lead to a more multifaceted appreciation of how legislative institutions and actors affect budget policy outcomes.

7.4 Taking lower level institutions seriously

A core argument of this book is that institutionalist research in public policy needs to move beyond broad constitutional parameters to incorporate the more detailed organisation of policy making. In contrast to macro-constitutional distinctions, which offer only rough classifications for political systems – such as unitary versus federal states or presidential versus parliamentary forms of government – I refer to these more detailed arrangements interchangeably as 'lower level' or 'finer grain' institutions. These institutions might affect only particular policy areas, become influential only under certain conditions, or be hidden away in secondary legislation. As the proverbial devilish detail, they are comparable to the small print in contracts: difficult to decipher and deceptively technical, but potentially decisive for the outcome.

Moreover, although derided by Weaver and Rockman (1993: 10) as 'secondary' with 'third tier' relevance, my work shows that such institutional characteristics can be of primary importance for explaining public policy outcomes, even exceeding the impact of macro-constitutional features. To be clear: I am not arguing that macro-level constitutional research is unimportant, but that it would benefit from incorporating additional features, in particular lower level or finer grain institutional variables such as amendment powers. There are already nascent signs that research on macro-constitutional features is developing in this direction. For instance, Cheibub (2006) qualifies the impact of presidentialism on fiscal policy with some variables that he suggests determine executive authority vis-à-vis the legislature. However, there ought to be much more systematic study of the interaction of macro-constitutional and lower level institutions to better understand how institutional design affects fiscal policy.

The incorporation of lower level or finer grain institutions into the research agenda does, however, pose challenges. One is that it requires more careful theorising about the effects expected from different institutional arrangements. Several of the fiscal institutionalist hypotheses lack the backing of formal theoretical analysis, as was the case with conjectures about the impact of sequencing on fiscal policy outcomes. The theoretical work in Chapter 2 suggests that few institutional arrangements are associated with clear-cut predictions in terms of an effect on relative spending levels, with the exception of amendment powers. The empirical results support this prediction. More careful theoretical modelling can clarify the effects of specific institutional arrangements and help to avoid unfounded or exaggerated claims.

Broadening the analysis to lower level institutions also has methodological implications. One of the key critiques levelled against the early fiscal institutionalist research is that it treats institutions as exogenous (Alesina and Perotti 1996: 4; Poterba 1996: 10). This might be a justifiable assumption for at least the short to medium term with regard to macro-constitutional variables, which tend to change rarely. Some lower level institutions, on the other hand, might be subject to more frequent adjustments – although this is not always the case, as the example of amendment powers highlights. Still, fiscal institutionalist research is challenged to develop its understanding of institutional change. One way of doing so is through methodological diversification, in particular detailed country studies of how budget systems adapt to changing conditions (Hallerberg 2004). Case study research cannot always fully resolve this debate, but the accounts of budget reform in Sweden and South Africa in Chapter 6 demonstrate that this type of work can complement quantitative analysis with a more in-depth understanding of how and why budget institutions change (see also Hallerberg, Scartascini and Stein 2009). Mixed methods research designs (Lieberman 2005) offer possibilities for tackling the methodological challenges involved in incorporating lower level institutions into the research agenda.

The systematic empirical study of how budget systems evolve has to be underpinned by high-quality institutional data. Up to now, the institutional data used is eclectic; there has been little concern with standardising various survey efforts. A number of different bodies are now conducting surveys of budget systems or particular aspects of them, including the European Commission (Deroose et al. 2006) and the OECD (2002b, 2006, 2007), as well as independent think tanks (International Budget Project 2006; International Budget Partnership 2009). While quality control remains a concern, these datasets are becoming increasingly sophisticated and more useful.[2] If a degree of standardisation were to be achieved, these surveys could yield consistent data on the institutional evolution of budget systems over time and for a larger set of countries. This, in turn, would greatly enhance the possibilities for detailed quantitative analysis. Overall, the growing popularity of these surveys augurs well for the empirical prospects of the fiscal institutionalist research agenda.

There are a number of possible next steps for advancing this research agenda. One of the primary challenges to the fiscal institutionalist literature is to develop its theoretical analysis of institutional arrangements. Institutional arrangements that are included in multi-item indices are often selected on the basis of conjectures and short informal arguments. This theoretical underinvestment is underscored by the negative results presented here in relation to a number of institutionalist hypotheses. Much more careful work is needed to properly theorise individual institutional arrangements. This will help researchers to focus on the truly relevant institutions and to better understand the conditions under which particular mechanisms have a certain effect. Of the features analysed in Chapter 2, the reversionary budget in particular deserves further attention, because of the number of papers that attribute a fiscal impact to this variable (e.g. Alesina et al. 1996; Hallerberg and Marier 2004; Cheibub 2006). In the medium term, a better balance between theory and empirical work would greatly enhance the credibility of fiscal institutionalist research. In turn, this would offer more useful guidance to those who seek to reform budget institutions and strengthen fiscal discipline.

The analysis in Chapter 5 in particular provides a very strong basis for further empirical work and suggests several possibilities. In particular, the finding that only legislative powers of amendment have a significant effect on expenditure levels among a range of legislative institutions may disappoint the purveyors of indices, but it is good news for comparative research. The relative simplicity of this measure, compared with complex indices, greatly reduces data requirements and reliance on elaborate survey tools. When extending this work to a large number of developing countries, it will be important to revisit the underlying concept of institutions. On average, formal institutions are probably meaningful structures in OECD countries. However, to what extent can we stretch this analysis to what Acemoglu (2005: 1045) refers to as 'weakly institutionalized polities'? Are formal institutions – constitutions, laws and regulations – as meaningful in Swaziland as they are in Switzerland? In developing countries, formal budgetary rules and procedures are often undermined by informal institutions, such as patronage networks (Rakner et al. 2004). Hence, while we should seek to expand empirical analysis beyond the usual suspects – the advanced industrialised democracies – it is important not to take for granted the relevance of formal institutional structures. How to understand the policy making process in weakly institutionalised polities is thus a fundamental challenge that future research in this area will have to tackle more systematically.

While the focus of this book is on institutions, there is substantial scope for integrating party political variables into the analysis. For example, several authors investigate the direct effects of partisan fragmentation on budget outcomes (Volkerink and De Haan 2001; Perotti and Kontopoulos 2002). A related question is whether the fiscal effects of partisan fragmentation can be neutralised or mitigated by institutional arrangements. In the legislative context, the literature on budget institutions would lead us to expect that the fiscal effects of partisan fragmentation in the legislature are conditional upon the extent of legislative authority in the budget process. While some authors explicitly pose this question (Fabrizio and Mody 2006), it has been largely ignored in empirical work. Elsewhere, I provide the first in-depth analysis of this interaction and discuss the potential for further work along these lines (Wehner 2010).

Moreover, there is a lack of research about institutional effects on the composition of budgets. The analysis in Chapter 2 suggests that a number of institutional features affect decisions about the mix of public spending, as well as or rather than aggregate fiscal policy outcomes, which I did not test empirically in this book. A proper exploration of this issue requires combining institutional data with information on legislative and executive preferences in different policy areas, which is empirically messy (Bräuninger 2005). Moreover, there is a range of measurement issues that have to be considered in comparing spending categories across countries. For instance, the measurement of social expenditure is complicated by the use of tax expenditures rather than direct expenditures, the effect of taxation of social benefits and indirect taxes on net social transfers as well as the use of private mandatory schemes (Joumard et al. 2003: 116; see also Kraan 2004; Kühner 2007). While these are difficult data issues that have to be acknowledged, they should not detract researchers from tackling this challenge. There are few studies of partisan effects on the composition of budgets (Tsebelis and Chang 2004; Bräuninger 2005). Further work in this neglected area should incorporate budget institutions into the analysis (Kraan and Kelly 2005).

Finally, research on legislative budgeting would benefit greatly from a cohesive body of methodologically rigorous comparative case studies. As the studies of budget reform in Sweden and South Africa demonstrated, this method is particularly well suited for exploring the dynamics of institutional change over time, as well as causal mechanisms. The available body of case study research on this topic is outdated, eclectic in approach and lacks analytical grounding. Crucial for the success of this element of the research agenda is the issue of case selection, which should be based on an explicit framework rather than convenient reversion to the usual suspects of comparative legislative studies. One particularly promising approach, as developed in this book, is to focus on those countries that underwent institutional reforms affecting the budgetary role of the legislature. This selection approach is particularly suitable for studying institutional change. The study of within-unit change also controls for time-invariant country-specific factors, which can eliminate a number of rival hypotheses. Pursued in this way, a set of well-structured and carefully selected case studies has the potential to complement the quantitative elements of this research agenda.

The study of the design of political institutions and their effects on public policy is a burgeoning field of research in both economics and political science. Thus far, most of the attention has been paid to macro-level constitutional distinctions. In future, increasing attention needs to be paid to studying the more detailed machinery for policy making and how its design affects outcomes in particular policy areas. The research on fiscal institutions is one example where this approach has already yielded some dividends, but much more can be done. Research that takes lower level institutional details seriously is likely to qualify or challenge some of the results from macro-constitutional research, and it should be central for the future of the institutionalist project in political economy.

7.5   Conclusions

Parliamentary control of the budget is difficult to attain if not elusive. Many national legislatures have neither the institutional means nor the political independence to be influential budgetary actors. In such cases, the annual ritual of budget approval amounts to little more than a constitutional myth. Active legislative bodies, on the other hand, are prone to suffer from a pro-spending bias. This analysis suggests a likely trade-off between legislative control of the budget process and a budget that is under control. To some, the fiscal cost of parliamentary activism may simply be an acceptable side effect of democracy. Others, surely, will disagree. Yet it may not be impossible for legislatures to be both powerful as well as fiscally responsible. This requires carefully engineered institutions that force legislators to fix prudent aggregate parameters and to focus debate on allocative choices within a hard budget constraint. Seemingly minor procedural details play a major role in any attempt to achieve this goal.

Appendix I
Data

A OECD dataset

AGE OF DEMOCRACY: Age of democracy, calculated as (2000–first year of democratic rule)/200, ranges from 0 to 1. Source: Variable AGE from Persson and Tabellini (2003).

AMENDMENTS: Occurrence of legislative amendments to the executive budget proposal. This measure indicates whether the legislature typically amends the budget as proposed by the executive (but not the nature and extent of any amendments). Coding: 0=typically no amendments, 1=typically some amendments. Source: OECD and World Bank (2003: Q2.7.i), OECD (2007: Q41).*

AUDIT COMMITTEE: Committee capacity for the consideration of audit reports. Coding: 0=no specialised audit committee, 1.7=audit subcommittee, 3.3=specialised audit committee. Source: OECD and World Bank (2003: Q4.5.m), OECD (2007: Q68), parliamentary websites.*

BICAMERALISM: Dummy variable, equal to 1 if there is a second chamber of the legislature with equal powers in budgetary matters as the lower house, 0 otherwise. Source: Heller (1997), Tsebelis and Money (1997), constitutions.

BUDGET COMMITTEE: Consideration of the draft budget by a specialised budget or finance committee. Coding: 0=no budget committee, 3.3=budget committee. Source: OECD and World Bank (2003: Q2.10.a), OECD (2007: Q33).*

CEILING: Dummy variable, equal to 1 if a legislature sets a hard spending ceiling before debating individual expenditure items, 0 otherwise. Source: OECD and World Bank (2003: Q2.7.j), OECD (2007: Q37).*

COMMITTEES: Committee capacity. Coding: Sum of BUDGET, SECTORAL and AUDIT, ranges from 0=no committee capacity to 10=full committee capacity. Source: Variables AUDIT, BUDGET and SECTORAL.

DIVIDED GOVERNMENT: Divided government index, calculated as x/10, where x=number of years in the period 1993–2002 in which the government did not have a legislative majority in the lower house, ranges from 0=always majority support to 1=never majority support. Source: Europa Publications Limited (various), Beck et al. (2001).

FLEXIBILITY: Executive flexibility during budget execution. Coding: Sum of WITHHOLD, VIREMENT and RESERVE, ranges from 0=full executive flexibility to 10=no executive flexibility. Source: Variables RESERVE, VIREMENT and WITHHOLD.

FORMER BRITISH COLONY: Dummy variable, equal to 1 if a country is a former British colony (excluding the US), 0 otherwise. Source: Variable COL_UK from Persson and Tabellini (2003).

INDEX: Index of legislative budget institutions. Sum of POWERS, REVERSION, FLEXIBILITY, TIME, COMMITTEES and RESEARCH, rescaled to range from 0=no legislative capacity to 100=full legislative capacity.

MAJORITARIAN ELECTIONS: Dummy variable for electoral systems equal to 1 if all seats of the lower house are elected under plurality rule, 0 otherwise. Source: Variable MAJ from Persson and Tabellini (2003).

ORGANISATION SUB-INDEX: Organisational capacity of the legislature in budgetary matters. Sum of TIME, COMMITTEES and RESEARCH, rescaled to range from 0=no organisational capacity to 50=full organisational capacity.

OUTLAYS: General government total outlays as a percentage of GDP, averaged over the period 2001–5. Source: OECD (2008).

POPULATION 15–64: Percentage of the population between the ages 15 and 64 in the total population, averaged over the period 2001–5. Source: World Bank (2007).

POPULATION 65+: Percentage of the population over the age of 65 in the total population, averaged over the period 2001–5. Source: World Bank (2007).

POWERS: Formal powers of the legislature to amend budgets. Coding: 0=accept or reject, 2.5=cuts only or other severe restrictions, 5=aggregate spending constraint, 7.5=deficit constraint, 10=unfettered. Source: OECD and World Bank (2003: Q2.7.d), OECD (2007: Q40).*

POWERS SUB-INDEX: Formal powers of the legislature in budgetary matters. Sum of POWERS, REVERSION and FLEXIBILITY, rescaled to range from 0=no formal powers to 50=full formal powers.

PRESIDENTIAL SYSTEM: Dummy variable for form of government, equal to 1 for presidential regimes, 0 otherwise. Only regimes where the confidence of the assembly is not necessary for the survival of the executive are included among presidential regimes. Source: Variable PRES from Persson and Tabellini (2003).

RESEARCH: Specialised legislative budget research office. Coding: 0=none, 2.5=less than ten professional staff, 5=ten to 25 professional staff, 7.5=26 to 50 professional staff, 10=US Congressional Budget Office. Source: OECD and World Bank (2003: Q2.10.e), OECD (2007: Q34).*

RESERVE: Power of the central budget authority/executive to fund new policy initiatives from a reserve fund. Coding: 0=reserve fund, 3.3=no reserve fund. Source: OECD and World Bank (2003: Q3.2.c.1), OECD (2007: Q61).*

REVERSION: Reversionary budget. Coding: 0=executive budget proposal, 3.3=vote on account, 6.7=last year's budget, 10=legislature approves interim measures. Source: OECD and World Bank (2003: Q2.7.c), OECD (2007: Q43).*

SECTORAL COMMITTEES: Consideration of the draft budget by sectoral or departmental committees. Coding: 0=departmental committees have no substantive role, 3.3=departmental committees decide sectoral budgets. Source: OECD and World Bank (2003: Q2.10.a), OECD (2007: Q33).*

TIME: Amount of time the budget is tabled ahead of the fiscal year. Coding: 0=up to two months, 3.3=up to four months, 6.7=up to six months, 10=more than six months. Source: OECD and World Bank (2003: Q2.7.b), OECD (2007: Q39).*

TRADE: Sum of imports and exports as a percentage of GDP, averaged over the period 2001–5. Source: World Bank (2007).

VIREMENT: Power of the central budget authority/executive to reallocate appropriated funds from one programme to another. Coding: 0=central budget authority may reallocate funds without legislative approval, 3.3=central budget authority may not reallocate funds or only with legislative approval. Source: OECD and World Bank (2003: Q3.2.a.4), OECD (2007: Q53).*

WITHHOLD: Power of the central budget authority/executive to withhold appropriated funds that are not available on a legal or entitlement basis. Coding: 0=central budget authority may withhold funds without legislative approval, 3.3=central budget authority may not withhold funds or only with legislative approval. Source: OECD and World Bank (2003: Q3.1.c), OECD (2007: Q52).*

Note: *Data are from OECD and World Bank (2003) for all countries with the exception of Luxembourg, Poland and Switzerland. Data for these three countries are from OECD (2007), which contained identical or highly equivalent items. Refer to Table 3.3 and Table 3.4 for details.

B   Global datasets

ACCEPT-OR-REJECT LIMIT: Dummy variable, equal to 1 if AMENDMENT LIMIT=1, 0 otherwise. Source: AMENDMENT LIMIT.

AFRICA: Regional dummy variable, equal to 1 if a country is in Africa, 0 otherwise. Source: Variable AFRICA from Persson and Tabellini (2003).

AGE OF DEMOCRACY: Age of democracy, calculated as (2000–first year of democratic rule)/200, ranges from 0 to 1. Source: Variable AGE from Persson and Tabellini (2003).

AMENDMENT LIMIT: Restrictions on the power of the legislature to amend budgets tabled by the executive. Coding: 0=none, .25=deficit constraint, .5=aggregate spending constraint, .75=cuts only or other severe restrictions, 1=accept or reject. Calculated as 1–POWERS. Source: Table 5.2.

BRITISH COLONIAL ORIGIN: British colonial origin, discounted by the years since independence. Source: Variable COL_UKA from Persson and Tabellini (2003).

CUTS ONLY LIMIT: Dummy variable, equal to 1 if AMENDMENT LIMIT=.75, 0 otherwise. Source: AMENDMENT LIMIT.

DEFICIT LIMIT: Dummy variable, equal to 1 if AMENDMENT LIMIT=.25, 0 otherwise. Source: AMENDMENT LIMIT.

DEMOCRACY: Average of Freedom House indices for civil liberties and political rights, where each index is measured on a scale from 1 to 7, with 1 representing the highest degree of freedom and 7 the lowest. Source: Variable GASTIL from Persson and Tabellini (2003).

EAST ASIA: Regional dummy variable, equal to 1 if a country is in East Asia, 0 otherwise. Source: Variable ASIAE from Persson and Tabellini (2003).

ELECTIONS: Dummy variable for legislative elections, equal to 1 in the year the (lower house of the) legislature is elected. Source: Variable ELLEG from Persson and Tabellini (2003).

EXPENDITURES: Central government expenditures as a percentage of GDP. Source: Variable CGEXP from Persson and Tabellini (2003).

FEDERALISM: Dummy variable, equal to 1 if the country has a federal political structure, 0 otherwise. Source: Variable FEDERAL from Persson and Tabellini (2003).

GDP PER CAPITA: Natural log of per capita real GDP. Source: Variable LYP from Persson and Tabellini (2003).

LATIN AMERICA: Regional dummy variable, equal to 1 if a country is in Latin America, Central America or the Caribbean, 0 otherwise. Source: Variable LAAM from Persson and Tabellini (2003).

MAJORITARIAN ELECTIONS: Dummy variable for electoral systems, equal to 1 if all seats of the lower house are elected under plurality rule, 0 otherwise. Source: Variable MAJ from Persson and Tabellini (2003).

OECD: Dummy variable, equal to 1 for all countries that were members of OECD before 1993, 0 otherwise (except for Turkey, which is coded as 0 even though it was an OECD member before the 1990s). Source: Variable OECD from Persson and Tabellini (2003).

OTHER COLONIAL ORIGIN: Non-Spanish and non-British colonial origin, discounted by the years since independence. Source: Variable COL_OTHA from Persson and Tabellini (2003).

POLITY: Interpolated version of Polity scores, rescaled so that higher values denote worse democracies. Source: Variable POLITY_GT from Persson and Tabellini (2003).

POPULATION 15–64: Percentage of the population between the ages 15 and 64 in the total population. Source: Variable PROP1564 from Persson and Tabellini (2003).

POPULATION 65+: Percentage of the population over the age of 65 in the total population. Source: Variable PROP65 from Persson and Tabellini (2003).

POWERS: Formal powers of the legislature to amend budgets. Coding: 0=accept or reject, .25=cuts only or other severe restrictions, .5=aggregate spending constraint, .75=deficit constraint, 1=unfettered. Source: Table 5.2.

PRESIDENTIAL SYSTEM: Dummy variable for form of government, equal to 1 for presidential regimes, 0 otherwise. Only regimes where the confidence of the assembly is not necessary for the survival of the executive are included among presidential regimes. Source: Variable PRES from Persson and Tabellini (2003).

SPANISH COLONIAL ORIGIN: Spanish colonial origin, discounted by the years since independence. Source: Variable COL_ESPA from Persson and Tabellini (2003).

TOTAL POPULATION: Natural log of the total population (in millions). Source: Variable LPOP from Persson and Tabellini (2003).

TOTAL SPENDING LIMIT: Dummy variable, equal to 1 if AMENDMENT LIMIT=.5, 0 otherwise. Source: AMENDMENT LIMIT.

TRADE: Sum of exports and imports of goods and services measured as a share of GDP. Source: Variable TRADE from Persson and Tabellini (2003).

Note: Variables are averaged over the 1990–8 period for the 80-country cross section, while the panel consists of annual observations for 58 countries over the 1960–98 period. All panel results use data from Persson and Tabellini's (2003) corrected panel dataset as posted on their personal websites (see their errata dated June 2003), not the older version used for their book.

Appendix II: Selected legal provisions

A   Sweden

Article 12

The Riksdag may decide in an act of law to allocate State spending to expenditure areas.

If the Riksdag has taken a decision under paragraph one, it determines for the next following budget year, by means of a single decision,

> an expenditure limit for each expenditure area, indicating the highest figure to which the sum total of expenditure falling within the expenditure area may amount; and

> an estimate of State revenue under the national budget.

Decisions concerning appropriations or other expenditure under the national budget year may not be taken before a decision has been taken under paragraph two. Appropriations or other expenditure under the national budget shall be determined for each expenditure area by means of a single decision.

Decisions concerning appropriations for the current budget year which affect expenditure limits may not be taken before a decision has been taken approving adjustment of the expenditure limits.

Supplementary provision

5.12.1

State expenditure shall be referred to the following expenditure areas:

1   The government of the Realm;
2   Economy and fiscal administration;
3   Taxes, customs and enforcement;
4   The judicial system;
5   International co-operation;
6   Defence and contingency measures;
7   International development cooperation;
8   Migration;

9	Health care, medical care and social services;
10	Financial security for the sick and disabled;
11	Financial security for the elderly;
12	Financial security for families and children;
13	The labour market;
14	Working life;
15	Financial support for students;
16	Education and academic research;
17	Culture, the media, religious communities and leisure activities;
18	Community planning, housing supply, construction and consumer policy;
19	Regional development;
20	General environmental protection and nature conservation;
21	Energy;
22	Transport and communications;
23	Agriculture, forestry, fisheries and related industries;
24	Industry and trade;
25	General grants to local government;
26	Interest on the national debt, etc.; and
27	The contribution to the European Community.

Decisions relating to the purposes and activities to be included in an expenditure area are taken in conjunction with decisions relating to the Spring Fiscal Policy Bill.

Source: Chapter 5, Article 12 of the Riksdag Act (SFS 1974: 153), as amended on 1 July 2007.

B   South Africa

B.1   *Original constitutional provisions on money bills*

77. Money Bills

(1)   A Bill that appropriates money or imposes taxes, levies or duties is a money Bill. A money Bill may not deal with any other matter except a subordinate matter incidental to the appropriation of money or the imposition of taxes, levies or duties.

(2)   All money Bills must be considered in accordance with the procedure established by section 75. An Act of Parliament must provide for a procedure to amend money Bills before Parliament.

Source: Section 77 of the Constitution of the Republic of South Africa, Act No. 108 of 1996.

B.2 Amended constitutional provisions on money bills

77. Money Bills

(1) A Bill is a money Bill if it—
    (a) appropriates money;
    (b) imposes national taxes, levies, duties or surcharges;
    (c) abolishes or reduces, or grants exemptions from, any national taxes, levies, duties or surcharges; or
    (d) authorises direct charges against the National Revenue Fund, except a Bill envisaged in section 214 authorising direct charges.

(2) A money Bill may not deal with any other matter except—
    (a) a subordinate matter incidental to the appropriation of money;
    (b) the imposition, abolition or reduction of national taxes, levies, duties or surcharges;
    (c) the granting of exemption from national taxes, levies, duties or surcharges; or
    (d) the authorisation of direct charges against the National Revenue Fund.

(3) All money Bills must be considered in accordance with the procedure established by section 75. An Act of Parliament must provide for a procedure to amend money Bills before Parliament.

Source: Section 77 of the Constitution of the Republic of South Africa, Act No. 108 of 1996, as amended by the Constitution of the Republic of South Africa Second Amendment Act, Act No. 61 of 2001.

B.3 Principles for amending the fiscal framework and money bills

8. Adopting the fiscal framework and revenue proposals

[...]

(5) When amending the fiscal framework, a money Bill or taking any decision in terms of this Act, Parliament and its committees must—
    (a) ensure that there is an appropriate balance between revenue, expenditure and borrowing;
    (b) ensure that debt levels and debt interest cost are reasonable;
    (c) ensure that the cost of recurrent spending is not deferred to future generations;
    (d) ensure that there is adequate provision for spending on infrastructure development, overall capital spending and maintenance;
    (e) consider the short, medium and long term implications of the fiscal framework, division of revenue and national budget on the long-term growth potential of the economy and the development of the country;

    (f)   take into account cyclical factors that may impact on the prevailing fiscal position; and

    (g)   take into account all public revenue and expenditure, including extra-budgetary funds, and contingent liabilities.

[...]

Source: Section 8 of the Money Bills Amendment Procedure and Related Matters Act, Act No. 9 of 2009.

Notes

1 Perspectives on Legislative Budgeting

1. Reported by Reuters on 5 May 2000 and quoted from http://www.slate.com/id/76886/.
2. I use the terms 'parliament' and 'legislature' interchangeably.
3. During the 1990s, there was a short-lived experiment with unifying expenditure and revenue proposals and tabling them at the same time, bringing the country more into line with most of the rest of the world, but the Labour government discontinued this practice upon gaining power in 1997 (Dorrell 1993).
4. Stourm (1917), Einzig (1959), Harriss (1975) and Webber and Wildavsky (1986) provide detailed historical accounts. Also refer to Schick (2002) for an excellent summary.
5. A 'scutage' was a tax paid in lieu of military service in feudal times, and was used by the king to maintain a paid army. In times of emergency and on special occasions, such as the marriage of his eldest daughter, he could also impose a levy known as an 'aid'.
6. The history of state audit in France can be traced back as far as the reign of Philippe V in the fourteenth century (Stourm 1917: 551). Feudal monarchs used early forms of audit to protect themselves against excessive theft from revenue collection agents.
7. René Stourm (1917: 595) reminisces about the debates of the laws on regulation during the 1820s: 'Not only did each discussion terminate in a proper resolution, but the general rules resulting from it brought our system of budgetary accounting to a high degree of perfection in a short time.' By the end of the nineteenth century, however, the interest of parliamentarians had waned. They paid scant attention and the approval of the law on regulation frequently took place more than a decade following the end of the relevant fiscal year. To this day, however, refusal to grant discharge can be a serious political threat. When the European Parliament rejected the discharge motion for the 1996 budget, this eventually led to the resignation of the entire commission in March 1999 (Miller and Ware 1999).
8. A similar committee had been appointed in 1690 under the Act for Appointing and Enabling Commissions to Examine, Take and State the Publick Accounts of the Kingdom (Einzig 1959: 168). However, it appears that the abuse of the committee for political purposes undermined its reputation and effectiveness, and the practice of parliamentary audit lapsed under Walpole's administration.
9. The term covers appropriation and tax bills, although this is an oversimplification. The full definition is rather more intricate (May 1997: 806): 'Section 1(2) of the Act defines a "money bill" as a public bill which in the

151

opinion of the Speaker of the House of Commons contains *only* provisions dealing with all or any of the following subjects, namely, the imposition, repeal, remission, alteration, or regulation of taxation; the imposition for the payment of debt or other financial purposes of charges on the Consolidated Fund or the National Loans Fund, or on money provided by Parliament or the variation or repeal of any such charges; Supply; the appropriation, receipt, custody, issue or audit of accounts of public money; the raising of guarantee of any loan or the repayment thereof; or subordinate matters incidental to those subjects or any of them. For the purposes of this definition the expressions "taxation", "public money", and "loan" respectively do not include any taxation, money, or loan raised by local authorities or bodies for local purposes, matters which, on the other hand, *are* included within the scope of Commons financial privilege.'

10. In contrast, Einzig concludes his analysis of parliamentary amendment activity during this period by pointing out that 'in many instances criticisms by the House drew the Government's attention to the possibility of justifiable economies' (Einzig 1959: 276).

11. Article 40 of the 1958 French Constitution now prohibits members from introducing bills or amendments 'where their adoption would have as a consequence either a diminution of public resources or the creation or increase of an item of public expenditure'. See also Hoffman (1959: 339) and Loewenstein (1959: 223).

12. Examples include Young (1999) on Australia; Lalumière (1976), Chinaud (1993) and Amselek (1998) on France; Friauf (1976), Gerster (1984), Sturm (1988) and Eickenboom (1989) on Germany; LeLoup (2004) on Hungary and Slovenia; Premchand (1963) on India; Leston-Bandeira (1999) on Portugal; Krafchik and Wehner (1998) and Verwey (2009) on South Africa; Chubb (1952), Einzig (1959) and Reid (1966) on the UK; Burnell (2001) on Zambia. Refer also to the collections by Coombes (1976) as well as Olson and Mezey (1991).

13. Schick (1986, 1988a) distinguishes between macro and micro-budgetary institutions. He defines the former as institutions that affect aggregate spending and the latter as those that affect particular programmes and decisions. I do not make this distinction here.

14. For a critique, see Primo and Snyder (2005).

15. Hallerberg (2004: 24) notes that 'ministers are often judged by how well they protect the interests of the constituents of their particular ministry. ... [W]here one stands on budget issues within one's party depends on where one sits at the cabinet table'.

16. Mahoney and Goertz (2006: 245–6) challenge these labels, which in their view 'do a poor job capturing the real differences between the traditions. Quantitative analysis inherently involves the use of numbers, but all statistical analyses also rely heavily on words for interpretation. Qualitative studies quite frequently employ numerical data; many qualitative techniques in fact require quantitative information. ... [Better labels] would be statistics versus logic, effect estimation versus outcome explanation, or population-oriented versus case-oriented approaches'.

2 Institutional Foundations of Legislative Control

1. Line item vetoes are exceptionally rare at the national level. Shugart and Haggard (2001: 80) find that only two out of 23 countries with pure presidential systems use a version of the line item veto with extraordinary majority override, namely Argentina and the Philippines. The US also had a short-lived experiment with presidential line item veto authority. In 1996, Congress passed the Line Item Veto Act, which gave the president a form of item veto. President Clinton claimed it would 'prevent Congress from enacting special interest provisions under the cloak of a 500 or 1000-page bill' (quoted from Schick 2000: 94–5). This veto was ruled unconstitutional in 1998, by which time Clinton had used it 82 times with 38 overrides. Clinton claimed that this had resulted in savings of \$2 billion, which was equivalent to 0.12 per cent of federal outlays in the 1997 fiscal year (\$1.6 trillion).
2. In addition to the excellent paper by Carter and Schap (1990), relevant work includes Abney and Lauth (1985), Holtz-Eakin (1988), Kiewiet and McCubbins (1988). Nice (1988), Dearden and Husted (1990), Dearden and Schap (1994), Byrd (1998), Baldez and Carey (1999), Cameron (2000), Gabel and Hager (2000) as well as Primo (2006).
3. Up to the 2005 fiscal year, Congress considered 13 regular appropriations bills. In 2005, a reorganisation of the Appropriations Committees cut the number of subcommittees to ten in the House of Representatives and 12 in the Senate, and the House had 11 such bills and the Senate 12 (Streeter 2006a). More recently, the House and Senate Appropriations Committees each had 12 subcommittees and a corresponding number of appropriations bills.
4. Towards the end of the nineteenth century, a view gained strength that only the executive could have 'so extensive and impartial a view of the mass of these details, and no one can compromise the conflicting interests with so much competence and precision' (Stourm 1917: 54). The US Congress held out longest compared with other legislatures by denying the president a formal role in preparing budgets, but finally conceded the establishment of an executive budget process with the Budget and Accounting Act in 1921 (Webber and Wildavsky 1986: 411–16). Modern budgeting made many parliaments more reactive and, eventually, passive recipients of financial proposals. As Schick (2002: 21) puts it, executive budgets became 'the authoritative metric for measuring legislative action'.
5. According to Streeter (2006b: 1), 'offset amendments generally change spending priorities in a pending appropriations measure by increasing spending for certain activities (or creating spending for new activities not included in the bill) and offsetting the increase(s) by decreasing or striking funding for other activities in the bill'.
6. At the time of writing, Standing Order No. 48 of the House of Commons reads: 'This House will receive no petition for any sum relating to public service or proceed upon any motion for a grant or charge upon

the public revenue, whether payable out of the Consolidated Fund or the National Loans Fund or out of money to be provided by Parliament, or for releasing or compounding any sum of money owing to the Crown, unless recommended from the Crown.'

7. The budget line connects the points that represent the maximum amounts that could be spent on item X or Y respectively if spending were concentrated on one item only (Pereira and Mueller 2004: 792). When modelling outputs the slope of the budget line depends on the price ratio of the relevant goods or services. However, appropriations on an output basis are very rare (Schick 2003).

8. Note that the analysis put forward here has relevance for a growing debate about the effectiveness of different types of fiscal policy rules. Fiscal rules are multi-annual constraints on a fiscal aggregate (Kopits and Symansky 1998), such as the 3 per cent deficit ceiling imposed by the European Union's Stability and Growth Pact. Anderson and Minarik (2006: 194) argue that deficit-based fiscal policy rules are less effective: 'Violations of a spending rule are transparent and incontrovertible. In contrast, non-compliance with a deficit rule ... can be hidden behind optimistic economic assumptions or unlikely plans for future spending and revenue discipline.'

9. The impoundment scenario depicted in Figure 2.5 illustrates an exception. Here, the executive prefers higher overall spending than the legislature, but the legislature prefers higher spending than the executive on one of the two spending items. With this constellation of preferences, and assuming strategic interaction, cuts only powers result in higher spending than unfettered powers of amendment.

10. I ignore the theoretically entertaining but practically largely irrelevant possibility of budgetary gatekeeping. Constitutions or other legislation typically *require* the executive to table a proposal for approval by the legislature on an annual basis (Lienert and Jung 2004). Biannual budgeting is used in some sub-national governments (Whalen 1995), but it is rare at the national level (Kraan and Wehner 2005: 60–2). Its strict periodicity distinguishes the budget process from most other policy-making processes in modern governments.

11. I assume full information. While deliberate misrepresentation is possible, its potential is limited by electoral considerations (Kiewiet and McCubbins 1988: 722).

12. This is obvious with reversion to zero, but last year's budget is likely to be less than the executive's preferred budget, too. Total nominal expenditure typically expands from year to year (Davis et al. 1966), in which case spending on each dimension will be slightly higher than last year in nominal terms, unless there is a substantial shift in relative priorities between the two years. A nominal increase can still imply fiscal retrenchment in real terms, when the amount by which an item increases fails to fully compensate for inflation, so this scenario even accommodates real cutbacks.

13. When the outcome budgeting framework was introduced at the turn of the century, the Australian Department of Defence had just a single outcome: 'To defend Australia and Australia's interests.' It later introduced seven outcomes, the three biggest of which related to the Army, the Navy and the Air Force (Blöndal et al. 2008: 155).

14. Peru provides an egregious example. Santiso (2004: 68) cites a World Bank study according to which, over the period January 1994 to March 2001, the legislature passed 1152 laws or resolutions, while the president issued 870 decrees. Of the latter, 86 per cent were urgency decrees, two-thirds of which either directly amended the budget or otherwise affected public finances.

15. The importance of legislative committees is widely recognised, although their primary function is disputed between proponents of distributive, informational and partisan explanations (Shepsle 1979; Krehbiel 1990; Cox and McCubbins 1993). In Chapters 5 and 6, I investigate the fiscal implications of committee structures.

3 Assessing the Power of the Purse

1. In addition, but without specific reference to budgetary matters, the index also considers whether the executive has gatekeeping powers over some types of legislation.

2. In the seventeenth century, the House of Commons increasingly used a Committee of the Whole House, which allowed it to appoint their own chairperson. This reduced the influence of the Speaker, who at the time was generally regarded as aligned with the monarch (Reid 1966: 45). The committee procedure allowed each member to speak more than once and thus facilitated much freer debate. It became easier for the Commons to delay passing the bill to grant subsidies to the Crown until the end of a session. Initially, the procedure may not have been intended as 'a weapon against the Crown' (Smith 1999: 73); it was convenient to remove portions of the debate from the floor. Once established, however, the strategic possibilities of this arrangement were soon discovered.

3. Clearly ignorant of practices elsewhere, Erskine May (1997: 794) still attempts to rationalise the late approval of the budget by venturing that 'the impracticality of framing Estimates too long in advance' makes it impossible to pass the budget by the beginning of a financial year. More appropriate is Schick's (2002: 18) interpretation that tardy approval minimises parliamentary involvement: 'With appropriations voted after the fiscal year was underway, Parliament came to merely endorse spending that had already been incurred.'

4. This practice is referred to as 'interim supply' in Canada, 'supply' in Australia and 'imprest supply' in New Zealand.

5. Note that there is no uniform definition of what constitutes a 'programme' and their number varies across countries (Kraan 2007). In general, the higher the level of aggregation in budgets, the less constrained is the executive by any limits on virement. Ideally, therefore, this item should be considered

in conjunction with the number of programmes in the budget, but this degree of precision is not possible with the available data.

6. Governments for a long time objected to the establishment of a committee to review the estimates, arguing that this would interfere with the financial initiative of the Crown (Einzig 1959: 256). When such a committee was set up in 1912 it did not live up to expectations (Chubb 1952: 198–210). Reforms in 1979 devolved the consideration of estimates to the departmental select committees (Flegmann 1986). Although these have powers to examine the expenditure of relevant government departments, as well as their policy and administration, less than a tenth of select committee inquiries during the 1997–8 and 1998–9 sessions specifically examined the estimates (Hansard Society Commission on Parliamentary Scrutiny 2001: 160). On the revenue side, all finance bill committee stages were taken on the floor of the House in the Committee of Ways and Means up until 1967. To save time, a standing committee stage for the finance bill was introduced in 1968 to deal with the less controversial aspects of the legislation (House of Commons Information Office 2003: 3). To this day, the House of Commons has no specialised committees to scrutinise appropriation and finance bills.

7. In 1919 the Commons, in what the Chancellor criticised as a 'virtuous outburst of economy', denied the Lord Chancellor funding for a second bathroom and other amenities, and the last government defeat over estimates was in 1921 over members' travelling expenses (Einzig 1959: 274–5). Amendment experience in many other Westminster type parliaments is similarly dated. The last time an allocation was reduced in the New Zealand Parliament, for instance, was in 1930 and involved the reduction of the vote for the Department of Agriculture by five pounds. At the time, a minority government had to rely on shifting coalitions (Finance and Expenditure Committee 2002: 11).

4   Explaining Cross-National Patterns

1. Elgie (2001: 7) distinguishes this arithmetical definition from a behavioural definition, where divided government refers to 'divisiveness' or 'conflict between the executive and legislative branches of government whatever the support for the executive in the legislature'. I use the arithmetical definition.

2. I used the margin of majority (MAJ) variable in the *Database of Political Institutions* (Beck et al. 2001) to assign scores. This variable is not to be confused with the electoral system dummy by Persson and Tabellini (2003), which has the same name. Where I discovered inconsistencies between the World Bank data and the *Europa World Yearbook*, I gave preference to the latter.

3. In fact, this institutional feature is no less durable than macro-constitutional characteristics. In a sample of 60 countries over the period 1960–98, Persson and Tabellini (2003: 88) find no significant change from a majoritarian to

a proportional representation electoral system during the 1960s and 70s, and only two incidents of such change in the 1980s (France and Cyprus). The 1990s saw more change in electoral systems. In terms of forms of government, they observe hardly any change over the entire sample period, except in Bangladesh, which adopted a presidential system in 1991, and a short-lived experiment with parliamentary government in Brazil between 1961 and 1963 (Persson and Tabellini 2003: 98).

5 Legislative Institutions and Fiscal Policy Outcomes

1. Conceptual distinctions vary. Herrnson (1995: 452) refers to *reanalysis* as the broader category, which entails a study of the same problem investigated by the initial investigator, using either the same database (*verification*) or independently collected data (*replication*). In contrast, Hamermesh (2007: 1) distinguishes *pure replication*, which involves checking the results in published papers using their data and models, from *scientific replication*, using a 'different sample, different population and perhaps similar, but not identical model'.

2. A later version uses a different disaggregation (Alesina et al. 1999).

3. Velasco (2000) considers implications in terms of deficits and debt.

4. An exceptional effort in this regard is the over-time analysis of the evolution of budget institutions in the European Union documented in Hallerberg, Strauch and Von Hagen (2007, 2009).

5. In addition, the Greek Parliament receives a different score for the amendment powers variable in Table 5.2 than in Table 3.3. I was unable to identify the precise timing of this institutional adjustment, but it appears that it occurred in the late 1990s, as suggested by the data in Hallerberg, Strauch and Von Hagen (2009: 64). Hence, the Greek Parliament is scored as having unlimited amendment powers in the global dataset, which covers an earlier period, and accept-or-reject authority in the OECD dataset, which covers a later period.

6. A potential problem of dynamic models with fixed effects is Nickell bias (Nickell 1981), but this is less of a concern with long time periods (Beck and Katz 2004: 15). Also, the Fisher test (Maddala and Wu 1999) did not indicate that it is problematic to assume stationarity in this sample.

7. The Hausman specification test can be used to test the null hypothesis that the fixed and random effects estimators do not differ substantially (Gujarati 2003: 651; Baltagi 2005: 19). Here, I conclude that random effects are not appropriate.

8. The effects of Accept-or-reject limit and Cuts only limit in non-election years cannot be estimated with a fixed effects specification, as there is no within-variation at all on these variables in this sample. I do report coefficients on Amendment limit, Total spending limit and Deficit limit. However, these are all based on very little information, in one instance a single country year. For this reason, I do not provide a substantive interpretation of these estimates.

6   The Promise of Top-Down Budgeting

1. I deliberately eschew referring to 'the case study method', since it is possible to distinguish several distinct methods using case studies (Gerring 2005: 343).
2. This applies more broadly to the empirical research on the policy effect of political institutions (March and Olsen 1984: 740; Acemoglu 2005: 1033; Congleton and Swedenborg 2006b: 17).
3. Shepsle (1978) and Weingast and Marshall (1988) support the argument that committee members are preference outliers relative to the floor of the house, although Krehbiel (1990, 1991) challenges this.
4. For discussions of earlier reform efforts, see Eriksson (1983) and Wilkes (1995).
5. Wehner (2007: 327–8) also discusses more recent reforms of *ex post* accountability arrangements, including the creation of the new Swedish National Audit Office in 2003.
6. The relevant formal rules are contained in article 12 of Chapter 5 of the Riksdag Act.
7. Articles 5 and 6 of Chapter 5 of the Riksdag Act deal with the voting procedure.
8. Changes made by the *Riksdag* to the government proposal are documented in the Finance Committee report on the budget (FiU10) that is handed to the Speaker and forwarded to the government. Recent reports are available on the parliamentary website at http://www.riksdagen.se.
9. The exception is the 2003 budget, which was passed after an election and had to be adjusted to reflect the co-operation agreement between the Social Democrats and their legislative allies. When the budget proposal was submitted to parliament in early October the Social Democrats had only reached an agreement with the Left Party. Negotiations continued and a few weeks later the Social Democrats, the Left Party and the Green Party presented a joint motion (2002/03:Fi230) suggesting a number of financially neutral changes. However, when the Finance Committee scrutinised these proposals it emerged that some of the indirect effects of an income tax change on local communities had been omitted, which amounted to 443 million Kronor.
10. A constitutional amendment in 2001 added further detail, but left intact the demand for legislation on an amendment procedure in place, now in section 77(3) of the Constitution. Refer to Appendix II for full details.
11. Together with the South African Council of Churches and non-governmental organisations, they formed a People's Budget Campaign in 2000. Over the following years, it released alternative budget proposals and continued to call for legislation to allow parliament to amend money bills.
12. The accounting officer in a department may only shift a saving of up to eight per cent of the amount appropriated for a programme to another programme within the same vote. In addition, amounts that are specifically and exclusively allocated for a purpose mentioned under a main division

within a vote may not be reduced, transfers to institutions may not be adjusted and capital expenditure may not be reduced in order to defray current expenditure.

13. In October 2002, the National Assembly resolved to establish a Joint Budget Committee with 15 of its members plus eight members of the National Council of Provinces, the regional chamber of parliament. The mandate of this committee was to scrutinise the Medium Term Expenditure Framework and appropriation bill tabled with the annual budget, monthly in-year expenditure and revenue statements and the pre-budget Medium Term Budget Policy Statement, with the exception of macroeconomic and revenue issues. Moreover, the committee was to consider Parliament's role in the development of budgets 'in accordance with constitutional requirements'.

14. The Political Committee is charged with providing strategic direction to the party in parliament and liaising with its National Working Committee.

15. This provision was inspired by the example of the German *Bundestag*, which has powers to apply a 'qualified freeze' so that the Federal Ministry of Finance has to obtain parliamentary consent before the budgeted amount for a particular item, or a certain percentage thereof, may be spent. This requires the provision of additional information to the Budget Committee, until parliamentarians are satisfied and release the funds (Eickenboom 1989: 1208).

16. For additional background and initial analysis of the legislation adopted in 2009, refer to the contributions in Verwey (2009).

7 Beyond the Myth of Fiscal Control

1. In addition, any type of fiscal indicator is associated with numerous measurement issues (e.g. Blejer and Cheasty 1991).

2. The Open Budget Initiative of the International Budget Partnership (IBP) at the Center on Budget and Policy Priorities (CBPP) in Washington, DC provides an excellent example of a high quality and rigorous multi-country study. This survey includes an independent peer review process. The organisation publishes the results from each country survey along with the comments of the reviewers on each survey item as well as a response explaining its final editorial decision.

Bibliography

Abedian, I., T. Ajam and L. Walker (1997). *Promises, Plans and Priorities: South Africa's Emerging Fiscal Structures*. Cape Town, Idasa.

Abney, G. and T. P. Lauth (1985). 'The Line-Item Veto in the States: An Instrument for Fiscal Restraint or an Instrument for Partisanship?' *Public Administration Review* 45(3): 372–7.

Acemoglu, D. (2005). 'Constitutions, Politics, and Economics: A Review Essay on Persson and Tabellini's *The Economic Effects of Constitutions*'. *Journal of Economic Literature* 43(4): 1025–45.

Acemoglu, D., S. Johnson and J. A. Robinson (2001). 'The Colonial Origins of Comparative Development: An Empirical Investigation'. *American Economic Review* 91(5): 1369–401.

Ad Hoc Joint Sub-Committee on Oversight and Accountability (2002). Final Report. Cape Town, Parliament of South Africa.

Adonis, A. (1993). *Parliament Today*. Manchester, Manchester University Press.

African National Congress (1994). *The Reconstruction and Development Programme: A Policy Framework*. Johannesburg, Umanyano Publications.

Alesina, A. and R. Perotti (1996). 'Budget Deficits and Budget Institutions'. NBER Working Paper 5556.

Alesina, A., R. Hausmann, R. Hommes and E. Stein (1996). 'Budget Institutions and Fiscal Performance in Latin America'. NBER Working Paper 5586.

Alesina, A., R. Hausmann, R. Hommes and E. Stein (1999). 'Budget Institutions and Fiscal Performance in Latin America'. *Journal of Development Economics* 59(2): 253–73.

Alt, J. E. and D. D. Lassen (2006). 'Transparency, Political Polarization, and Political Budget Cycles in OECD Countries'. *American Journal of Political Science* 50(3): 530–50.

Alt, J. E. and R. C. Lowry (1994). 'Divided Government, Fiscal Institutions, and Budget Deficits: Evidence from the States'. *American Political Science Review* 88(4): 811–28.

Amselek, P. (1998). 'Le Budget de l'État et le Parlement sous la Ve République'. *Revue du Droit Publique* (Supp.): 1444–73.

Anderson, B. (2008). 'The Value of a Nonpartisan, Independent, Objective Analytical Unit to the Legislative Role in Budget Preparation'. *Legislative Oversight and Budgeting: A World Perspective*. R. Stapenhurst, R. Pelizzo, D. M. Olson and L. von Trapp. Washington, DC, World Bank: 131–9.

Anderson, B. and J. J. Minarik (2006). 'Design Choices for Fiscal Policy Rules'. *OECD Journal on Budgeting* 5(4): 159–208.

Arter, D. (1984). *The Nordic Parliaments: A Comparative Analysis*. New York, St Martin's Press.

Bagehot, W. (1867 [1963]). *The English Constitution*. London, Collins.

Baldez, L. and J. M. Carey (1999). 'Presidential Agenda Control and Spending Policy: Lessons from General Pinochet's Constitution'. *American Journal of Political Science* 43(1): 29–55.

Baltagi, B. H. (2005). *Econometric Analysis of Panel Data*. Chichester, J. Wiley and Sons.

Bastida, F. and B. Benito (2007). 'Central Government Budget Practices and Transparency: An International Comparison'. *Public Administration* 85(3): 667–716.

Bawn, K. (1997). 'Choosing Strategies to Control the Bureaucracy: Statutory Constraints, Oversight, and the Committee System'. *Journal of Law, Economics, and Organization* 13(1): 101–26.

Bechberger, E. K. (2007). 'Regaining Control of the Social Budgets: Fiscal Commitment and Social Insurance Reform in France and Germany 1990–2005'. Doctoral dissertation. London, Government Department, London School of Economics and Political Science.

Beck, N. (2001). 'Time-Series-Cross-Section Data: What Have We Learned in the Past Few Years?' *Annual Review of Political Science* 4: 271–93.

Beck, N. and J. N. Katz (1995). 'What to Do (and Not to Do) With Time-Series Cross-Section Data'. *American Political Science Review* 89(3): 634–47.

Beck, N. and J. N. Katz (2004). 'Time-Series-Cross-Section Issues: Dynamics'. Unpublished manuscript.

Beck, T., G. Clarke, A. Groff, P. Keefer and P. Walsh (2001). 'New Tools in Comparative Political Economy: The Database of Political Institutions'. *World Bank Economic Review* 15(1): 165–76.

Bendor, J., S. Taylor and R. van Gaalen (1985). 'Bureaucratic Expertise versus Legislative Authority: A Model of Deception and Monitoring in Budgeting'. *American Political Science Review* 79(4): 1041–60.

Benito, B. and F. Bastida (2009). 'Budget Transparency, Fiscal Performance, and Political Turnout: An International Approach'. *Public Administration Review* 69(3): 403–17.

Bennett, A. and C. Elman (2006). 'Qualitative Research: Recent Developments in Case Study Methods'. *Annual Review of Political Science* 9: 455–76.

Bergman, T. (2004). 'Sweden: Democratic Reforms and Partisan Decline in an Emerging Separation-of-Powers System'. *Scandinavian Political Studies* 27(2): 203–25.

Berry, W. D. (1993). *Understanding Regression Assumptions*. London, Sage Publications.

Berry, W. D. and S. Feldman (1985). *Multiple Regression in Practice*. London, Sage Publications.

Blais, A., D. Blake and S. Dion (1993). 'Do Parties Make a Difference? Parties and the Size of Government in Liberal Democracies'. *American Journal of Political Science* 37(1): 40–62.

Blejer, M. I. and A. Cheasty (1991). 'The Measurement of Fiscal Deficits: Analytical and Methodological Issues'. *Journal of Economic Literature* 29(4): 1644–78.

Blöndal, J. R. (2001a). 'Budgeting in Canada'. *OECD Journal on Budgeting* 1(2): 39–84.

Blöndal, J. R. (2001b). 'Budgeting in Sweden'. *OECD Journal on Budgeting* 1(1): 27–57.

Blöndal, J. R. (2003). 'Budget Reform in OECD Member Countries: Common Trends'. *OECD Journal on Budgeting* 2(4): 7–25.

Blöndal, J. R., C. Goretti and J. K. Kristensen (2003). 'Budgeting in Brazil'. *OECD Journal on Budgeting* 3(1): 97–131.

Blöndal, J. R., D.-J. Kraan and M. Ruffner (2003). 'Budgeting in the United States'. *OECD Journal on Budgeting* 3(2): 7–54.

Blöndal, J. R., D. Bergvall, I. Hawkesworth and R. Deighton-Smith (2008). 'Budgeting in Australia'. *OECD Journal on Budgeting* 8(2): 127–90.

Bohrnstedt, G. W. and D. Knoke (1994). *Statistics for Social Data Analysis*. Itasca, IL, F. E. Peacock Publishers.

Bozeman, B. and J. D. Straussman (1982). 'Shrinking Budgets and the Shrinkage of Budget Theory'. *Public Administration Review* 42(6): 509–15.

Bradbury, J. C. and M. W. Crain (2001). 'Legislative Organization and Government Spending: Cross-Country Evidence'. *Journal of Public Economics* 82(3): 309–25.

Brambor, T., W. R. Clark and M. Golder (2006). 'Understanding Interaction Models: Improving Empirical Analyses'. *Political Analysis* 14(1): 63–82.

Bräuninger, T. (2005). 'A Partisan Model of Government Expenditure'. *Public Choice* 125(3–4): 409–29.

Brazier, A. and V. Ram (2005). Inside the Counting House: A Discussion Paper on Parliamentary Scrutiny of Government Finance. London, Hansard Society.

Brender, A. and A. Drazen (2005). 'Political Budget Cycles in New Versus Established Democracies'. *Journal of Monetary Economics* 52(7): 1271–95.

Breton, A. (1996). *Competitive Governments: An Economic Theory of Politics and Public Finance*. Cambridge, Cambridge University Press.

Burnell, P. (2001). 'Financial Indiscipline in Zambia's Third Republic: The Role of Parliamentary Scrutiny'. *Journal of Legislative Studies* 7(3): 34–64.

Byrd, R. C. (1998). 'The Control of the Purse and the Line Item Veto Act'. *Harvard Journal on Legislation* 35(2): 297–333.

Calland, R. (1997). *All Dressed up with Nowhere to Go? The Rapid Transformation of the South African Parliamentary Committee System (in Comparative Theoretical Perspective)*. Bellville, School of Government, University of the Western Cape.

Calland, R. (1999). *The First Five Years: A Review of South Africa's Democratic Parliament*. Cape Town, Idasa.

Calland, R. (2006). *Anatomy of South Africa: Who Holds the Power?* Cape Town, Zebra Press.

Cameron, C. M. (2000). *Veto Bargaining: Presidents and the Politics of Negative Power*. Cambridge, Cambridge University Press.

Campos, E. and S. Pradhan (1996). 'Budgetary Institutions and Expenditure Outcomes: Binding Governments to Fiscal Performance'. World Bank Policy Research Working Paper 1646.

Carey, J. M. and M. S. Shugart, Eds (1998). *Executive Decree Authority*. Cambridge, Cambridge University Press.

Carter, J. R. and D. Schap (1990). 'Line-Item Veto: Where is Thy Sting?' *Journal of Economic Perspectives* 4(2): 103–18.

Chabert, G. (2001). 'La Réforme de l'Ordonnance de 1959 sur la Procédure Budgétaire: Simple Aménagement Technique ou Prélude à des Véritables Bouleversements?' *Regards sur l'Actualité* 275: 13–25.

Chang, E. C. C. (2008). 'Electoral Incentives and Budgetary Spending: Rethinking the Role of Political Institutions'. *Journal of Politics* 70(4): 1086–97.

Cheibub, J. A. (2006). 'Presidentialism, Electoral Identifiability, and Budget Balances in Democratic Systems'. *American Political Science Review* 100(3): 353–68.

Cheibub, J. A. and F. Limongi (2002). 'Democratic Institutions and Regime Survival: Parliamentary and Presidential Democracies Reconsidered'. *Annual Review of Political Science* 5: 151–79.

Chinaud, R. (1993). 'Loi de Finances – Quelle Marge de Manœuvre Pour le Parlement?' *Pouvoirs* 64: 99–108.

Chubb, B. (1952). *The Control of Public Expenditure: Financial Committees of the House of Commons*. Oxford, Clarendon Press.

Cogan, J. F. (1994). 'The Dispersion of Spending Authority and Federal Budget Deficits'. *The Budget Puzzle: Understanding Federal Spending*. J. F. Cogan, T. J. Muris and A. Schick. Stanford, CA, Stanford University Press: 16–40.

Congleton, R. D. and B. Swedenborg (2006a). *Democratic Constitutional Design and Public Policy: Analysis and Evidence*. Cambridge, MA, MIT Press.

Congleton, R. D. and B. Swedenborg (2006b). 'Introduction: Rational Choice Politics and Political Institutions'. *Democratic Constitutional Design and Public Policy: Analysis and Evidence*. R. D. Congleton and B. Swedenborg. Cambridge, MA, MIT Press: 1–36.

Congress of South African Trade Unions (1997). COSATU Submission on the Money Bills Amendment Procedure Bill, presented to the Portfolio Committee on Finance, 22 October 1997. Cape Town, Congress of South African Trade Unions.

Coombes, D. L., Ed. (1976). *The Power of the Purse: The Role of European Parliaments in Budgetary Decisions*. London, George Allen and Unwin.

Corder, H., S. Jagwanth and F. Soltau (1999). Report on Parliamentary Oversight and Accountability, July 1999. Cape Town, Faculty of Law, University of Cape Town.

Cox, G. W. and M. D. McCubbins (1993). *Legislative Leviathan: Party Government in the House*. Berkeley, CA, University of California Press.

Crain, M. W. and T. J. Muris (1995). 'Legislative Organization of Fiscal Policy'. *Journal of Law and Economics* 38(2): 311–33.

Crombez, C., T. Groseclose and K. Krehbiel (2006). 'Gatekeeping'. *Journal of Politics* 68(2): 322–34.

Cusack, T. R. (1997). 'Partisan Politics and Public Finance: Changes in Public Spending in the Industrialized Democracies, 1955–1989'. *Public Choice* 91: 375–95.

Cusack, T. R. (1999). 'Partisan Politics and Fiscal Policy'. *Comparative Political Studies* 32(4): 464–86.

Davey, E. (2000). *Making MPs Work for our Money: Reforming Parliament's Role in Budget Scrutiny*. London, Centre for Reform.

Davis, O. A., M. A. H. Dempster and A. Wildavsky (1966). 'A Theory of the Budgetary Process'. *American Political Science Review* 60(3): 529–47.

De Renzio, P. (2006). 'Aid, Budgets and Accountability: A Survey Article'. *Development Policy Review* 24(6): 627–45.

Dearden, J. A. and D. Schap (1994). 'The First Word and the Last Word in the Budgetary Process: A Comparative Institutional Analysis of Proposal and Veto Authorities'. *Public Choice* 81(1–2): 35–53.

Dearden, J. A. and T. A. Husted (1990). 'Executive Budget Proposal, Executive Veto, Legislative Override and Uncertainty: A Comparative Analysis of the Budgetary Process'. *Public Choice* 65(1): 1–19.

Dempster, M. A. H. and A. Wildavsky (1979). 'On Change: Or, There is No Magic Size for an Increment'. *Political Studies* 27: 371–89.

Demsetz, H. and K. Lehn (1985). 'The Structure of Corporate Ownership: Causes and Consequences'. *Journal of Political Economy* 93(6): 1155–77.

Department of Finance (1996). Growth, Employment and Redistribution: A Macroeconomic Strategy. Pretoria, Government Printer.

Department of Finance (1997). Medium Term Budget Policy Statement. Pretoria, Government Printer.

Deroose, S., L. Moulin and P. Wierts (2006): 'National Expenditure Rules and Expenditure Outcomes: Evidence for EU Member States'. *Wirtschaftspolitische Blätter* 53(1): 27–41.

Dewald, W. G., J. G. Thursby and R. G. Anderson (1986). 'Replication in Empirical Economics: The Journal of Money, Credit and Banking Project'. *American Economic Review* 76(4): 587–603.

Dharmapala, D. (2003). 'Budgetary Policy with Unified and Decentralized Appropriations Authority'. *Public Choice* 115: 347–67.

Dharmapala, D. (2006). 'The Congressional Budget Process, Aggregate Spending, and Statutory Budget Rules'. *Journal of Public Economics* 90(1–2): 119–41.

Diaz-Cayeros, A., K. M. McElwain, V. Romero and K. A. Siewierski (2002). 'Fiscal Decentralization, Legislative Institutions and Particularistic Spending'. Unpublished manuscript.

Döring, H., Ed. (1995a). *Parliaments and Majority Rule in Western Europe*. Frankfurt, Campus.

Döring, H. (1995b). 'Time as a Scarce Resource: Government Control of the Agenda'. *Parliaments and Majority Rule in Western Europe*. H. Döring. Frankfurt, Campus: 223–46.

Döring, H. and M. Hallerberg, Eds (2004). *Patterns of Parliamentary Behavior: Passage of Legislation across Western Europe*. Aldershot, Ashgate.

Dorotinsky, B. (2008). 'A Note on What Happens if No Budget Is Passed before the Fiscal Year Begins'. *Legislative Oversight and Budgeting: A World Perspective*. R. Stapenhurst, R. Pelizzo, D. M. Olson and L. von Trapp. Washington, DC, World Bank: 111–15.

Dorrell, S. (1993). 'Budgetary Reform'. *Fiscal Studies* 14(1): 89–94.

Dunleavy, P. (1991). *Democracy, Bureaucracy and Public Choice: Economic Explanations in Political Science*. London, Prentice Hall.

Dunleavy, P. and F. Boucek (2003). 'Constructing the Number of Parties'. *Party Politics* 9(3): 291–315.

Economist (2004). 'Mexico's Budget Wrangles: Show Us the Money'. *The Economist* 373(8405), 11 December, London edition: 54.

Edin, P.-A. and H. Ohlsson (1991). 'Political Determinants of Budget Deficits: Coalition Effects Versus Minority Effects'. *European Economic Review* 35(8): 1597–603.

Ehrhart, K.-M., R. Gardner, J. von Hagen and C. Keser (2007). 'Budget Processes: Theory and Experimental Evidence'. *Games and Economic Behavior* 59(2): 279–95.

Eickenboom, P. (1989). 'Haushaltsausschuß und Haushaltsverfahren'. *Parlamentsrecht und Parlamentspraxis in der Bundesrepublik Deutschland: Ein Handbuch*. H.-P. Schneider and W. Zeh. Berlin, De Gruyter: 1183–220.

Einzig, P. (1959). *The Control of the Purse: Progress and Decline of Parliament's Financial Control*. London, Secker and Warburg.

Elgie, R., Ed. (2001). *Divided Government in Comparative Perspective*. Oxford, New York, Oxford University Press.

Engstrom, E. J. and S. Kernell (1999). 'Serving Competing Principals: The Budget Estimates of OMB and CBO in an Era of Divided Government'. *Presidential Studies Quarterly* 29(4): 820–30.

Ensor, L. (2001). 'Manuel and MPs Agree on Powers to Affect Budget'. *Business Day*, 27 June. Johannesburg: 2.

Ensor, L. (2002). 'Hogan Resigns from Finance Committee'. *Business Day*, 29 May. Johannesburg: 1.

Epstein, D. and S. O'Halloran (1999). *Delegating Powers: A Transaction Cost Politics Approach to Policy Making under Separate Powers*. Cambridge, Cambridge University Press.

Eriksson, B. (1983). 'Sweden's Budget System in a Changing World'. *Public Budgeting and Finance* 3(3): 64–80.

Esaiasson, P. and K. Heidar, Eds (2000). *Beyond Westminster and Congress: The Nordic Experience*. Columbus, OH, Ohio State University Press.

Europa Publications Limited (various). *Europa World Yearbook*. London, Europa Publications Limited.

European Commission Economic Policy Committee (2006). The Impact of Ageing on Public Expenditure: Projections for the EU25 Member States on Pensions, Health Care, Long-term Care, Education and Unemployment Transfers (2004–50). Brussels, European Commission Directorate-General for Economic and Financial Affairs.

Fabrizio, S. and A. Mody (2006). 'Can Budget Institutions Counteract Political Indiscipline?' IMF Working Paper WP/06/123.

Feinstein, A. (2007). *After the Party: A Personal and Political Journey Inside the ANC*. Johannesburg, Jonathan Ball.

Ferejohn, J. and K. Krehbiel (1987). 'The Budget Process and the Size of the Budget'. *American Journal of Political Science* 31(2): 296–320.

Filc, G. and C. Scartascini (2004). 'Budget Institutions and Fiscal Outcomes: Ten Years of Inquiry on Fiscal Matters at the Research Department'. Paper presented at the IADB Research Department Ten-Year Anniversary Conference, Washington, DC, 17 September.

Filc, G. and C. Scartascini (2007). 'Budgetary Institutions'. *The State of State Reform in Latin America*. E. Lora. Stanford, CA, Stanford University Press: 157–84.

Finance and Expenditure Committee (2002). Report on the Standard Estimates Questionnaire 2002/2003. Wellington, New Zealand House of Representatives.

Finansdepartement (2000). Utvärdering och vidareutveckling av budget-processen. Stockholm, Ministry of Finance.

Fiorino, N. and R. Ricciuti (2007). 'Legislature Size and Government Spending in Italian Regions: Forecasting the Effects of a Reform'. *Public Choice* 131: 117–25.

Fish, S. M. (2006). 'Stronger Legislatures, Stronger Democracies'. *Journal of Democracy* 17(1): 5–20.

Flegmann, V. (1986). *Public Expenditure and the Select Committees of the Commons*. Aldershot, Gower.

Fölscher, A., Ed. (2002). *Budget Transparency and Participation: Five African Case Studies*. Cape Town, Idasa.

Fölscher, A. (2007). 'Country Case Study: South Africa'. *Budgeting and Budgetary Institutions*. A. Shah. Washington, DC, World Bank: 501–34.

Fölscher, A., W. Krafchik and I. Shapiro (2000). *Transparency and Participation in the Budget Process*. Cape Town, Idasa.

Ford, W. C., G. Hunt, J. C. Fitzpatrick, R. R. Hill, K. E. Harris and S. D. Tilley, Eds (1904–37). *Journals of the Continental Congress, 1774–1789*. Washington, DC, Government Printing Office.

Fox, J. (1991). *Regression Diagnostics*. London, Sage Publications.

Franzese, R. J. (1999). 'Electoral and Partisan Manipulation of Public Debt in Developed Democracies, 1956–90'. *Institutions, Politics and Fiscal Policy*. R. R. Strauch and J. von Hagen. Boston, MA, Kluwer Academic Publishers: 61–83.

Franzese, R. J. (2002). 'Electoral and Partisan Cycles in Economic Policies and Outcomes'. *Annual Review of Political Science* 5: 369–421.

Freedom House (2008). Freedom in the World Country Ratings 1972–2008. Available on the Internet: http://www.freedomhouse.org [last accessed October 2008].

Frey, B. and L. J. Lau (1968). 'Towards a Mathematical Model of Government Behaviour'. *Journal of Economics* 28(3): 355–80.

Friauf, K. H. (1976). 'Parliamentary Control of the Budget in the Federal Republic of Germany'. *The Power of the Purse: The Role of European Parliaments in Budgetary Decisions*. D. L. Coombes. London, George Allen and Unwin: 66–84.

Friedrich, R. J. (1982). 'In Defense of Multiplicative Terms in Multiple Regression Equations'. *American Journal of Political Science* 26(4): 797–833.

Gabel, M. J. and G. L. Hager (2000). 'How to Succeed at Increasing Spending Without Really Trying: The Balanced Budget Amendment and the Item Veto'. *Public Choice* 102: 19–23.

George, A. L. and A. Bennett (2005). *Case Studies and Theory Development in the Social Sciences*. Cambridge, MA, MIT Press.

Gerring, J. (2004). 'What Is a Case Study and What Is It Good for?' *American Political Science Review* 98(2): 341–54.

Gerring, J. (2005). 'Causation: A Unified Framework for the Social Sciences'. *Journal of Theoretical Politics* 17(2): 163–98.

Gerster, J. (1984). *Der Berichterstatter im parlamentarischen Haushaltsverfahren*. Regensburg, Verlag Recht, Verwaltung, Wirtschaft.

Gilligan, T. W. and J. G. Matsusaka (2001). 'Fiscal Policy, Legislature Size, and Political Parties: Evidence from State and Local Governments in the First Half of the 20th Century'. *National Tax Journal* 54(1): 57–82.

Gleich, H. (2003). 'Budget Institutions and Fiscal Performance in Central and Eastern European Countries'. European Central Bank Working Paper 215.

Goodin, R. E. (1996). 'Institutions and Their Design'. *The Theory of Institutional Design*. R. E. Goodin. Cambridge, Cambridge University Press: 1–53.

Government Commission on Budget Law (1996). Proposal for a State Budget Act in Sweden. Stockholm.

Gujarati, D. N. (2003). *Basic Econometrics*. Boston, MA, McGraw Hill.

Haggard, S. and M. D. McCubbins, Eds (2001). *Presidents, Parliaments, and, Policy*. Cambridge, Cambridge University Press.

Hall, P. A. and R. C. R. Taylor (1996). 'Political Science and the Three New Institutionalisms'. Max-Planck-Institut für Gesellschaftsforschung Discussion Paper 96/6.

Hallerberg, M. (1999). 'The Role of Parliamentary Committees in the Budgetary Process within Europe'. *Institutions, Politics and Fiscal Policy*. R. R. Strauch and J. von Hagen. Boston, MA, Kluwer Academic Publishers: 87–106.

Hallerberg, M. (2004). *Domestic Budgets in a United Europe: Fiscal Governance from the End of Bretton Woods to EMU*. Ithaca, NY, Cornell University Press.

Hallerberg, M. and J. von Hagen (1997). 'Sequencing and the Size of the Budget: A Reconsideration'. Centre for Economic Policy Research Discussion Paper 1589.

Hallerberg, M. and P. Marier (2004). 'Executive Authority, the Personal Vote, and Budget Discipline in Latin American and Caribbean Countries'. *American Journal of Political Science* 48(3): 571–87.

Hallerberg, M., C. Scartascini and E. Stein, Eds (2009). *Who Decides the Budget? A Political Economy Analysis of the Budget Process in Latin America*. Washington, DC, Inter-American Development Bank.

Hallerberg, M., R. R. Strauch and J. von Hagen (2001). The Use and Effectiveness of Budgetary Rules and Norms in EU Member States. Report Prepared for the Dutch Ministry of Finance by the Institute of European Integration Studies.

Hallerberg, M., R. R. Strauch and J. von Hagen (2007). 'The Design of Fiscal Rules and Forms of Governance in European Union Countries'. *European Journal of Political Economy* 23(2): 338–59.

Hallerberg, M., R. R. Strauch and J. von Hagen (2009). *Fiscal Governance in Europe*. Cambridge, Cambridge University Press.

Hamermesh, D. S. (2007). 'Replication in Economics'. NBER Working Paper 13026.

Hansard Society Commission on Parliamentary Scrutiny (2001). *The Challenge for Parliament: Making Government Accountable*. London, Vacher Dod.

Hardin, G. (1968). 'The Tragedy of the Commons'. *Science* 162(3859): 1243–8.

Harriss, G. L. (1975). *King, Parliament, and Public Finance in Medieval England to 1369*. Oxford, Clarendon Press.

Hawkesworth, I., D. Bergvall, R. Emery and J. Wehner (2008). 'Budgeting in Greece'. *OECD Journal on Budgeting* 8(3): 70–119.

Heald, D. (2003). 'Fiscal Transparency: Concepts, Measurement and UK Practice'. *Public Administration* 81(4): 723–59.

Hebert, R. S., S. M. Wright, R. S. Dittus and T. A. Elasy (2002). 'Prominent Medical Journals Often Provide Insufficient Information to Assess the Validity of Studies With Negative Results'. *Journal of Negative Results in BioMedicine* 1(1).

Helland, L. (1999). 'Fiscal Constitutions, Fiscal Preferences, Information and Deficits: An Evaluation of 13 West-European Countries 1978–95'. *Institutions, Politics and Fiscal Policy*. R. R. Strauch and J. von Hagen. Boston, NY, Kluwer Academic Publishers: 107–38.

Heller, P. S. (2003). *Who Will Pay? Coping with Aging Societies, Climate Change, and Other Long-Term Fiscal Challenges*. Washington, DC, International Monetary Fund.

Heller, W. B. (1997). 'Bicameralism and Budget Deficits: The Effect of Parliamentary Structure on Government Spending'. *Legislative Studies Quarterly* 22(4): 485–516.

Heller, W. B. (2001). 'Political Denials: The Policy Effect of Intercameral Partisan Differences in Bicameral Parliamentary Systems'. *Journal of Law, Economics, and Organization* 17(1): 34–61.

Herrnson, P. S. (1995). 'Replication, Verification, Secondary Analysis, and Data Collection in Political Science'. *PS: Political Science & Politics* 28(3): 452–5.

Hibbs, D. A. (1977). 'Political Parties and Macroeconomic Policy'. *American Political Science Review* 71(4): 1467–87.

Hindmoor, A. (2006). *Rational Choice*. New York, Palgrave Macmillan.

Hjalmarsson, Å. (2005). Comments presented at a CEF [Center of Excellence in Finance] Seminar on Results-Based Budgeting and Management. Unpublished manuscript.

Hjalmarsson, Å. and G. Jonsson (2003). Accountability and Control in the Central Government Sector. Stockholm, Ministry of Finance.

Hoffmann, S. H. (1959). 'The French Constitution of 1958: I. The Final Text and Its Prospects'. *American Political Science Review* 53(2): 332–57.

Hogwood, B. W. (1992). *Trends in British Public Policy*. Buckingham, Open University Press.

Holtz-Eakin, D. (1988). 'The Line Item Veto and Public Sector Budgets: Evidence from the States'. *Journal of Public Economics* 36(3): 269–92.

Horn, M. J. (1995). *The Political Economy of Public Administration: Institutional Choice in the Public Sector*. Cambridge, Cambridge University Press.

House of Commons Information Office (2003). *Financial Procedure*. London, House of Commons.

Huber, J. D. (1996). *Rationalizing Parliament: Legislative Institutions and Party Politics in France*. Cambridge, Cambridge University Press.

Huber, J. D. and C. R. Shipan (2002). *Deliberate Discretion: The Institutional Foundations of Bureaucratic Autonomy*. Cambridge, Cambridge University Press.

Hudson, A. and C. Wren (2007). 'Parliamentary Strengthening in Developing Countries'. Final Report for DFID. London, Overseas Development Institute.

Huntington, S. P. (1991). *The Third Wave: Democratization in the Late Twentieth Century*. Norman, OK, University of Oklahoma Press.

Inter-Parliamentary Union (1986). *Parliaments of the World: A Comparative Reference Compendium*. Aldershot, Gower.

International Budget Partnership (2009). *Open Budgets. Transform Lives. The Open Budget Survey 2008*. Washington, DC, International Budget Partnership.

International Budget Project (2006). Open Budget Index. Available on the Internet: http://www.openbudgetindex.org [last accessed November 2006].

International Monetary Fund (1998). Code of Good Practices on Fiscal Transparency. Washington, DC, International Monetary Fund.

International Monetary Fund (2001). Revised Code of Good Practices on Fiscal Transparency. Washington, DC, International Monetary Fund.

International Monetary Fund (2003). South Africa: Staff Report for the 2003 Article IV Consultation. Washington, DC, International Monetary Fund.

International Monetary Fund (2007a). Code of Good Practices on Fiscal Transparency. Washington, DC, International Monetary Fund.

International Monetary Fund (2007b). Manual on Fiscal Transparency. Washington, DC, International Monetary Fund.

Jackman, R. W. (1985). 'Cross-National Statistical Research and the Study of Comparative Politics'. *American Journal of Political Science* 29(1): 161–82.

Johnson, J. K. and R. Stapenhurst (2008). 'Legislative Budget Offices: International Experience'. *Legislative Oversight and Budgeting: A World Perspective*. R. Stapenhurst, R. Pelizzo, D. M. Olson and L. von Trapp. Washington, DC, World Bank: 141–58.

Joint Committee of Public Accounts and Audit (2002). Review of the Accrual Budget Documentation, Report No. 388. Canberra, Parliament of Australia.

Joumard, I., P. M. Kongsrud, Y. Nam and R. Price (2003). 'Enhancing the Cost Effectiveness of Public Spending: Experience in OECD Countries'. *OECD Economic Studies* 37(2): 109–61.

Kam, C. D. and R. J. Franzese (2007). *Modeling and Interpreting Interactive Hypotheses in Regression Analysis*. Ann Arbor, MI, University of Michigan Press.

Keith, R. (2000). 'Preventing Federal Government Shutdowns: Proposals for an Automatic Continuing Resolution'. CRS Report RL30339. Washington, DC, Congressional Research Service.

Kiewiet, D. R. and M. D. McCubbins (1988). 'Presidential Influence on Congressional Appropriations Decisions'. *American Journal of Political Science* 32(3): 713–36.

Kim, J. M. and C.-K. Park (2006). 'Top-down Budgeting as a Tool for Central Resource Management'. *OECD Journal on Budgeting* 6(1): 87–125.

King, G. (1995). 'Replication, Replication'. *PS: Political Science & Politics* 28(3): 444–52.

King, G., R. Keohane and S. Verba (1996). *Designing Social Inquiry: Scientific Inference in Qualitative Research*. Princeton, NJ, Princeton University Press.

Kirchgässner, G. (2001). 'The Effects of Fiscal Institutions on Public Finance: A Survey of the Empirical Evidence'. CESifo Working Paper 617.

Kittel, B. (1999). 'Sense and Sensitivity in Pooled Analysis of Political Data'. *European Journal of Political Research* 35(2): 225–53.

Kopits, G. and J. Craig (1998). 'Transparency in Government Operations'. IMF Occasional Paper 158.

Kopits, G. and S. A. Symansky (1998). 'Fiscal Policy Rules'. IMF Occasional Paper 162.

Kotzé, H. (1996). 'The New Parliament: Transforming the Westminster Heritage'. *South Africa: Designing New Political Institutions*. M. Faure and J.-E. Lane. London, Sage: 252–68.

Kraan, D.-J. (1996). *Budgetary Decisions: A Public Choice Approach*. Cambridge, Cambridge University Press.

Kraan, D.-J. (2004). 'Off-Budget and Tax Expenditures'. *OECD Journal on Budgeting* 4(1): 121–42.

Kraan, D.-J. (2007). 'Programme Budgeting in OECD Countries'. *OECD Journal on Budgeting* 7(4): 1–41.

Kraan, D.-J., D. Bergvall and I. Hawkesworth (2007). 'Budgeting in Turkey'. *OECD Journal on Budgeting* 7(2): 7–58.

Kraan, D.-J. and J. Kelly (2005). *Reallocation: The Role of Budget Institutions*. Paris, Organisation for Economic Co-operation and Development.

Kraan, D.-J. and J. Wehner (2005). 'Budgeting in Slovenia'. *OECD Journal on Budgeting* 4(4): 55–98.

Kraan, D.-J. and M. Ruffner (2005). 'Budgeting in Switzerland'. *OECD Journal on Budgeting* 5(1): 37–78.

Krafchik, W. and J. Wehner (1998). 'The Role of Parliament in the Budgetary Process'. *South African Journal of Economics* 66(4): 512–41.

Krehbiel, K. (1990). 'Are Congressional Committees Composed of Preference Outliers?' *American Political Science Review* 84(1): 149–63.

Krehbiel, K. (1991). *Information and Legislative Organization*. Ann Arbor, MI, University of Michigan Press.

Kristensen, J. K., W. S. Groszyk and B. Bühler (2002). 'Outcome-Focused Management and Budgeting'. *OECD Journal on Budgeting* 1(4): 7–34.

Kühner, S. (2007). 'Country-Level Comparisons of Welfare State Change Measures: Another Facet of the Dependent Variable Problem Within the Comparative Analysis of the Welfare State?' *Journal of European Social Policy* 17(1): 5–18.

Laakso, M. and R. Taagepera (1979). '"Effective" Number of Parties: A Measure with Application to West Europe'. *Comparative Political Studies* 12(1): 3–27.

Lalumière, P. (1976). 'Parliamentary Control of the Budget in France'. *The Power of the Purse: The Role of European Parliaments in Budgetary Decisions*. D. L. Coombes. London, George Allen and Unwin: 124–47.

Laver, M. and K. A. Shepsle (1991). 'Divided Government: America is Not "Exceptional"'. *Governance* 4(3): 250–69.

Lehrer, D., J. Leschke, S. Lhachimi, A. Vasiliu and B. Weiffen (2007). 'Negative Results in Social Science'. *European Political Science* 6(1): 51–68.

LeLoup, L. T. (2004). 'Uloga parlamenata u određivanju proračuna u Mađarskoj i Sloveniji' [Parliamentary Budgeting in Hungary and Slovenia]. *Financijska teorija i praksa* 28(1): 49–72.

Leston-Bandeira, C. (1999). 'The Role of the Portuguese Parliament Based on a Case Study: The Discussion of the Budget, 1983–95'. *Journal of Legislative Studies* 5(2): 46–73.

Levy, A. and N. Lovegrove (2009). 'Reforming the Public Sector in a Crisis: An Interview with Sweden's Former Prime Minister'. *McKinsey Quarterly* 2009(3): 39–46.

Lieberman, E. S. (2005). 'Nested Analysis as a Mixed-Method Strategy for Comparative Research'. *American Political Science Review* 99(3): 435–52.

Lienert, I. (2003). 'A Comparison Between Two Public Expenditure Management Systems in Africa'. IMF Working Paper WP/03/2.

Lienert, I. (2005). 'Who Controls the Budget: The Legislature or the Executive?' IMF Working Paper WP/05/115.

Lienert, I. and M.-K. Jung (2004). 'The Legal Framework for Budget Systems: An International Comparison'. *OECD Journal on Budgeting* Special Issue 4(3).

Lijphart, A. (1984). *Democracies: Patterns of Majoritarian and Consensus Government in Twenty-One Countries*. New Haven, CT, Yale University Press.

Lijphart, A., Ed. (1992). *Parliamentary Versus Presidential Government*. Oxford, Oxford University Press.

Lijphart, A. (1999). *Patterns of Democracy: Government Forms and Performance in Thirty-Six Countries*. New Haven, CT, Yale University Press.

Linz, J. J. (1990). 'The Perils of Presidentialism'. *Journal of Democracy* 1(1): 51–69.

Loewenstein, K. (1959). 'The Constitution of the Fifth Republic: A Preliminary Report'. *Journal of Politics* 21(2): 211–33.

Longley, L. D. and R. H. Davidson, Eds (1998). *The New Roles of Parliamentary Committees*. London, Frank Cass.

Mackintosh, J. P. (1962). *The British Cabinet*. London, Stevens.

Maddala, G. S. and S. Wu (1999). 'A Comparative Study of Unit Root Tests with Panel Data and a New Simple Test'. *Oxford Bulletin of Economics and Statistics* 61(S1): 631–52.

Mahoney, J. and G. Goertz (2006). 'A Tale of Two Cultures: Contrasting Quantitative and Qualitative Research'. *Political Analysis* 14(3): 227–49.

March, J. G. and J. P. Olsen (1984). 'The New Institutionalism: Organizational Factors in Political Life'. *American Political Science Review* 78(3): 734–49.

Mattson, I. and K. Strøm (1995). 'Parliamentary Committees'. *Parliaments and Majority Rule in Western Europe*. H. Döring. Frankfurt, Campus: 249–307.

May, E. (1997). *Treatise on the Law, Privileges, Proceedings and Usage of Parliament*. London, Butterworths.

McCubbins, M. D. and T. Schwartz (1984). 'Congressional Oversight Overlooked: Police Patrols versus Fire Alarms'. *American Journal of Political Science* 28(1): 165–79.

McGee, D. G. (2002). *The Overseers: Public Accounts Committees and Public Spending*. London, Commonwealth Parliamentary Association and Pluto Press.

Messick, R. E. (2002). 'Strengthening Legislatures: Implications from Industrial Countries'. World Bank PREM Note 63. Washington, DC, World Bank.

Meyers, R. T. (1994). Strategic Budgeting. Ann Arbor, MI, University of Michigan Press.

Meyers, R. T. (1997). 'Late Appropriations and Government Shutdowns: Frequency, Causes, Consequences, and Remedies'. *Public Budgeting and Finance*: 25–38.

Meyers, R. T. (2001). 'Will the US Congress's "Power of the Purse" Become Unexceptional?' Paper presented at the Annual Meeting of the American Political Science Association, San Francisco, CA, 30 August.

Meyers, R. T. and P. G. Joyce (2005). 'Congressional Budgeting at Age 30: Is It Worth Saving?' *Public Budgeting and Finance* 25(4): 68–82.

Mezey, M. L. (1979). *Comparative Legislatures*. Durham, NC, Duke University Press.

Mezey, M. L. (1983). 'The Functions of Legislatures in the Third World'. *Legislative Studies Quarterly* 8(4): 511–50.

Michie, J. and V. Padayachee (1998). 'Three Years after Apartheid: Growth, Employment and Redistribution?' *Cambridge Journal of Economics* 22: 623–35.

Milesi-Ferretti, G. M., R. Perotti and M. Rostagno (2002). 'Electoral Systems and Public Spending'. *Quarterly Journal of Economics* 117(2): 609–57.

Miller, G. J. and T. M. Moe (1983). 'Bureaucrats, Legislators, and the Size of Government'. *American Political Science Review* 77(2): 297–322.

Miller, V. and R. Ware (1999). The Resignation of the European Commission. London, House of Commons Library.

Ministry of Finance (2005). *The Central Government Budget Process*. Stockholm, Ministry of Finance.

Molander, P. (1992). Statsskulden och budgetprocessen. Stockholm, Ministry of Finance.

Molander, P. (1999). 'Reforming Budgetary Institutions: Swedish Experiences'. *Institutions, Politics and Fiscal Policy*. R. R. Strauch and J. von Hagen. Boston, MA, Kluwer Academic Publishers: 191–214.

Molander, P. (2001). 'Budgeting Procedures and Democratic Ideals'. *Journal of Public Policy* 21(1): 23–52.

Morgenstern, S. (2002a). 'Towards a Model of Latin American Legislatures'. *Legislative Politics in Latin America*. S. Morgenstern and B. Nacif. Cambridge, Cambridge University Press: 1–19.

Morgenstern, S. (2002b). 'Explaining Legislative Politics in Latin America'. *Legislative Politics in Latin America*. S. Morgenstern and B. Nacif. Cambridge, Cambridge University Press: 413–45.

Morgenstern, S. and B. Nacif (2002). *Legislative Politics in Latin America*. Cambridge, Cambridge University Press.

Moussa, Y. (2004). 'Public Expenditure Management in Francophone Africa: A Cross-Country Analysis'. IMF Working Paper WP/04/42.

Mueller, D. C. (2003). *Public Choice III*. Cambridge, Cambridge University Press.

Mueller, D. C. and T. Stratmann (2003). 'The Economic Effects of Democratic Participation'. *Journal of Public Economics* 87: 2129–55.

Murray, C. and L. Nijzink (2002). *Building Representative Democracy: South Africa's Legislatures and the Constitution*. Cape Town, European Union Parliamentary Support Programme.

Murray, C. M. and R. Simeon (1999). 'From Paper to Practice: The National Council of Provinces after its First Year'. *SA Public Law* 14(1): 96–141.

National Audit Office (2001). *State Audit in the European Union*. London, NAO.

Newham, G. (1997). Legislature Battles the Budget. *Parliamentary Whip*, 11 August. Cape Town, Idasa: 2–3.

Nice, D. C. (1988). 'The Item Veto and Expenditure Restraint'. *Journal of Politics* 50(2): 487–99.

Nickell, S. (1981). 'Biases in Dynamic Models with Fixed Effects'. *Econometrica* 49(6): 1417–26.

Niskanen, W. A. (1971). *Bureaucracy and Representative Government*. Chicago, IL, Aldine Atherton.

Niskanen, W. A. (1973). *Bureaucracy – Servant or Master? Lessons from America*. London, Institute of Economic Affairs.

Niskanen, W. A. (1975). 'Bureaucrats and Politicians'. *Journal of Law and Economics* 18(3): 617–43.

Nordhaus, W. D. (1975). 'The Political Business Cycle'. *The Review of Economic Studies* 42(2): 169–90.

Norton, P. (1993). *Does Parliament Matter?* New York, Harvester Wheatsheaf.

O'Donnell, G. (1998). 'Horizontal Accountability in New Democracies'. *Journal of Democracy* 9(3): 112–26.

Olson, D. M. (1994). *Democratic Legislative Institutions: A Comparative View*. Armonk, NY, M. E. Sharpe.

Olson, D. M. and M. L. Mezey, Eds (1991). *Legislatures in the Policy Process: The Dilemmas of Economic Policy*. Cambridge, Cambridge University Press.

Olson, M. (1965). *The Logic of Collective Action: Public Goods and the Theory of Groups*. Cambridge, Harvard University Press.

Oppenheimer, B. I. (1983). 'How Legislatures Shape Policy and Budgets'. *Legislative Studies Quarterly* 8(4): 551–97.

Organisation for Economic Co-operation and Development (1998). Survey of Budgeting Developments – Country Responses. Paris, Organisation for Economic Co-operation and Development.

Organisation for Economic Co-operation and Development (2002a). 'OECD Best Practices for Budget Transparency'. *OECD Journal on Budgeting* 1(3): 7–14.

Organisation for Economic Co-operation and Development (2002b). 'The OECD Budgeting Database'. *OECD Journal on Budgeting* 1(3): 155–171.

Organisation for Economic Co-operation and Development (2006). Results of the OECD 2006 Budget Survey for Latin American Countries. Available on the internet: http://www.oecd.org/gov/budget/database [last accessed March 2007].

Organisation for Economic Co-operation and Development (2007). International Budget Practices and Procedures Database. Available on the Internet: http:// www.oecd.org/gov/budget/database [last accessed October 2008].

Organisation for Economic Co-operation and Development (2008). *OECD Economic Outlook* 83. Paris, Organisation for Economic Co-operation and Development.

Organisation for Economic Co-operation and Development and European Commission Joint Research Centre (2008). *Handbook on Constructing Composite Indicators: Methodology and User Guide*. Paris, Organisation for Economic Co-operation and Development.

Organisation for Economic Co-operation and Development and World Bank (2003). Results of the Survey on Budget Practices and Procedures. Available on the Internet: http://www.oecd.org/gov/budget/database [last accessed October 2006].

Osborne, D. and T. Gaebler (1992). *Reinventing Government: How the Entrepreneurial Spirit is Transforming the Public Sector*. New York, Plume.

Ostrom, E. (1990). *Governing the Commons: The Evolution of Institutions for Collective Action*. Cambridge, Cambridge University Press.

Parliamentary Review Commission (2001). Sweden's Parliamentary Review Commission: Summary in English. Stockholm, Sveriges Riksdag.

Patterson, S. C. and A. Mughan, Eds (1999). *Senates: Bicameralism in the Contemporary World (Parliaments and Legislatures)*. Columbus, OH, Ohio State University Press.

Patterson, S. C. and A. Mughan (2001). 'Fundamentals of Institutional Design: The Functions and Powers of Parliamentary Second Chambers'. *Journal of Legislative Studies* 7(1): 39–60.

Pelizzo, R. and F. C. Stapenhurst (2004). 'Tools for Legislative Oversight: An Empirical Investigation'. World Bank Policy Research Working Paper 3388.

Pelizzo, R., R. Stapenhurst, V. Sahgal and W. Woodley (2006). 'What Makes Public Accounts Committees Work? A Comparative Analysis'. *Politics and Policy* 34(4): 774–93.

Pereira, C. and B. Mueller (2004). 'The Cost of Governing: Strategic Behavior of the President and Legislators in Brazil's Budgetary Process'. *Comparative Political Studies* 37(7): 781–815.

Perotti, R. and Y. Kontopoulos (2002). 'Fragmented Fiscal Policy'. *Journal of Public Economics* 86(2): 191–222.

Persson, G. (1997). *Den som är satt i skuld är fri: Min berättelse om hur Sverige återfick sunda statsfinanser*. Uddevalla, Atlas.

Persson, T. and G. Tabellini (2000). *Political Economics: Explaining Economic Policy*. Cambridge, MA, MIT Press.

Persson, T. and G. Tabellini (2002). 'Do Constitutions Cause Large Governments? Quasi-Experimental Evidence'. *European Economic Review* 46: 908–18.

Persson, T. and G. Tabellini (2003). *The Economic Effects of Constitutions*. Cambridge, MA, MIT Press.

Persson, T. and G. Tabellini (2004). 'Constitutional Rules and Fiscal Policy Outcomes'. *American Economic Review* 94(1): 25–45.

Persson, T. and G. Tabellini (2006). 'Constitutions and Economic Policy'. *Democratic Constitutional Design and Public Policy: Analysis and Evidence.* R. D. Congleton and B. Swedenborg. Cambridge, MA, MIT Press: 81–110.

Persson, T., G. Roland and G. Tabellini (2003). 'How Do Electoral Rules Shape Party Structures, Government Coalitions, and Economic Policies?' Unpublished manuscript.

Persson, T., G. Roland and G. Tabellini (2005). 'Electoral Rules and Government Spending in Parliamentary Democracies'. Unpublished manuscript.

Pierson, P. (1995). 'Fragmented Welfare States: Federal Institutions and the Development of Social Policy'. *Governance* 8(4): 449–78.

Pierson, P. (2000). 'Increasing Returns, Path Dependence, and the Study of Politics'. *American Political Science Review* 94(2): 251–67.

Pierson, P. and T. Skocpol (2002). 'Historical Institutionalism in Contemporary Political Science'. *Political Science: State of the Discipline.* I. Katznelson and H. V. Milner. New York, W. W. Norton: 693–721.

Plümper, T. and V. E. Troeger (2007). 'Efficient Estimation of Time-Invariant and Rarely Changing Variables in Finite Sample Panel Analyses with Unit Fixed Effects'. *Political Analysis* 15(2): 124–39.

Porritt, E. (1910). 'The Struggle over the Lloyd-George Budget'. *Quarterly Journal of Economics* 24(2): 243–78.

Poterba, J. M. (1996). 'Do Budget Rules Work?' NBER Working Paper 5550.

Poterba, J. M. and J. von Hagen, Eds (1999). *Fiscal Institutions and Fiscal Performance.* Chicago, IL, University of Chicago Press.

Premchand, A. (1963). *Control of Public Expenditure in India: A Historical and Analytical Account of the Administrative, Audit and Parliamentary Processes.* New Delhi, Allied Publishers.

Primo, D. M. (2006). 'Stop Us Before We Spend Again: Institutional Constraints on Government Spending'. *Economics and Politics* 18(3): 269–312.

Primo, D. M. (2007). *Rules and Restraint: Government Spending and the Design of Institutions.* Chicago, IL, University of Chicago Press.

Primo, D. M. and J. M. J. Snyder (2005). 'Public Goods and the Law of 1/n'. Unpublished manuscript.

Probyn, J. W., Ed. (1877). *Correspondence Relative to the Budgets of Various Countries.* London, Cassell Petter and Galpin.

Public Expenditure and Financial Accountability Secretariat (2005). Public Financial Management Performance Measurement Framework. Washington, DC, Public Expenditure and Financial Accountability Secretariat.

Publius (1961 [1788]). *The Federalist Papers.* Edited by Clinton Lawrence Rossiter. New York, New American Library.

Quigley, J. M. and D. L. Rubinfeld (1996). 'Federalism and Reductions in the Federal Budget'. *National Tax Journal* 49(2): 289–302.

Ragin, C. C. (1987). *The Comparative Method: Moving Beyond Qualitative and Quantitative Strategies.* Berkeley, CA, University of California Press.

Ragin, C. C. (2000). *Fuzzy-Set Social Science.* Chicago, IL, University of Chicago Press.

Rakner, L., L. Mukubvu, N. Ngwira, K. Smiddy and A. Schneider (2004). 'The Budget as Theatre: The Formal and Informal Institutional Makings of the Budget Process in Malawi'. Unpublished manuscript.

Reid, G. (1966). *The Politics of Financial Control: The Role of the House of Commons*. London, Hutchinson University Library.

Ricciuti, R. (2004). 'Legislatures and Government Spending: Evidence From Democratic Countries'. Unpublished manuscript.

Rodrik, D. (1998). 'Why Do More Open Economies Have Bigger Governments?' *Journal of Political Economy* 106(5): 997–1032.

Romer, T. and H. Rosenthal (1978). 'Political Resource Allocation, Controlled Agendas, and the Status Quo'. *Public Choice* 33(4): 27–43.

Rothstein, B. (1996). 'Political Institutions: An Overview'. *A New Handbook of Political Science*. R. E. Goodin and H.-D. Klingemann. Oxford, Oxford University Press: 133–66.

Roubini, N. and J. D. Sachs (1989). 'Political and Economic Determinants of Budget Deficits in the Industrial Democracies'. *European Economic Review* 33(5): 903–34.

Rubin, I. (1989). 'Aaron Wildavsky and the Demise of Incrementalism'. *Public Administration Review* 49(1): 78–81.

Ruffner, M., J. Wehner and M. Witt (2005). 'Budgeting in Romania'. *OECD Journal on Budgeting* 4(4): 27–54.

Sakurai, K. (2004). 'Analysis of Budget System'. *Government Auditing Review* 11: 55–64.

Santiso, C. (2006). 'Banking on Accountability? Strengthening Budget Oversight and Public Sector Auditing in Emerging Economies'. *Public Budgeting and Finance* 26(2): 66–100.

Santiso, C. (2004). 'Politics of Budgeting in Peru: Legislative Budget Oversight and Public Finance Accountability in Presidential Systems'. SAIS Working Paper WP/01/04.

Scartascini, C. and E. Stein (2009). 'A New Framework'. *Who Decides the Budget? A Political Economy Analysis of the Budget Process in Latin America*. M. Hallerberg, C. Scartascini and E. Stein. Washington, DC, Inter-American Development Bank: 1–21.

Schick, A. (1983). 'Incremental Budgeting in a Decremental Age'. *Policy Sciences* 16(1): 1–25.

Schick, A. (1986). 'Macro-Budgetary Adaptations to Fiscal Stress in Industrialized Democracies'. *Public Administration Review* 46(2): 124–34.

Schick, A. (1988a). 'Micro-Budgetary Adaptations to Fiscal Stress in Industrialized Democracies'. *Public Administration Review* 48(1): 523–33.

Schick, A. (1988b). 'An Inquiry into the Possibility of a Budgetary Theory'. *New Directions in Budget Theory*. I. Rubin. Albany, NY, State University of New York: 59–69.

Schick, A. (2000). *The Federal Budget: Politics, Policy, Process*. Washington, DC, Brookings Institution Press.

Schick, A. (2002). 'Can National Legislatures Regain an Effective Voice in Budget Policy?' *OECD Journal on Budgeting* 1(3): 15–42.

Schick, A. (2003). 'The Performing State: Reflection on an Idea Whose Time Has Come But Whose Implementation Has Not'. *OECD Journal on Budgeting* 3(2): 71–103.

Shah, A. (1994). *The Reform of Intergovernmental Fiscal Relations in Developing and Emerging Market Economies*. Washington, DC, World Bank.

Shepsle, K. A. (1978). *The Giant Jigsaw Puzzle: Democratic Committee Assignments in the Modern House*. Chicago, IL, University of Chicago Press.

Shepsle, K. A. (1979). 'Institutional Arrangements and Equilibrium in Multidimensional Voting Models'. *American Journal of Political Science* 23(1): 27–59.

Shepsle, K. A. and B. R. Weingast (1981). 'Political Preferences for the Pork Barrel: A Generalization'. *American Journal of Political Science* 25(1): 96–111.

Shugart, M. S. and J. M. Carey (1992). *Presidents and Assemblies: Constitutional Design and Electoral Dynamics*. Cambridge, Cambridge University Press.

Shugart, M. S. and S. Haggard (2001). 'Institutions and Public Policy in Presidential Systems'. *Presidents, Parliaments, and Policy*. S. Haggard and M. D. McCubbins. Cambridge, Cambridge University Press: 64–102.

Shi, M. and J. Svensson (2002). 'Conditional Political Budget Cycles'. Centre for Economic Policy Research Discussion Paper 3352.

Siaroff, A. (2003). 'Comparative Presidencies: The Inadequacy of the Presidential, Semi-Presidential and Parliamentary Distinction'. *European Journal of Political Research* 42(3): 287–312.

Sigelman, L. (2006). 'The Coevolution of American Political Science and the American Political Science Review'. *American Political Science Review* 100(4): 463–78.

SIGMA (2002). Relations Between Supreme Audit Institutions and Parliamentary Committees. Paris, Organisation for Economic Co-operation and Development.

Smith, D. L. (1999). *The Stuart Parliaments, 1603–1689*. London, Arnold.

South African Reserve Bank (various). Quarterly Bulletin. Pretoria, South African Reserve Bank.

Sparks, A. (1995). *Tomorrow is Another Country: The Inside Story of South Africa's Negotiated Revolution*. London, Heinemann.

Stapenhurst, F. C. and R. Pelizzo (2002). 'A Bigger Role for Legislatures'. *Finance and Development* 39(4): 46–8.

Stasavage, D. and D. Moyo (2000). 'Are Cash Budgets a Cure for Excessive Fiscal Deficits (and at What Cost)?' *World Development* 28(12): 2105–22.

Staskiewicz, W. (2002). 'Budget Analysis for Parliaments: The Case of Poland'. Paper presented at the 68th International Federation of Library Associations and Institutions Council and General Conference, Glasgow, 18–24 August.

Stein, E., E. Talvi and A. Grisanti (1998). 'Institutional Arrangements and Fiscal Performance: The Latin American Experience'. NBER Working Paper 6358.

Steunenberg, B. (2005). 'The Interaction Between Departments and the Treasury: A Model of Budgetary Decision Making in the UK'. Unpublished manuscript.

Stourm, R. (1917). *The Budget*. New York, London, D. Appleton for the Institute for Government Research.

Strauch, R. R. and J. von Hagen, Eds (1999). 'Institutions, Politics and Fiscal Policy'. *ZEI Studies in European Economics and Law* Vol. 2. Boston, MA, Kluwer Academic Publishers.

Streak, J. (2004). 'The Gear Legacy: Did Gear Fail or Move South Africa Forward in Development?' *Development Southern Africa* 21(2): 271–88.

Streeter, S. (2006a). 'The Congressional Appropriations Process: An Introduction'. CRS Report 97-684 GOV. Washington, DC, Congressional Research Service.

Streeter, S. (2006b). 'House Offset Amendments to Appropriations Bills: Procedural Considerations'. CRS Report RL31055. Washington, DC, Congressional Research Service.

Strøm, K. (1990). *Minority Government and Majority Rule*. Cambridge, Cambridge University Press.

Strøm, K., W. C. Müller and T. Bergman, Eds (2003). *Delegation and Accountability in Parliamentary Democracies*. Oxford, Oxford University Press.

Sturm, R. (1988). *Der Haushaltsausschuß des Deutschen Bundestages: Struktur und Entscheidungsprozeß*. Opladen, Leske und Budrich.

Tarschys, D. (2002). 'Time Horizons in Budgeting'. *OECD Journal on Budgeting* 2(2): 77–103.

Ter-Minassian, T., Ed. (1997). *Fiscal Federalism in Theory and Practice*. Washington, DC, International Monetary Fund.

Tollini, H. (2009). 'Reforming the Budget Formulation Process in the Brazilian Congress'. *OECD Journal on Budgeting* 9(1): 7–35.

Tsebelis, G. (2002). *Veto Players: How Political Institutions Work*. Princeton, NJ, Princeton University Press.

Tsebelis, G. and E. Alemán (2005). 'Presidential Conditional Agenda Setting in Latin America'. *World Politics* 57(3): 396–420.

Tsebelis, G. and E. C. C. Chang (2004). 'Veto Players and the Structure of Budgets in Advanced Industrialized Countries'. *European Journal of Political Research* 43: 449–76.

Tsebelis, G. and J. Money (1997). *Bicameralism*. Cambridge, Cambridge University Press.

Tufte, E. R. (1978). *Political Control of the Economy*. Princeton, NJ, Princeton University Press.

United Kingdom Department for International Development (2004). Poverty Reduction Budget Support: A DFID Policy Paper. London, DFID.

United Kingdom Department for International Development (2006). Making Governance Work for the Poor: A White Paper on International Development. London, DFID.

United States Agency for International Development (2000). USAID Handbook on Legislative Strengthening. Washington, DC, United States Agency for International Development.

Velasco, A. (2000). 'Debts and Deficits with Fragmented Fiscal Policymaking'. *Journal of Public Economics* 76(1): 105–25.

Verwey, L., Ed. (2009). *Parliament, the Budget and Poverty in South Africa: A Shift in Power*. Cape Town, Idasa.

Volkerink, B. and J. de Haan (2001). 'Fragmented Government Effects on Fiscal Policy: New Evidence'. *Public Choice* 109(3–4): 221–42.

Von Hagen, J. (1991). 'A Note on the Empirical Effectiveness of Formal Fiscal Restraints'. *Journal of Public Economics* 44(2): 199–210.

Von Hagen, J. (1992). Budgeting Procedures and Fiscal Performance in the European Communities. Brussels, Commission of the European Communities Directorate-General for Economic and Financial Affairs.

Von Hagen, J. and I. J. Harden (1995). 'Budget Processes and Commitment to Fiscal Discipline'. *European Economic Review* 39: 771–9.

Walker, L. and B. Mengistu (1999). *Spend and Deliver: A Guide to the Medium-Term Expenditure Framework*. Cape Town, Idasa.

Walters, R. H. and R. Rogers (2004). *How Parliament Works*. New York, Longman.

Weaver, R. K. and B. A. Rockman (1993). 'Assessing the Effects of Institutions'. *Do Institutions Matter? Government Capabilities in the United States and Abroad*. R. K. Weaver and B. A. Rockman. Washington, DC, The Brookings Institution: 1–41.

Webber, C. and A. B. Wildavsky (1986). *A History of Taxation and Expenditure in the Western World*. New York, Simon and Schuster.

Weeks, J. (1999). 'Stuck in Low GEAR? Macroeconomic Policy in South Africa, 1996–1998'. *Cambridge Journal of Economics* 23(6): 795–811.

Wehner, J. (2000). 'Fiscal Federalism in South Africa'. *Publius: The Journal of Federalism* 30(3): 47–72.

Wehner, J. (2003). 'Principles and Patterns of Financial Scrutiny: Public Accounts Committees in the Commonwealth'. *Commonwealth and Comparative Politics* 41(3): 21–36.

Wehner, J. (2006). 'Assessing the Power of the Purse: An Index of Legislative Budget Institutions'. *Political Studies* 54(4): 767–85.

Wehner, J. (2007). 'Budget Reform and Legislative Control in Sweden'. *Journal of European Public Policy* 14(2): 315–34.

Wehner, J. (2009). 'Cabinet Structure and Fiscal Policy Outcomes'. *European Journal of Political Research* (forthcoming).

Wehner, J. (2010). 'Institutional Constraints on Profligate Politicians: The Conditional Effect of Partisan Fragmentation on Budget Deficits'. *Comparative Political Studies* 43(2): 208–29.

Weingast, B. R. and W. J. Marshall (1988). 'The Industrial Organization of Congress; or, Why Legislatures, Like Firms, Are Not Organized as Markets'. *Journal of Political Economy* 96(1): 132–63.

Weingast, B. R., K. A. Shepsle and C. Johnsen (1981). 'The Political Economy of Benefits and Costs: A Neoclassical Approach to Distributive Politics'. *Journal of Political Economy* 89(4): 642–64.

Whalen, C. J. (1995). 'Biennial Budgeting for the Federal Government: Lessons from the States'. *Policy Studies Review* 14(3–4): 303–22.

Wildavsky, A. B. (1961). 'Political Implications of Budgetary Reform'. *Public Administration Review* 21(4): 183–90.

Wildavsky, A. B. (1964). *The Politics of the Budgetary Process*. Boston, MA, Little Brown.

Wildavsky, A. B. (1988). *The New Politics of the Budgetary Process*. Glenview, IL, Scott Foresman.

Wildavsky, A. B. and N. Caiden (2001). *The New Politics of the Budgetary Process.* New York, Addison Wesley/Longman.

Wilks, S. (1995). 'Reform of the National Budget Process in Sweden'. *International Journal of Public Sector Management* 8(2): 33–43.

Williams, R. and E. Jubb (1996). 'Shutting Down Government: Budget Crises in the American Political System'. *Parliamentary Affairs* 49(3): 471–84.

Woo, J. (2003). 'Economic, Political, and Institutional Determinants of Public Deficits'. *Journal of Public Economics* 87: 387–426.

World Bank (2007). *World Development Indicators.* Washington, DC, World Bank.

Yläoutinen, S. (2004). Fiscal Frameworks in the Central and Eastern European Countries. Helsinki, Ministry of Finance.

Young, L. (1999). 'Minor Parties and the Legislative Process in the Australian Senate: A Study of the 1993 Budget'. *Australian Journal of Political Science* 34(1): 7–27.

Index